Teaching and Learning with Innovative Technologies in Higher Education

Teaching and Learning with Innovative Technologies in Higher Education provides a wealth of expertly curated case studies demonstrating how educators and technologists can leverage emerging digital technologies to enhance students' experiences. As university staff integrate transformative digital learning tools into their pedagogical practices with a mix of excitement and consternation, new insights are needed into the opportunities, success and limitations of these fast-evolving tools. This book presents real-world examples of effective, digitally enriched approaches to teaching delivery and standards, student engagement and inclusivity, immersive simulations and environments and beyond. Spanning a diverse, comprehensive range of digital technologies deployed in higher education, these practical case studies will guide novice and experienced academics across disciplines in updating their instructional skills and course content for new generations of learners.

Gelareh Roushan is Professor of Digital Transformation and Head of the Centre for Fusion Learning Innovation and Excellence at Bournemouth University, UK.

Martyn Polkinghorne is Associate Professor of Business and Management and was the Education Excellence Theme Leader at Bournemouth University, UK.

Uma Patel is Visiting Fellow and was Programme Leader for the Postgraduate Certificate in Education Practice at Bournemouth University, UK.

Teaching and Learning with Innovative Technologies in Higher Education

Real-World Case Studies

EDITED BY GELAREH ROUSHAN,
MARTYN POLKINGHORNE AND UMA PATEL

Routledge
Taylor & Francis Group

NEW YORK AND LONDON

Designed cover image: © Getty Images

First published 2025
by Routledge
605 Third Avenue, New York, NY 10158

and by Routledge
4 Park Square, Milton Park, Abingdon, Oxon, OX14 4RN

Routledge is an imprint of the Taylor & Francis Group, an informa business

Library of Congress Cataloging-in-Publication Data
Names: Roushan, Gelareh, editor. | Polkinghorne, Martyn, editor. | Patel, Uma, editor.
Title: Teaching and learning with innovative technologies in higher education: real-world case studies / Edited by Gelareh Roushan, Martyn Polkinghorne, and Uma Patel.
Description: New York, NY: Routledge, 2025. | Includes bibliographical references and index.
Identifiers: LCCN 2024043076 (print) | LCCN 2024043077 (ebook) | ISBN 9781032635262 (hardback) | ISBN 9781032627267 (paperback) | ISBN 9781032635248 (ebook)
Subjects: LCSH: Education, Higher—Effect of technological innovations on—Case studies. | Transformative learning. | Internet in higher education—Case studies. | Web-based instruction.
Classification: LCC LB2395.7 .T36 2025 (print) | LCC LB2395.7 (ebook) | DDC 378.1/7344678—dc23/eng/20241129
LC record available at https://lccn.loc.gov/2024043076
LC ebook record available at https://lccn.loc.gov/2024043077

ISBN: 978-1-032-63526-2 (hbk)
ISBN: 978-1-032-62726-7 (pbk)
ISBN: 978-1-032-63524-8 (ebk)

DOI: 10.4324/9781032635248

Typeset in Dante & Avenir
by codeMantra

Contents

Acknowledgments   ix

Introduction   1

1   Innovative Applications of Technology for Animation,
    Simulation and Visualization   12

Case Study 1.1: Using Digital Visualization Tools to
Create Virtual Field Trips   12
Amy L. Evans and Simon M. Hutchinson

Case Study 1.2: Using Virtual Laboratories to Develop
Problem-Solving Skills   20
Selva Mary G. and John Blesswin A.

Case Study 1.3: Engaging Emerging Technologies to Support
Teaching Practices   26
David Hunt and Stephen Pyne

Case Study 1.4: Learning Technology Designs for
Immersive Discussion   32
Anthony Basiel and Mike Howarth

Case Study 1.5: Using Holographic 3D Representations as Teaching Tools   38
Julie A. Lessiter and Helen Clare Taylor

Case Study 1.6: Using Immersive Technologies for Professional
Practice Learning   43
Liz Berragan and Simon Kersey

2   **Innovative Applications of Technology to Support Online Teaching**   **52**

Case Study 2.1: Applying Active Digital Education for the Design of Online Learning   52
Helen Caldwell, David Meechan and Emma Whewell

Case Study 2.2: Microsoft Teams as a Tool for Student Empowerment and Engagement   57
Sterling Rauseo and Raluca Marinciu

Case Study 2.3: Developing an Online Learning Ecosystem   63
Tom Ritchie

Case Study 2.4: A Pedagogical Model for Engaging Postgraduate Researchers Online   69
Kelly Louise Preece

Case Study 2.5: Ensuring Effective Asynchronous Curriculum Delivery   75
Claire Stocks, Dawne Irving-Bell, David Wooff and Scott Farrow

3   **Innovative Applications of Technology to Support Student Engagement and Inclusivity**   **84**

Case Study 3.1: Creating Microsystems to Improve Student Engagement   84
Angeline Dharmaraj-Savicks

Case Study 3.2: Using Technology to Support Online Presence and Student Engagement   91
Rosemary Pearce, Rachel Bancroft and Rachel Challen

Case Study 3.3: Using Technology to Direct Student Learning Behavior   96
Lynn Gribble and Janis Wardrop

Case Study 3.4: Effects of Learning Technologies on the Critical Reflection of Equity and Social Justice   102
Uma Patel

Case Study 3.5: Developing Solutions to Re-Engage Students with Low Attainment   109
Barry Avery, Rebecca Lees and Daniel Russell

Case Study 3.6: Enabling Students to Evaluate Their Academic Writing   114
Sonya McChristie

4   Innovative Applications of Technology within Virtual
    Learning Environments   124

    Case Study 4.1: Using Technology to Enhance the Learning
    Environment for Postgraduate Researchers (PGRs)   124
    Fiona Knight, Julia Taylor and Louise Bryant

    Case Study 4.2: Using Technology to Create a Flexible Learning Pathway   133
    Helen Keen-Dyer, Shannon Delport and Vivian Romero

    Case Study 4.3: Using a Learning Design Framework to Engage and
    Support Students   139
    Carina Buckley and Karen Heard-Lauréote

    Case Study 4.4: Embedding Proctoring Tools within the Virtual
    Learning Environment   144
    David Hunt, Tracey Webb and Stephen Pyne

    Case Study 4.5: Using an Experiential Digital Learning Platform to
    Enhance Student Employability   151
    Andrina Halder

5   Innovative Applications of Technology to Improve
    Teaching Standards   159

    Case Study 5.1: Using Online Platforms for Assessment
    and Feedback   159
    Linda Lefièvre and Mark Hancock

    Case Study 5.2: Using Technology to Evaluate Student Learning Gain   166
    Martyn Polkinghorne, Gelareh Roushan and Julia Taylor

    Case Study 5.3: Using Point-of-View Cameras to Support Teaching,
    Assessment and Feedback   172
    Graham French and Rhys Coetmor Jones

    Case Study 5.4: Supporting New Teaching Staff to Navigate the
    Virtual Learning Environment   177
    Mary Joy Guevarra, Scott Hedger and Allard Lummen

    Case Study 5.5: Implementing a Framework for Digital Pedagogies to
    Enhance Student Learning   182
    Tim Galling, Gelareh Roushan and Tracey Webb

6   Innovative Applications of Technology to Support the
    Student Learning Experience   192

    Case Study 6.1: Using Technology to Humanize Support for Students   192
    Lucinda Becker

    Case Study 6.2: Building a Bridge Between Analog and Digital with
    LEGO® Serious Play®   198
    Caitlin Kight and Holly Henderson

    Case Study 6.3: Creating Online Social Connections for PGRs   203
    Carol Azumah Dennis, Philippa Waterhouse and Inma Alvarez

    Case Study 6.4: Enhancing the Student Experience with
    Technological Added Value   209
    Mick Marriott and Anne Kellock

    Case Study 6.5 Using Synchronous Collaborative Platforms to
    Support Interdisciplinary Groups   215
    Uwe Matthias Richter

    Conclusion   **225**
    Martyn Polkinghorne, Gelareh Roushan and Uma Patel

    Notes on Contributors   232

    Glossary of Terms   248

    Index   251

Acknowledgments

The editors and authors would like to express their gratitude to the work of their colleagues and the learning journeys experienced by students, which together have made the creation of this book possible.

Introduction

The Higher Education sector is passing through a period of significant change and evolution. Clearly there is a need to develop the student experience in response to the increasing globalization and internationalization of education, alongside a requirement that we find ways to engage students more fully with the teaching materials provided. Furthermore, as the student cohorts become larger in size, and more diverse in nature, we need to explore different approaches that can be used to maximize learning opportunities for students, which also ensures the equity and inclusion of our educational provision.

In addition, it is necessary that the knowledge and skills being developed by each student will support their future employability, and so improve their life choices. All these dimensions of university education are happening against a backdrop of regulatory and funding pressures, and with stakeholders having an increasing awareness of the importance of sustainability and social responsibility. Together these drivers are shaping the strategic priorities and policies of Higher Education as universities operate in an ever-changing and increasingly competitive landscape.

Technology is not the solution to all these issues, but it does have a part to play, and so we have collected together a series of case studies that provide examples of how it can be used to support teaching, to improve student engagement, and to reduce the administrative burden on staff. Each case study provides the personal perspective, and lived experience, of those involved. As a result, we hope that you find them to be both interesting and inspiring.

In Chapter 1, we have included six case studies that consider how in Higher Education academics are increasingly using applications of technology, such

DOI: 10.4324/9781032635248-1

as animation, simulation and visualization, to bring their teaching 'to life', and to help their students to understand concepts and principles which are otherwise difficult to grasp.

Case Study 1.1, by Evans and Hutchinson, uses digital visualization tools to create Virtual Field Trips and considers how fieldwork is regarded as an essential educational experience for students studying certain disciplines. For these students, fieldwork often forms a core part of the teaching and learning experience. Virtual Field Trips were introduced *in extremis* during the COVID-19 pandemic when travel was restricted, but at that time, their pedagogical value was unclear. This case study reflects upon experiences of creating and employing Virtual Field Trips to support students studying at different levels, and explores how the use of digital visualization tools can be used to enhance the accessibility of fieldwork, thereby positively influencing diversity, equality / equity and inclusion.

Case Study 1.2, by Mary and Blesswin, focuses upon the use of virtual laboratories to develop problem-solving skills, and considers how digital fluency extends beyond mere consumption. As such, understanding the intricacies of programming becomes paramount as it can foster logical thinking and problem-solving acumen. The Technology-Enabled Laboratory was introduced with a vast repository of over 1,739 problem descriptions, mirroring real-world scenarios. Using this approach, each student embarks on a journey of extensive practice through personalized assignments and feedback, thereby ensuring that learners not only imbibe programming syntax, but also cultivate analytical prowess. The case study reflects upon how harmonizing structured learning and extensive practice through the Technology-Enabled Laboratory establish a new interactive and adaptive education paradigm from which the students can benefit.

Case Study 1.3, by Hunt and Pyne, discusses engaging with emerging technologies to support teaching practice. The case study considers the application of innovative teaching practices, using new technologies, to underpin educational delivery across a variety of disciplines. This case study focuses upon the journey from the conception of emerging technology workshops, through to curricul specific teaching seminars. Examples are used to evidence the interrelationships between emerging technologies, and their adaptation into multidisciplinary teaching, from which an enhanced learning experience can emerge to the benefit of both staff and students.

Case Study 1.4, by Basiel and Howarth, details learning technology designs for immersive discussion, and presents the implications of using a multi-cam model with innovative camera set-up, and a larger group webinar Socratic discussion model using a 360° immersive design. Although developed separately, merging both technologies together is demonstrated to have significant advantages in terms of learning and teaching. Together, the models are shown to promote interactive learning in hybrid classrooms. Effective changes to existing classroom design are discussed that have been seen to further facilitate the student learning experience.

Case Study 1.5, by Lessiter and Taylor, considers how the use of holographic 3D representations as teaching tools can help students who are challenged to understand concepts when presented only with theory, and the use of flat 2D imagery in textbooks. These students will often struggle to visualize and understand how natural and abstract concepts work. Dynamic digital imagery enhances the study of complex, integrated and internal processes. Holograms can be used to teach systems and formations in 3D, so that an object or organism, such as a tornado or human blood vessel, can be studied from different perspectives, and can be manipulated so that inner workings and pathways can be observed. This approach challenges our perceptions regarding what can be achieved in our teaching to enhance student learning.

Case Study 1.6, by Berragan and Kersey, investigates using immersive technologies for professional practice learning, and considers how simulation and immersive technologies continue to revolutionize Higher Education because they offer dynamic and contemporary ways of supporting and engaging with learners. This case study explores the experience of social work students and academics, and the role of simulation in developing and delivering learning and assessment through immersive virtual reality technology. New and innovative possibilities are highlighted, and the outcomes and impact of using immersive technologies in professional practice are discussed.

In Chapter 2 we have included five case studies that together consider innovative applications of technology to support online teaching. Online teaching presents particular challenges for both academics and students. However, increasingly technology can be used to facilitate this learning journey, thereby ensuring an improved experience for those involved.

Case Study 2.1, by Caldwell, Meechan and Whewell, discusses the application of Active Digital Education for the design of online learning. This case study considers how Active Digital Education places a strong emphasis on 'learning by doing' in a digital environment. Learners actively engage with content, make sense of ideas, represent them explicitly and build knowledge through dialog. This approach also draws upon the Universal Design for Learning Framework for making Active Digital Education inclusive. This approach enables learning to be designed, and modified, to ensure that it remains of interest to a wide diversity of learners. This case study demonstrates how digital tools can add pace, collaboration and engagement to synchronous and asynchronous online learning.

Case Study 2.2, by Rauseo and Marinciu, explores the use of Microsoft Teams as a tool for student empowerment and engagement. This case study reflects upon how the COVID-19 pandemic was a crisis that caused both disruptions and innovation, in Higher Education delivery. In the scramble that resulted from social distancing rules, Higher Education was forced behind screens, to deliver what was previously an intimate personal interaction between student and tutor. Online technologies became the only medium for student-tutor interaction. In the face of such a potentially distancing medium, it was necessary to consider how this might affect engagement, and so impact upon feelings of belongingness, and eventually student success. These reflections are based upon the personal experiences of academics in their attempts to maintain key beneficial aspects of the role while they delivered their personal tutoring.

Case Study 2.3, by Ritchie, focuses upon the development of an online learning ecosystem. This case study describes how Microsoft Teams was used to explore how a technology-led approach to module design resulted in a co-designed ecosystem that supported student success, and increased satisfaction. This case study discusses the importance of student support tools in online learning ecosystems, and the challenges in developing these during COVID-19. It then considers the design and implementation of the online learning ecosystem, with practical examples illustrating how this technology-based approach led to both pedagogical and assessment changes.

Case Study 2.4, by Preece, considers a pedagogical model for engaging postgraduate researchers online. This case study explores delivering online training and development for postgraduate researchers (PGRs), and shares the pedagogical model developed for creating an engaging, cross-campus, international learning community. Considering a Researcher Development Program for PGRs, the existing webinar program was developed into an innovative online learning experience with live, static and social elements based upon events, resources and social media. The model, the supporting technologies, and modes of delivery are all discussed.

Case Study 2.5, by Stocks, Irving-Bell, Wooff and Farrow, investigates an effective asynchronous curriculum, and explores the challenges faced when adopting this approach as a delivery model for staff induction within Higher Education. The approach taken includes participant engagement, checking understanding, ensuring that learning takes place in a timely way and evaluating the impact that such an approach has on student learning. This case study explores the use of gamification to address these challenges, and how asynchronous delivery can be utilized to support new lecturers to further understand how digital gamification can be applied in their own teaching practice.

In Chapter 3 we have included six case studies that consider the innovative applications of technology to support student engagement and inclusivity. In order to support students to learn, we need to ensure that they engage as much as possible in their studies. However, there are a wide range of challenges that many students need to overcome in order that they can achieve this. As educators, we therefore need to find ways of using technology to increase inclusivity by breaking down the barriers restricting student engagement.

Case Study 3.1, by Dharmaraj-Savicks, considers how microsystems can be created to increase student engagement, and the role that student engagement plays in Higher Education as it is a central feature of the student learning experience. The influence of technology, and its potential to increase the self-reliance and engagement of students in synchronous learning, has been widely reported, but there is little theoretical guidance to provide a meaningful understanding of how to operationalize such student engagement. This case study is based upon a student engagement framework that exemplifies the complex reciprocal interactions between students and the systems that shape their engagement. To do this, engagement is framed in two dimensions: (1) behavioral – which is the active response to learning activities that are perceived as continued participation and (2) affective engagement – where an emotional investment is observed through positive reactions to a combination of the learning environment and individuals.

Case Study 3.2, by Pearce, Bancroft and Challen, explores the use of technology to support online presence, and student engagement, during the period of remote teaching in response to the COVID-19 pandemic. This was a time when conversations about presence came to the forefront, and educators grappled with how to evolve a face-to-face community online while keeping students both present and engaged. Without using specialist tools, or state-of-the-art equipment, or requiring an unobtainable level of specialist technical knowledge, three examples of practice are included to demonstrate innovations in how teaching was adjusted in response to this ever-changing situation. While on-campus learning has since resumed, teaching has not returned to the pre-COVID-19 pandemic 'norm', but instead new pedagogy continues to emerge, building upon approaches that encourage student presence, whether online or on campus.

Case Study 3.3, by Gribble and Wardrop, discusses the use of technology to direct student learning behavior, and we explore how Personalized Learning Designer was employed through the Moodle Learner Management System to encourage students to undertake timely and appropriate learning behaviors. By mapping student behaviors aligned to successful student outcomes, including grades and completion, it was found that communication could be largely automated, freeing up the administrative burden placed upon the teaching team. Furthermore, this use of technology supported the use of care pedagogy at scale, thereby ensuring that students were encouraged, and at times directed, to undertake activities. Most importantly, it provided a digital guiding hand, leading students in a personal way to navigate the course materials and supporting them more directly as and when required. The use of such technology, while initially taking time to set up, was found to increase learning activity by students, reduce course failure rates and improve efficiency in academic administration.

Case Study 3.4, by Patel, reports on the effects of learning technologies used for critical reflection relating to equity and social justice. Specifically, it investigates the impact of integrating learning technologies into staff development workshops focused upon inclusive education practices. The workshops were built upon prior research into the Equity Compass Tool. Learning technologies used in this case study include online content, synchronous video conferencing, tools for collaboration and discussion and emerging Artificial Intelligence (AI) Avatars. The workshops delivered aimed to empower educators to contextualize and enhance their practice toward reaching more equitable outcomes. Three critical junctures offered insights: (1) that language is a social construct; (2) that every discipline has a 'history of the now' and that 'disciplines are disciplining'; and (3) that critical incident stories presented by AI Avatars can provide educators with context-specific experiences for student reflection and discussion.

Case Study 3.5, by Avery, Lees and Russell, considers the development of solutions to help re-engage students who have low attainment, and details their attempt at fostering engagement between different students. To do this they calculate an Aggregate Measure of Module Engagement for all students based upon their face-to-face class attendance, and participation in scheduled online activities. This measure then classifies learners as being low, medium or highly engaged, and based upon this understanding, a suite of differentiated formative tasks is offered that is tailored to each student's specific situation. By building early interventions like this, this study demonstrates approaches that can both recover students, who are identified as exhibiting low engagement, and reinforce good practice for those with stronger engagement.

Case Study 3.6, by McChristie, searches for ways to enable students to evaluate their own academic writing by using a new, and innovative, student support service that provides students with an opportunity to submit draft written work for personalized, professional feedback on the quality of their academic writing prior to submission. The feedback covers spelling, grammar, levelness and even referencing. This intervention was targeted at new undergraduate students, and those on integrated foundation years. Providing students with early feedback in this way helped to identify any potential issues which may later have become a barrier to their success in terms of academic success. This case study specifically discusses both the practical considerations and the technical hurdles that had to be overcome.

In Chapter 4 we have included five case studies that consider the innovative applications of technology within VLEs, and Learner Management Systems. These are both online software platforms that many universities use to facilitate learning and teaching activities within a virtual space. Via the VLE or Learner Management System, lecture materials can be shared, lectures themselves can be recorded and students' grades can be published. The VLE will often offer several additional software tools that can be used, and there may be opportunities to integrate external applications within it. Furthermore, the VLE typically provides resources to facilitate communication, collaboration and administrative tasks.

Case Study 4.1, by Knight, Taylor and Bryant, discusses using technology to enhance the learning environment to support the requirements of postgraduate researchers (PGRs). PGRs are students who are undertaking research degrees such as Master's degrees (level 7) and Doctorates (level 8). This case study is centered upon the transformative role that online administration and progression monitoring can have to support these PGRs. This study focuses upon the development and implementation of a bespoke online system integrated within the VLE. It provides a summary of the individual phases involved in the development, and this case study identifies the emergent key benefits, including streamlining and standardizing processes, efficient PGR-related data collection and analysis, effective monitoring of PGR progression and greater transparency in the individual postgraduate research student journey.

Case Study 4.2, by Keen-Dyer, Delport and Romero, explores how technology can be used to create a flexible learning pathway for students. This case study considers the steps taken to support the increasing number of international students within Higher Education. These steps include leveraging the Learner Management System to create specially designed learning objects which are curated into a guided flexible learning pathway. The resulting pathway supports a guided discovery approach, which affords students a level of autonomy and agency in their learning, but with the scaffolding in place to ensure they are supported throughout their learning journey.

Case Study 4.3, by Buckley and Heard-Laureote, considers using a Learning Design Framework to engage and support students. The application of a Learning Design Framework creates a structured and engaging learning environment. The Learning Design Framework itself is mediated through the VLE to enhance student learning. It draws together three distinct strands of engagement: (1) collaborative learning which is live, onsite and participative and seeks to maximize peer-to-peer learning in group settings; (2) directed learning which supports, and scaffolds, student autonomy through flexibly delivered on-demand resources that consolidate key concepts and theories; and (3) guided learning which adds value to the student experience by developing their skills, attributes and knowledge necessary for their future career. The Learning Design Framework brings together online and physical classrooms, the individual with their peers and the academic with professional services.

Case Study 4.4, by Hunt, Webb and Pyne, focuses upon embedding proctoring tools within the VLE. This case study considers how the pivot to online learning during the COVID-19 pandemic impacted upon the ability of Higher Education to meet the demands of Professional, Statutory, and Regulatory Bodies, many of which stipulate the use of proctored exams for summative assessments. This case study discusses the implementation of the Honorlock proctoring software for facilitating live online invigilated exams, and how the software was used to support summative assessments across a range of year groups. This study shows how online proctoring offers distinct advantages, and disadvantages, in relation to both the staff and student experience. However, it does provide the necessary flexibility to enable students to complete summative exams from home in a robust online environment.

Case Study 4.5, by Halder, uses an experiential digital learning platform to enhance student employability. This case study discusses an initiative undertaken to involve the students in the use of Riipen, which is an experiential digital learning platform, based upon a consultancy-based teaching module. Riipen was one of the initiatives adopted by the careers team in the Business School. Using this platform, the students were provided with an opportunity to work with business owners based in the USA and so gain hands-on experience of applying their theoretical knowledge. This also allowed them to demonstrate employability skills, and network with employers, and it therefore effectively brought the workplace into the classroom.

In Chapter 5 we have included five case studies that consider the innovative applications of technology to improve teaching standards. In today's Higher Education sector there is a constant drive to improve the quality of our teaching, and increasingly, technology can play an important part in this process, both in terms of what we deliver and how we deliver it.

Case Study 5.1, by Lefièvre and Hancock, considers the use of online platforms to support the assessment and feedback processes. This case study reflects upon how the COVID-19 public health crisis transformed the landscape of Higher Education which fast-tracked the digital adoption of technology to support both teaching and assessment, and which challenged the sector's traditional approaches. This rapid transition brought forth the swift embrace of digital tools, some previously underutilized and others procured with urgency.

Case Study 5.2, by Polkinghorne, Roushan and Taylor, explores the use of technology to evaluate student learning gain. This case study is centered upon the transformative role of the JISC Online Survey tool used in Higher Education. Through a series of pilot activities, a variety of assessment tasks were considered such as group work, individual assessments and autonomous project work. Notably, the tool facilitated efficient data collection and analysis, empowering educators to delve into nuanced insights that would otherwise have been unknown.

Case Study 5.3, by French and Jones, focuses upon the application of point-of-view cameras to support teaching, assessment and feedback. This case study considers how initial teacher education often relies upon direct experience. When the ability to engage in this type of practice was constrained due to the COVID-19 pandemic restrictions, it was necessary to develop alternatives that would enhance practice, as opposed to just being a substitute activity. Multiple point-of-view video cameras were used to record practical sessions from the student perspective, and this enabled academics to utilize the footage to exemplify critical incidents, and so enhance students' development of their own observation and evaluation skills.

Case Study 5.4, by Guevarra, Hedger and Lummen, investigates the ways of supporting new teaching staff to navigate a VLE. This case study delves into the implementation of an innovative training approach that aimed to enhance staff proficiency. A bespoke video guidance series was created titled 'Brightspace Foundations'. The videos offered an immersive learning experience, blending pertinent information with a friendly approach. Bite-sized, self-paced content, and formative self-assessments, enabled staff to learn anytime, anywhere and on any device.

Case Study 5.5, by Galling, Roushan and Webb, discusses the implementation of a framework for digital pedagogies which has been designed to enhance student learning. This case study considers the launch of an internally developed framework designed to establish a baseline level standard for the presentation of teaching content in a VLE. The aim of the framework was to support a drive for consistency leading to a more positive student experience, and to foster increased digital literacy across academic staff and students.

In Chapter 6 we have included five case studies that consider the innovative applications of technology to support the student learning experience. How we use technology to support the learning experience of our students is critical in terms of adding value. Technology itself is not simply the solution to all educational problems, however the right use of technology, at the right time and for the right students, can have a dramatic effect upon their ability to engage, learn and ultimately succeed.

Case Study 6.1, by Becker, explores how, over the last decade, educators have become increasingly used to answering students' queries with 'I have put the documents on the Virtual Learning Environment', or 'You can find your feedback on the system' or 'the links are there on the central support site, you just have to look'. Yet, over this time, students still fail to follow such assignment instructions, neglect to read their feedback and consequently become anxious over a perceived problem, or query, that is clearly answered on the online support sites. The projects in this case study share ways in which academics can humanize the technology, so that students find it more accessible and supportive, thereby increasing its overall impact and value.

Case Study 6.2, by Kight and Henderson, discusses how creative and playful activities can have many benefits for students. During the COVID-19 pandemic, these techniques were particularly helpful for responding to, and mitigating against, some of the biggest challenges associated with online teaching, i.e., difficulties associated with communication, engagement and building learning communities. A project called 'Serious Play, Serious Fun, Serious Skills' was initiated. Through this initiative, a LEGO® Serious Play® (LSP) facilitator trained colleagues across the institution in delivering LSP virtually. LEGO® is an inherently tactile, 'analog' activity, so it is somewhat ironic that it spread throughout the institutional teaching portfolio during a time when education was taking place in an entirely digital environment.

Case Study 6.3, by Dennis, Waterhouse and Alvarez, uses Cultural Historical Activity Theory as a lens to explore a key aspect of the recent COVID-19 global health crisis. The national lockdowns, which began in March 2020, forced the delivery of their doctoral program to shift to exclusively online learning. These changes induced contradictions, and tensions, related to the technical skills of the Postgraduate Team responsible for delivering the program. Microsoft Teams was used as a pedagogic meeting space for PGRs, in contrast to the university's required online platform, and what unexpectedly emerged was a series of auto-ethnographic-infused student-led seminars from a community of students who initially had little in common.

Case Study 6.4, by Marriott and Kellock, considers how technology has had an incredible impact upon society and Higher Education over the past few decades. However, the overuse of technology as a pedagogical approach can be as much a barrier to engagement as an aid. In this case study, an example of how technology has been applied to enhance the learning of computer science students is provided based upon Tinkercad Circuits. This illustrates how technology can be used effectively and demonstrates its value when supporting the development of relevant skill sets. This case study concludes with a critique of 'innovation for innovations sake' and considers if students are being bombarded with a myriad of technological solutions that could as easily be achieved using more conventional methods such as Post-it notes and pens.

Case Study 6.5, by Richter, details part of an online undergraduate module, in which students were tasked to address a problem of their choice while working in interdisciplinary groups. They had to produce sustainable solutions to their chosen problem as a digital artifact. Microsoft Teams and Microsoft Class Teams were used as synchronous collaborative platforms for timetabled webinars and private group channels. The group channel provided students with a space to meet virtually, chat, share files and collaborate synchronously.

The case studies presented in this book remind us of the importance of leveraging the benefits of technology to support student engagement, improve inclusivity, increase employability and enhance learning outcomes. These case studies represent applications that range from Virtual Field Trips to online learning communities. Regardless of ways in which technology has been incorporated in the learning and teaching approaches in these case studies, it is evident that its strategic integration into existing educational practices has enabled educators to respond to some of the challenges faced across Higher Education and beyond.

Innovative Applications of Technology for Animation, Simulation and Visualization

1

The following six case studies describe innovative applications of technology using animation, simulation and visualization. Each case study presents the personal perspectives of those involved.

Case Study 1.1: Using Digital Visualization Tools to Create Virtual Field Trips

AMY L. EVANS AND SIMON M. HUTCHINSON

Fieldwork can be defined as any component of the curriculum that requires exiting the physical classroom and learning via first-hand experiences (Gold et al., 1991). Relating specifically to the subject of this case study, Das and Chatterjea (2018) state that fieldwork is the hallmark of good geographical education. In the United Kingdom (UK) Higher Education sector, fieldwork is regarded as essential for students taking geography and environmental science degrees. It is also a prominent teaching approach in the national subject 'benchmark statements' for Earth Sciences, Environmental Sciences and Environmental Studies (ES3) (Quality Assurance Agency, 2022). However, the view that geography is primarily a field-based discipline

DOI: 10.4324/9781032635248-2

has been questioned. For many, there are personal and ethical barriers to participating in fieldwork which can be exclusionary and even a source of anxiety for students (Leyland *et al.*, 2022; Quality Assurance Agency, 2022).

At the University of Salford (UoS), we initially started using Digital Visualization Tools (DVTs) to develop Virtual Field Trips (VFTs) for ES3 students in 2020 when the COVID-19 pandemic shut down our ability to undertake in-person fieldwork. We subsequently discovered the benefits of the learning environment that VFTs can provide. Building on Hockings *et al.*'s (2012) description of inclusive learning and teaching, in which pedagogy, curricula and assessment are designed and delivered to be accessible to all students, we found that we were able to produce a more inclusive approach to fieldwork. The ability to revisit information, usually only accessed on the day of a field trip, provided an opportunity for more effective learning (Henderson *et al.*, 2015) and made field locations accessible to students who otherwise might have been unable to attend.

From first-hand conversations and targeted questionnaires, we have found that many of our students and staff alike consider fieldwork to be one of the most enjoyable and memorable aspects of their environmental sciences studies. Boyle *et al.* (2007) make the case that fieldwork is particularly important for the affective domain of student development in that the feelings, emotions and attitudes of individuals need to be engaged so that students do not just receive information, but also respond to it, value it and see themselves as practitioners of their subject. However, rising field trip costs may restrict some students' participation in fieldwork, which is an inclusivity issue that must be addressed. The carbon footprint of fieldwork should also be considered with regard to the current climate emergency (Hoolohan *et al.*, 2021). Based on these arguments and observations we observed the potential to develop the use of VFTs further while recognizing that their application warranted both the evaluation of student engagement with this technology and changes in attitude toward its use.

Description

While VFTs were much more widespread due to the COVID-19 pandemic, they have been used in a range of formats within Higher Education for some time. Fundamentally, a virtual field trip can be classified as being a digital resource that allows a person to visualize a remote location using images and materials such as maps, data and web links (Hurst, 1998; Stainfield *et al.*, 2000). Examples range from pre-recorded video tours to immersive e-gaming simulations such as Pringle's (2013) Virtual Geoscience

Trainer. They can also be virtual 'walk-throughs' accompanied by desktop studies using easily accessible online information and data (Mercer *et al.*, 2022). Examples include McDougall's (2019) Virtual Reality (VR) glaciated landscapes which enable the user to wear VR headsets to explore panoramic images of locations.

Our use of VFTs integrated many aspects of the above examples to produce cost-effective and easy-to-make teaching resources. Using ThingLink, an online visual learning platform, we can create interactive virtual environments that could be explored on any device with web browser capabilities. We employed digital assets such as photographs, 360-degree imagery, 3D models and videos, and then uploaded these to a ThingLink folder to patch them together in an interactive format that enabled the student to move through the environment at their own pace. The ability to embed additional and supporting information using web links, and datasets via 'clickable' icons, meant that the configuration possibilities of individual VFTs were enormous, and they could be designed to meet the specific learning outcomes for defined groups or activities.

Creating a VFT requires the collation of quality digital assets and a clear storyboard to facilitate an optimal and user-friendly experience. We used GoPro Max action cameras, which can take 360-degree photos and videos, with a tripod and DJI Mini 2 drones. They were selected as both were relatively affordable and readily available. They have proven to be both user-friendly and reliable. The decision to use smaller and cheaper drones to capture aerial photography partly reflects UK civil aviation rules which allow an operator to fly a drone under 250g with relatively few restrictions. 'GoPro MAX 360-degree' action cameras were selected due to their performance and reliability when used in the field where weather and mishandling can be a concern. Digital cameras and smartphone cameras were also used, often being a backup or a quick way to take an opportunistic shot.

Application

Across four academic year groups in Levels 4–7 of their university studies on the University of Salford's Geography and Environmental Management (GEM) modules, we created five ThingLink-based VFTs during the 2020–2023 academic cycles to initially replace, and later accompany, in-person field trips. In 2020, when fieldwork was not possible due to the global COVID-19 pandemic, we rapidly prepared alternatives for two undergraduate modules where fieldwork was essential. Once travel was re-opened, we began to use our VFTs as accompanying study tools for three more modules where fieldwork was required for summative assessment. The initial two VFTs were progressively enhanced with newly captured drone images, videos, 360-degree images and 3D models.

Enabling students to visit locations remotely, when travel was restricted, allowed us to replace in-person field courses with VFTs. While also acknowledging through student feedback that they can never fully replace real experiences, it was apparent that they can provide a viable alternative when this is not possible. Currently, we use VFTs to enhance the learning experience, and inclusivity, of in-person field trips by preparing students for the field both academically and psychologically. Cognitive loads differ from student to student, reflecting personal factors such as health, gender, culture and previous experiences. We therefore consider VTFs as being essential to provide diverse pedagogical resources to help navigate any personal anxieties that students may have (Petterson *et al.*, 2021). By enabling students to review field conditions, and possible residential trip accommodation, through VFTs before the event, we can help to reduce levels of anxiety, and the cognitive load, for those less familiar or comfortable with fieldwork.

Within each of the VFTs we have created, we have also embedded a live questionnaire for students to provide feedback on their experience to help us to make informed decisions on their further use going forward.

Impact

We wanted to learn what our students thought about the use of VFTs so we could determine their value, and to try to improve their application. We assessed 123 student opinions collected via online questionnaires during three academic cycles between 2020 and 2023 and evaluated the perceived usefulness of VFTs as a teaching tool, their ease of use and their impact on inclusivity. From the responses we identified three key themes around students' perceptions and experiences when using VFTs: (1) the features and functionality of the VFT; (2) the use of VFTs as a pre-field trip guide; and (3) the use of VFTs as a study tool. We were also able to pick out key comments and thoughts related to Equality / Equity, Diversity and Inclusivity (EDI).

Most students either strongly agreed, or agreed, that our VFTs were easy to access and navigate. When asked what they enjoyed about their experience of using a VFT, most students commented on the wealth of information provided and strongly agreed that this was both relevant and clear. Examples of student feedback comments are provided below:

> *The links to websites, that explained certain parts in more detail, were very helpful.*
>
> Anonymous student

> *[I liked] the multiple buttons that lead to external sites which can provide more information.*
>
> Anonymous student

> *Links to source material [were useful].*
>
> Anonymous student

The quality of the digital assets used in creating each VFT was determined as being significant in the success of the resulting virtual experience. Our students stated that having visual aids was useful, and that the quality of the visual media made the VFT fun to use, and the subject matter easier to understand. The interactive aspect of each VFT being an enjoyable resource highlighted that using an engaging approach is necessary for any VFT to be successful.

> *[I enjoyed] how interactive it was, and the fact it wasn't just a word document describing the place with photos.*
>
> Anonymous student

> *I liked how it was really interactive.*
>
> Anonymous student

> *Really useful interactive tool.*
>
> Anonymous student

We also asked students what would improve the quality of each VFT. Clearer instructions were suggested as being important to enable full access, making the VFT a more inclusive and effective learning tool.

> *Clearer signposting for what each of the buttons leads to [would help with] easier navigation.*
>
> Anonymous student

As a result of these initial comments, we subsequently provided sessions to introduce the students to the best approach and help them to engage with the various aspects of the VFT, to ensure that each of them had maximized their experience.

When asked what they did not enjoy when using the VFT, a key response from students was the inability to virtually interact with the lecturer throughout the experience. One student stated:

> *Maybe an interactive feature where you could ask additional questions [would help]. For instance, a text box where the lecturer could answer any questions.*
> Anonymous student

Learning from this, the need for teacher-student engagement throughout the use of a VFT is required for students to fully benefit from the tool.

Survey results showed that our students felt more confident about attending in-person field trips after engaging with the associated VFT, and that they found it to be a useful tool when preparing for an upcoming in-person trip. Student responses included:

> *[The VFT] helped me to visualize, and in turn understand, what we were meant to do on the in-person trip.*
> Anonymous student

> *[The VFT] informed you about the site before you went, and you could refer to it BEFORE and AFTER which was super useful especially for a site that is across a wide area.*
> Anonymous student

Students' responses showed that they would revisit the VFT after the in-person field trip for studying purposes, and so would like to see more use of VFTs in their university course. Responses from students included:

> *Really useful interactive tool. It definitely has its place alongside in-person field trips. Especially, if you wanted to discuss the trip in advance of going, or refer back to it for an assignment.*
> Anonymous student

> *[The VFT] provided knowledge useful to revise if you missed the notes for it which is good for exam revision.*
> Anonymous student

> *Virtual Field Trips can be introduced as an important element in this module. It was possible to gain practical knowledge through it.*
> Anonymous student

By providing our students access to virtual field trips we feel that we have fostered a more inclusive teaching environment for those with disabilities (Chiarella and Vurro, 2020).

Responses selected from student surveys regarding EDI included:

I think it would be helpful to make the virtual field trips more comprehensive for students with accessibility needs that might be unable to visit in person.
                                                                   Anonymous student

Virtual field trips would [be] helpful for people with accessibility needs.
                                                                   Anonymous student

For myself, being a disabled student, I know some areas are not possible for me to visit, but I would still love to see what they look like.
                                                                   Anonymous student

Fieldwork can be a barrier for certain groups of students, and the factors raising such barriers can be both visible and hidden, ranging from physical disabilities to neurodivergent needs (Chiarella and Vurro, 2020). Producing a VFT as part of a module that has fieldwork, or site visits, enables us to identify potential barriers, and so find ways to overcome them.

We have a diverse group of students, and a large international cohort, on our postgraduate courses, and not all our students have fieldwork experience, or awareness of the British climate. Being mindful not to make assumptions about ability and experience, a VFT can provide a digital visualization illustrating factors such as the terrain, or possible adverse weather conditions, and information regarding accessibility, thereby allowing students to make informed decisions, and so be better prepared for an in-person field trip. When working outdoors, the weather, group size and location can make hearing the teacher difficult or, for neurodivergent students, harder to follow. Although it is great to see something first-hand, a VFT provides a way to revisit information that may have been missed on the day.

Providing details within the VFT regarding access to toilet facilities, walking distances, activities and length of stay on the day of the physical trip can be extremely beneficial in informing students with pre-existing conditions and potential anxieties. This can also provide an opportunity for such students to identify possible participation issues so they can alert staff to potential problems beforehand.

Learning from our initial VFTs that were produced as a response to the COVID-19 pandemic, and the subsequent iterations alongside students' comments, we have built on our practice, and now ensure that EDI considerations are addressed when planning fieldwork. However, it seems very clear from our students' feedback that although they see the value of VFTs as a study tool, and as a way to support EDI, they do not want to see VFTs entirely replace the in-person field trip experience. Student responses included:

> *I do not think virtual field trips should be used as a replacement for site visits, but rather as a resource for additional information, or contextualizing the area. The resource is still very useful however.*
>
> Anonymous student

> *Being on the field trip helps me understand the assessment better. The virtual field trip was able to provide me with some knowledge of the area before we visited it.*
>
> Anonymous student

> *You can never better the real experience of a nature-based field trip, however, these virtual field trips definitely support learning in times of social restrictions, or as extra-educational materials towards lectures.*
>
> Anonymous student

Case Study Conclusion

COVID-19's restrictions on field trips are now largely over, and many students and staff members have welcomed back 'real' field trips over virtual alternatives. However, poor accessibility and inclusion in Geoscience at many levels remain, and there is a role for the use of DVTs in helping to open up the environmental sciences. VFTs need not be seen as a replacement for in-person field-based activities, e.g., as a means of cost saving, but if well-designed, they can usefully augment the learning experience and enhance the traditional field trip.

Students' expectations of the use, and availability, of technology in Higher Education are changing, and such technology can provide a powerful means of enhancing engagement.

Going forward, VFTs are likely to become quicker, and simpler to create. For example, commercially available action-type cameras and lightweight drones are becoming more affordable, and the images that they record are improving, negating the need for expensive and specialist equipment. It is also likely that it will become easier to create VFTs via game engine-driven applications to make virtual excursions more immersive. This may include Augmented Reality (AR) and Extended Reality (XR) features.

Case Study 1.2: Using Virtual Laboratories to Develop Problem-Solving Skills

SELVA MARY G. AND JOHN BLESSWIN A.

At the SRM Institute of Science and Technology's Directorate of Learning and Development, one of our primary responsibilities is guiding first-year undergraduates through the pivotal 'Programming for Problem Solving' course. At its core, this course is not just about introducing students to programming languages, but more crucially it is an avenue for students to hone their logical reasoning, analysis and higher-order thinking skills.

In the past, we observed that our students' practical sessions were centered around a static set of standard questions. While these questions did serve a purpose, they offered limited exposure, leading to a constrained understanding of the vast realm of programming. We realized that to empower our students we needed to transcend traditional learning boundaries. Our focus shifted toward understanding the nuances of how individuals learn, especially in the context of problem-solving.

Description

Our introspection culminated in our vision for the Technology-Enabled Laboratory (TEL) tool. This was not just another e-learning platform, instead it was our brainchild to ensure that students' learning trajectories remained ascendant, even outside the confines of the classroom. We designed the TEL tool as an interactive platform for enhanced programming lab practices, ensuring a more dynamic, adaptive and comprehensive learning experience.

For this project we had multiple primary objectives including the need to foster self-directed learning by empowering students to take charge of their education, allowing them to delve deeper into topics, transcend the confines of the traditional curriculum, and that would encourage them to seek knowledge actively. We also wanted to enhance analytical capabilities by providing learners with comprehensive analytics and dashboards, enabling them to gauge their strengths, identify areas for improvement and thereby tailor their learning journey effectively.

We knew that promoting reflective learning, by creating an environment where students are not just passive recipients of information, but active participants in the learning process, consistently reflecting on their progress and understanding, would be an important achievement. However, we also wanted to cultivate lifelong learning skills by equipping students with the tools and mindset to view learning as a continuous journey, honing their problem-solving skills and instilling a genuine passion for knowledge that persists beyond formal education.

Finally, personalizing the learning experience ensured that the platform could adapt to the diverse needs of the student population, recognizing individual skills, learning abilities and interests and thereby offering a tailored educational experience was a prerequisite. The resulting TEL tool is a robust, web-based platform tailored to enrich the learning experience for students undertaking the 'Programming for Problem Solving' course. At its core, the TEL tool's architecture comprises of:

1. Problem statement repository, which is a vast repository hosting over 2,500 problem descriptions meticulously curated to mirror real-world scenarios and challenges.
2. Student workspace, which is an intuitive interface where learners can draft, modify and submit solutions using a wide range of programming languages.
3. Real-time compilation server, which is a server-side component that compiles and evaluates submitted solutions in real time, ensuring immediate feedback to learners.
4. Analytics dashboard function that provides educators and learners with key insights into performance metrics, areas of interest and progress tracking.

By sharing our journey and experiences with TEL, we hope to shed light on how technology can significantly enhance the learning experience in Higher Education.

The true strength of the TEL tool lies in its robust operational framework which we meticulously designed to meet the diverse needs of both educators and students. Far from being just a bank of problem statements, or a mere automated code-checking tool, we conceptualized TEL as an all-encompassing learning ecosystem.

We provide each registered learner with a specially curated set of 300 problem statements organized into easy, medium and hard difficulty levels. The 'Editor' workspace serves as a playground and a testing ground for students. Here, they can freely write and modify their code, benefiting from our system's real-time compilation and feedback.

We have also integrated a dynamic color-coding system to visualize progress, complemented by badges and ranks to motivate and reward effort. Our analytics dashboard informs students of their performance metrics, helping them identify their strengths and areas for improvement. Beyond the technical aspects, we designed TEL to emphasize self-directed learning. We encourage students to actively participate in their educational journey, prompting them to reflect on their progress and adapt their learning strategies as needed. Once all test cases are successfully evaluated, the learner has effectively solved the challenge.

We allow course facilitators to create, and introduce, new problem sets into our expansive repository. Each set can be further enriched with various test cases, which can be visible, invisible and/or mandatory, to ensure the solutions' accuracy. Our dynamic feedback system allows us, and other facilitators, to monitor student progress in real time. This capability enables us to offer personalized guidance adapted to each learner's cognitive and academic needs.

We have also integrated CDIO (Conceive-Design-Implement-Operate) frameworks into TEL, supporting activity-based learning, and helping students master complex cognitive tasks. Additionally, our plagiarism detection engine maintains the course's academic integrity by ensuring the originality of each submission.

The course facilitator can see each learner's progress and completion levels, which helps the facilitator identify learners who are struggling. Hence, facilitators can invest their time and efforts in mentoring and helping academically challenged learners to develop their logical reasoning abilities and programming skills.

Application

Our journey with the TEL tool began with its integration into the 'Programming for Problem Solving' course at our main campus. The overwhelming success of this initial application suggested that TEL had a broader role to play in our academic ecosystem.

The efficacy of TEL wasn't just proven at one campus, as it soon became an integral part of the curriculum across all campuses of the SRM Institute of Science and Technology. With over 52,000 full-time students, and more than 3,200 academics, spread across our multiple campuses, the wide-reaching adoption of TEL is a testament to its scalability and universal applicability.

What sets TEL apart is its versatility in accommodating a wide array of programming languages. We have incorporated 23 programming languages, including C, C++, Java, Python, C#, GO, Haskell, Ruby, R and Octave. This extensive language support makes TEL a truly adaptable tool, catering to diverse academic needs. Furthermore, TEL's application is not confined to a single course, and we have successfully integrated it into an array of practical courses including:

- Data structures;
- Design and analysis of algorithms;
- Computer networks;
- Operating systems;
- Database management systems with SQL (Structured Query Language).

The tool's expansive application across multiple disciplines underscores its utility as a multifaceted educational resource. To facilitate a smooth transition to using this new technology, we organized academic training sessions across all campuses. The positive initial feedback we received from both students and academics necessitated only minor adjustments to the system.

TEL's design allows for extensive customization. Academics can tailor problem sets and other features to meet the specific objectives of their courses, making it a truly adaptable educational tool. Through its widespread campus adoption, versatile language support and integration into various courses, TEL has proven to be more than just an educational platform. It is a catalyst for academic innovation, enriching the educational experience for both academics and students alike.

Impact

The introduction of TEL has been nothing short of revolutionary. Garnering participation from over 37,000 learners within our own institution, its reach has now transcended beyond our university to many other engineering institutions in India.

Feedback mechanisms, coupled with rewards such as badges and ranks, have instilled motivation and a sense of accomplishment among students. Through our continuous engagement and feedback, we have witnessed learners transition from programming novices to experts, ready to take on industry challenges.

We evaluate the impact of TEL using a range of metrics. The widespread adoption of TEL has seen participation from over 68,000 learners, not just within SRM Institute of Science and Technology, but also in various other engineering institutions across India. Instructor efficacy for facilitators has been possible using TEL's real-time analytics and feedback system which allow more effective monitoring of student progress. This targeted approach aids struggling students without compromising the pace of more advanced learners.

High completion rates have been achieved with over 10,000 learners already successfully completing each level and being certified by the university. This is a testament to the effectiveness of the TEL tool in engaging students and ensuring their academic development. Reduced drop-out rates have been noticeable with a reduction in the number of students dropping out of the 'Programming for Problem-Solving' course, as the adaptive and personalized nature of TEL accommodates diverse learning styles and paces.

Enhancement of the traditional learning experience is now possible due to the interactive and dynamic nature of TEL which has contributed to a more enriching learning experience. Students report a higher level of engagement and comprehension, as corroborated by anonymous feedback and course evaluations. Skills development has occurred beyond programming, as the platform fosters essential 21st-century skills such as critical thinking, problem-solving and self-directed learning. The real-world challenges presented in the problem statements prepare students for industry demands.

Fostering collaboration has been achieved as the platform has encouraged not just individual learning, but also collaborative problem-solving, thereby creating a sense of community among learners. Motivation and confidence of students have been enhanced with the introduction of badges, ranks and other gamified elements that instill motivation and a sense of accomplishment, thereby increasing student confidence.

Accessibility has been improved with TEL's web-based architecture, which makes quality education more accessible, potentially benefiting learners who may not have had the opportunity for such exposure otherwise. Lifelong learning goals have been supported as TEL inculcates a culture of continuous learning. Students are therefore more prepared and willing to take charge of their educational journey, a skill that will benefit them long after their formal education is complete.

External recognition has been achieved as the success of TEL has attracted attention from educational bodies and industry stakeholders, opening avenues for partnerships, research and further development.

Setting new educational standards has been accomplished as TEL's success has prompted other institutions to reconsider their pedagogical approaches, thereby raising educational standards across the sector.

The impact of the TEL tool has been profound. With numbers reflecting widespread adoption and high completion rates, we have tangible proof of the tool's efficacy in enhancing the educational experience. The drastic reduction in drop-out rates, and the overwhelmingly positive feedback received, underlines the platform's success in accommodating diverse pace and learning styles of students.

In summary, we have worked to ensure that TEL is not merely a technological tool, but a harmonious blend of technological sophistication and pedagogical innovation. Through TEL, we are redefining the landscape of programming education, making it more dynamic, interactive and effective.

Case Study Conclusion

In a rapidly evolving educational landscape, the need for innovative, effective and scalable learning solutions has never been more urgent. Our work with the TEL tool demonstrates how technology can be seamlessly integrated into traditional academic settings to create a more dynamic, interactive and effective learning environment.

What started as a localized project for first-year students at SRM Institute of Science and Technology has blossomed into a comprehensive educational tool adopted across multiple campuses and courses, impacting learners, and enriching the educational experience for academics and students alike. The platform's impact extends beyond programming proficiency, nurturing essential skills such as critical thinking, problem-solving and lifelong learning. For educators, the tool provides invaluable insights into student performance, enabling targeted interventions and personalized guidance.

As we look to the future, the success of TEL serves as an encouraging prototype for similar initiatives. Its adaptability and scalability hint at its potential application in other disciplines and educational settings. Moreover, it opens avenues for additional research into personalized, technology-enabled education, offering a promising direction for educationalists, policymakers and technologists to explore collaboratively. In essence, the TEL tool is not just an end-point, but instead it is a milestone in the ongoing journey toward redefining the contours of modern education. By leveraging technology to serve pedagogical aims, we have changed how we teach and revolutionized what it means to learn in the process.

Case Study 1.3: Engaging Emerging Technologies to Support Teaching Practices

DAVID HUNT AND STEPHEN PYNE

The need was identified to guide teaching staff in the adoption of emerging, and evolving, industry-led technologies. Specifically, this applied to the technology applications available to staff and students to support teaching. Following institutional restructuring, a new more user-friendly Virtual Learning Environment (VLE) was implemented, which reduced reliance on technical support from the learning technology team. The changes enabled the team to expand their role, providing a mechanism for investigating developments in emerging technologies. This detailed review subsequently led to the conception of the Pedagogies Innovation Lab (PIL) which established structured time for learning technologists to focus on easily adopted emerging technologies. Investigations centered around pedagogical benefits to underpin academically led teaching practices, creating direct pathways to feed into curricular based activities.

Description

Initially the PIL provided a test environment for learning technologists to:

- Identify and procure equipment;
- Explore and evaluate specific functionalities of the technologies;
- Compare technologies against alternative options;
- Review the institutional technology landscape;
- Produce cost analysis reports;
- Identify stakeholder interest within specific areas of educational focus.

Once the initial investigations were finalized, and software/hardware testing was completed, a baseline educational use for each technology was established. Combining our comprehension of technology, pedagogy and industry, the learning technologists established a series of practical innovation workshops, and drop-in sessions, targeted at academic staff.

These sessions were initially structured around a 'show and tell' approach to introduce the technologies, build academic appetite and increase user confidence. As well as highlighting the technologies and their application within education, the sessions also helped to empower teaching staff in becoming early adopters (Armstrong, 2019) engendering an institutional community of practice. A notable outcome from the workshops was that staff were inspired to identify how they would/could use the technologies in their own teaching practice, thereby precipitating the adoption of the technologies into the curriculum.

On request from academic staff, and in consultation with them, we designed bespoke pedagogically led student-facing workshops to explore the application of specific innovative technologies. The sessions were tailored around intended learning outcomes and academic discipline, and had a specific focus on student assessment. Each workshop consisted of an initial presentation to introduce the technologies, demonstrating how they could be applied within different industry practices, as well as providing tangible examples of ways they could be effectively used to enhance student assessments.

The presentations included technical demonstrations showcasing the functionalities of each technology, followed by the facilitation of practical hands-on exercises in using the equipment. Overall, the workshops were received well by students, and each encouraged open in-class discussion in which students were particularly interested in the practical aspects.

Application

Through the discovery stages in the creation of the PIL, several barriers were identified in its development from concept to delivery. These barriers provided important lessons in futureproofing any further procurement projects. The initial funding requirements were realized though capital expenditure as opposed to fully funded research projects. Therefore, securing funding proved difficult to justify at this stage as there were uncertainties around the functionalities of the untested equipment and how the technologies would be adopted by staff at the institution (Rogers, 2000). This proved to be the case with the procurement of two handheld 3D scanners, as it was found that the devices were challenging to use, and maintain, due to the supporting software being unreliable and prone to errors. Consequently, the output results, and 3D scans obtained, were disappointing, and the devices were deemed unsuitable for practical use.

Initial difficulties were also experienced when setting up Virtual Reality-Head-Mounted Displays (VR-HMDs) which required stable Wi-Fi connectivity. Issues were identified with the network infrastructure around our campus which prevented a consistent connection. Additionally, operational changes, and system updates, implemented by platforms and manufacturers, resulted in access problems. The purchase of Oculus by Facebook, and then the subsequent rebranding from Facebook to Meta, resulted in frequent changes to account management processes. This complicated the process of updating software and maintaining an unfailing end user experience.

Procuring the appropriate number of VR-HMDs for each student was not financially feasible. As an alternative, a large quantity of Google Cardboards was purchased as they had already proven to be an effective, yet economical, option for demonstrating VR and 360-degree video, albeit at a more rudimentary level. The Cardboards were used prolifically in the workshops, and enabled every student to engage, and experience, the technology. However, Google has since withdrawn support, and the viewing option on YouTube has subsequently been removed, rendering the Cardboards ineffective within a short period.

The ongoing enhancements, and developments, in how technology is used, and maintained, have resulted in some equipment becoming obsolete very quickly, thereby reducing its serviceable life and cost effectiveness. This was exacerbated by the impact of the COVID-19 pandemic, and the resulting national lockdowns, when the shift to online teaching rendered practical demonstrations impossible. This was especially relevant when devices were expected to be worn and shared around student cohorts. Working from home, and unable to access equipment, also impacted upon the evaluation, development and maintenance of these devices.

While digital badges and awards are not exactly an emerging technology, adoption has been slow in the Higher Education sector and has not yet achieved their full potential. In our Faculty of Media and Communication, students on programs under the Department of Media Production were required to complete a series of self-managed learning tasks, prior to being permitted to book out loan equipment from the kit room, and with over 1,300 students requiring equipment in support of their study, this was proving difficult to manage. To find a technological solution to this, and in consultation with department staff, we developed the Media Skills Passport by creating a module within a departmental area of the VLE. Initially this module consisted of three sections: (1) Safe Production Certificate; (2) Kit Safety Certificate; and (3) Mains Lighting Certificate.

Each section contained a series of subsections with subject-specific learning materials followed by online Multiple-Choice Questions (MCQs). As each subsection was completed, the student was issued a digital badge and on completion of the main section, with all badges obtained, a downloadable PDF certificate awarded. This introduced an element of gamification to encourage student engagement with learning (Whitton and Moseley, 2012). Production of the appropriate badge or certificate would then permit the student to book the related equipment. Automated VLE reports called Intelligent Agents were set up so that program- and level-specific reports could be produced to show student completion status. This allowed the awards to be cross-checked by the Kit Room staff, and for teaching staff to monitor student progress.

The Media Skills Passport has proven to be highly effective, and the awards extremely popular with students. Later, similar systems using this sense of play (Emin and Ney, 2013) have been developed within the Nursing and Physiotherapy departments where they are also popular with students and staff and are increasing student engagement.

Eye tracking glasses are wearable devices equipped with infrared cameras which monitor and record the user's eye movements. Data is then produced and can be analyzed to determine the user's gaze point. The glasses are supplied with a tethered mobile device which hosts eye tracking software. Once the wearer has completed their session, they are provided with a digital recording which is overlaid with eye tracking data.

As part of the Advertising Management program in the Faculty of Media and Communication, students were tasked with producing dissertation projects involving the creation of websites and marketing materials. Initially, learning technologists were approached to facilitate a technology innovation workshop introducing students to various emerging technologies. Building upon our previous successes, an additional tailored workshop was created to support student research projects. This workshop explored the adoption and analysis of eye tracking technologies. Students were encouraged to examine the interrelationships between the design of effective marketing strategies and materials from the perspective of the end user experience.

Wearing the glasses, students were initially given an opportunity to track the campus, understand the functionalities of the technology and interpret eye tracking data. Students were then placed into groups to critically analyze advertising campaigns and web resources using a variety of different sized screens. This approach enabled the students to make comparisons, and draw conclusions, on the effectiveness of eye tracking in different environments. The integration of this technology into the teaching session cultivated student-led discussions that supported a constructivist approach to achieve the desired learning outcomes (Taylor and Hsueh, 2005).

It was encouraging to see how students immediately adapted to using the technology and recognized the direct benefits of using eye tracking data to elevate their research. Students provided peer feedback on their project proposals producing qualitative data which would later feed into their final dissertations. Two final-year students arranged follow-up appointments with the learning technologists to generate metric-driven reports produced by the software. One of the projects involved the construction of a website. Using eye tracking glasses on focus group participants, the student was able to elicit qualitative and quantitative data pinpointing which areas had greater visual appeal. The results were then used to justify the redesign of their website, and this was evidenced in their dissertation.

The second student project involved the creation of marketing materials, both physical and digital. Eye tracking was used on a smaller sample to capture and report on specific areas of interest to the participants. The software produced heat maps of physical materials, generating engagement patterns, which visually demonstrated the intensity of interest. Captured data was then aggregated to enable students to adapt their marketing materials based upon the evidence gathered.

Following an emerging technologies staff workshop, a PhD student from the Midwifery department was awarded research funding to investigate virtual worlds in immersive training. Having decided on a platform, and engaging with the provider, the learning technologists were assigned to the project to support the development and delivery of the content. Viewable via computer, mobile devices, Google Cardboards and VR-HMDs, the content was designed for trainee midwives and related to how to correctly conduct urinalysis on expectant mothers (King et al., 2018).

Using avatars to represent midwives and patients in a virtual medical examination room, students were led through approved Nursing and Midwifery Council procedures. Learning technologists designed interactive digital artifacts, including video demonstrations, hand-washing procedures, pop-up images of urology comparison charts and patient interactions. The simulation was designed to replace existing teaching methods and create a safe learning space thereby mitigating physical patient risks. Feedback recorded at the seminars was extremely positive, and students described the interactive experiential learning (Sternberg and Zhang, 2001) activity as more engaging and preferable compared to standard delivery.

The successful use of virtual worlds was documented and disseminated across the university. Subsequently, another PhD nursing student expanded this practice by developing an enriched virtual scenario for managing a critically deteriorating diabetic patient. The learning technologists were again approached to support the project, and we undertook training, facilitated by the software supplier, that provided us with the necessary skills in creating these digital assets.

Impact

In co-ordination with the PhD student, we produced micro formative quizzes, which were integrated into the virtual scenario. The quizzes directed the students through a different course of action, and, depending on their preceding choice, resulted in a range of patient outcomes. We also supported teaching seminars by demonstrating how to use the technology and providing first-hand technical guidance.

Nursing students were placed into two control groups, virtual and non-virtual, in which they undertook alternate teaching and assessment activities. The original non-virtual seminars were completed using lecture-style presentations and in-class written tests, whereas the virtual control group undertook comparable learning and assessment exercises using the virtual worlds. Overall feedback was positive, although a small number of students experienced issues with seeing other participants' avatars in their virtual world. This was reported back to the software supplier who quickly resolved the issue. Students were verbally enthusiastic when using VR and they understood how to use the technology to navigate through the scenario.

Student attainment levels demonstrated positive variances between the two assessment methods with virtual control group students demonstrating deeper cognizance. Students also identified the increased safety of treating interactive virtual patients. Outcomes from both groups were evidenced as part of the PhD research favoring the adoption of virtual worlds in medical training. The software supplier ceased trading due to COVID-19; however, results from the virtual world projects have been viewed as a catalyst for future developments in medical education within the institution.

Case Study Conclusion

Adopting emerging technologies in Higher Education represents a transformative shift that holds the potential to revolutionize the way students learn. The PIL has proven to be an important initiative at Bournemouth University where it has encouraged and supported the inclusion of innovative technologies, equipping students with the necessary skills required for the modern workforce. Successful implementation has required robust planning, academic engagement and infrastructure support. Facilitating simple workshops and drop-in sessions to demonstrate technology concepts has required minimal resources compared to significant advancements of learning outcomes.

Developing close partnerships with teaching teams has proven to be fundamental in progressing the PIL, creating academic communities of engagement and increasing digital literacies. Furthermore, introducing students to the concepts and benefits of emerging technologies has influenced curricula modifications fostering student-centered and experiential learning. Student research into the application of emerging technologies has resulted in the re-evaluation of assignment briefs beyond essays and dissertations, and the inclusion of appropriate technologies has shaped both formative and summative assessments.

As learning technologists, we believe the future disrupter of technology innovations in education will center around advancements in Artificial Intelligence (AI) (Andriessen and Sandberg, 1999). Staff in the Faculty of Health and Social Sciences at Bournemouth University have procured a license for an AI-generated training video platform. The technology is currently being used to create demonstration scenarios for medical students dealing with distressed patients.

The advantage of this approach is that no real actors are required, removing the need for role-play, which many students find uncomfortable performing. There are also no additional costs or equipment required for creating and editing content. Additionally, the avatars are AI-generated making it easier for the students to remain emotionally detached. This encourages calm discussion, engagement and reflection around dealing with emotive issues. Although evaluations are still ongoing, initial findings indicate that students find this form of interaction extremely constructive and engaging.

Case Study 1.4: Learning Technology Designs for Immersive Discussion

ANTHONY BASIEL AND MIKE HOWARTH

This case study summarizes the development of two models for using online teaching technologies that were investigated before, during and after the COVID-19 period. The first model is a multi-cam desk for tutors working from home. The second model is a 360-degree camera with the tutor and students in the classroom and with other students online. Because of COVID-19, the first model took priority and work began before 2019. Only later in 2020, during the relaxation of the lockdown restrictions, could we start testing the second model. Since this time, we have focused on further developments following a return to a hybrid teaching environment in 2022 in which we use both an online and classroom presence. This approach provides a platform for immersive teaching and formative assessments, which has been made possible due to technological advancement in terms of web video servers and storage capacity.

Description

The first breakthrough came when we started teaching from home during the enforced campus closures during the COVID-19 pandemic. Using an ironing board as a make-shift desk, with my laptop at one end and myself at the other, I unexpectedly discovered that there was a large space visible in front of the wide-angle web camera. Suddenly I had space for creative demonstrations, the use of props for interactive engagement such as a miniature easel for a blackboard, and to prop up an iPad in full view of the students. The result was the development of a new relationship between me and the students called 'classroom proxemics' (Martinez-Maldonado *et al.*, 2020). The distance between us was no longer the usual and disturbing experience of being a disembodied head and shoulders. Also, the wide-angle web camera lens provided a sense of natural depth and perspective, resulting in a significant ease of tension across the class. These are my professional 'trade methods' of media camerawork learned working at University College, London. I published my first attempts at this in collaboration with a practicing tutor who was having to make a video demonstration for the first time (Howarth, 2022).

There are various methods for providing video feedback to students including highlighting subject content and changing academic style. I encourage students to read out sections of their work and answer the inevitable questions, 'Did you really mean to say that?' with a follow-up question of 'How could you change the words around to make your point easier for the reader to understand?' In this way, the session becomes a 'show and tell' experience. After each session I always send the Zoom video recording to the students for their reflection, and to help them to build confidence.

In the autumn of 2021, an inexpensive commercial 'switcher', which is a mini studio linking cameras together, called the Blackmagic ATEM became available. It is designed for home TV production. As a result of this addition, I was now able to move between the following range of technologies to support engagement:

- Input 1: Wide-angle webcam for informal conversation mode;
- Input 2: Wide view-to-student-camera for introductions and conclusions;

- Input 3: Main computer for resources, PowerPoint and other media;
- Input 4: iPad visual screen for student text, sketches, visualization and animation;
- Input 5: Over-the-shoulder point-of-view (POV) perspective of tutor demonstrations.

Together these various inputs provided a range of visual angles, and scenes, to reinforce key points. 'Show not tell' teaching for enhanced student engagement was now achievable from home. Also, the development of soft skills in terms of student involvement in discussions complemented the e-learning techniques used. The potential for using these different viewpoints within our teaching was explored further during 2021–2022 when we started to pilot these blended learning technologies.

Application

We responded to the return to campus and hybrid teaching, i.e., face-to-face lecturing with online streaming, by also considering students staying at home. We tested a live hybrid project during COVID-19 at a local village hall (https://littlehadhamvillagehall.com/). The National Health Service had financed live-streamed women's health sessions using three automatic cameras of the PTZ type (pan, tilt and zoom). The positions, and switching, on such a large scale, needed to be practiced. Cameras were placed in positions that would capture active participation of those present. These were placed just above average head height so that online viewers experienced a sensation of being 'in the room'. Many university cameras in teaching rooms are normally in high positions which can inadvertently create a feeling of isolation from events for the students watching.

We consider that the basic university hybrid classroom can be improved. A tutor can enhance engagement, both for online and face-to-face teaching, using just three cameras and a redesigned standard university podium. One large switcher control box on the podium allows both groups of students to see the five outputs of the resulting multi-cam model. The tutor then selects one scene for the digital projector and streams output simultaneously from the five scenes on the podium monitor. We found that the cameras needed to be carefully positioned. If we imagine a 180° line running diagonally across the room, then cameras must be located on one side of that line, and so must the podium where the tutor stands.

During the COVID-19 pandemic we wanted to provide the opportunity for exploring webinar designs for larger groups of learners in our university, and so undertook a pilot case study for a blended learning webinar design that aimed to foster creativity and innovation. My 360-degree immersive webinar design (https://abasiel.wordpress.com/elearning-r-d/) used a convergence of (1) a 2D digital video camera, (2) a 360-degree AR recording and (3) auxiliary devices such as smartphones, an omni-microphone and voice-to-text transcribed Word Clouds (https://angelastic.com/2020/08/01/audio-word-clouds/).

The pedagogic design underpinning a 360-degree immersive webinar learning experience was based on my view of a Socratic discussion circle. The goal of the Socratic method is to increase student understanding through inquiry, by freeing their desire for understanding which otherwise clings to the false security of their current understanding. Through the deconstruction of existing ideas, the classic style of Socratic discourse liberates people to think about basic principles and ideas resulting in an enhanced sense of both clarity and necessity. According to Maxwell (2019), the Socratic method only requires short answers that address specific points, and the discussion can't move on to more advanced or complicated topics, until an adequate understanding of basic principles has been achieved. I have found the classic Socratic method can be a profoundly useful tool to facilitate improvements in critical thinking, and to elevate the quality of human discourse regarding difficult and controversial issues.

Considering the Socratic method in a digital age begins with the room layout. First, an inner circle of key experts is created surrounded by a circle of face-to-face audience members. The seating therefore changes from a traditional classroom lecture with the 'sage on the stage' in front of rows of passive students. The outer circle is the online audience. The tutor introduces the open-ended problem to solve, or issue to debate, and becomes the discussion facilitator.

Socratic pedagogy is not about asking questions with specific answers in mind. Instead, it is an active engagement in dialog, asking students to think and be creative in their answers, while the instructor remains open to what the students might respond to, or ask about. It is not just about providing feedback on a particular situation or recently completed task, but instead it is about helping students learn to think, and to then apply that learning in the current moment, and to situations in the future.

One advantage of this Socratic discussion model is that it is a transdisciplinary approach to learning. It can be used for a variety of scenarios ranging from healthcare to performing arts. For example, a medical patient can be diagnosed by a circle of professional doctors, or a group of musicians can sit in a circle with instruments to compose songs for a concert. Benner *et al.* (2008, p. 89) argue that "critical reflection requires that the thinker examine the underlying assumptions and radically question or doubt the validity of arguments, assertions, and even facts of the case."

Socratic questioning seeks out and exposes false assumptions and gaps in knowledge. Comparing beliefs and assumptions of webinar participants they can:

> *Learn how to ask questions of other students and of themselves since students learn not merely to follow someone else's lead, but to lead others and to lead themselves in critical analysis.*
>
> (Bloch-Schulman, 2012, p. 15)

The host facilitator prompts the experts to address the questions. Each member of the inner circle can express their position on the topic of discussion. The live and online audiences are moderated by the live facilitator (LV). Online communication is undertaken using text chat which appears on the projector screen for all to see. In the center is a 360-degree AR camera. Additionally, an extra camera captures a standard 2D recording, and can zoom in on the speaker or audience members as needed. Very importantly, the omni-microphone also records all audio which is recorded, transcribed and converted into a dynamic tag cloud text summary. The in-class participants use their smartphone cameras to add their individual perspective of events on the main project screen. This meta-film approach, or film-in-a-film (https://abasiel.wordpress.com/elearn/), enhances this fishbowl design.

We piloted the use of these blended learning technologies with a small cohort of Computing Science User Experience and Interface Design undergraduate students who participated in a simplified version of the 360-degree (https://www.youtube.com/watch?v=ds-ev7kIYcs) immersive webinar design. The goal of the project was to promote collaboration with external partners of Solent University, to conduct a pilot study examining blended learning technologies, and to support peer and self-assessment review using a range of interactive discourse designs.

Our SMART Objectives were:

1. Establish a sound pedagogic design to use a Socratic discussion model in a blended learning model;
2. Develop the use of AR through a 360-degree camera in the middle of an open-ended discussion;
3. Explore the multi-cam model (https://www.mhmvr.co.uk/).

For examples of the Socratic discussion model filmed using the Insta 360 Pro AR camera please visit https://tinyurl.com/Socratic360.

As a pilot study using a small sample group, this investigation provided a sound technical and pedagogic model to promote and support the learning innovations. A survey was undertaken of the small sample group for this pilot study to collect their feedback data in three areas, these being (1) individual factors; (2) socio-technical factors; and (3) pedagogical factors. The feedback was positive and supportive.

> *The opportunity to feel more immersed in the conversation, with the ability to easily move angles, is a quick way to get engaged.*
>
> Anonymous student

> *I can learn to solve open-ended problems.*
>
> Anonymous student

Impact

The research was presented at City University, London's annual education conference (Basiel and Howarth, 2022). The session was our first live lecture theater session since the COVID-19 lockdowns. It became clear to us in a real-life situation that, for the Socratic discussion to work online, two elements needed to be addressed. First, the $180°$ rule had to be applied to the positioning of the cameras. Second, the live facilitator had to position themselves on the correct side of the line and have a multi-cam control desk. In the session, even though the event cameras could not be located at the right height or position, the microphones were superb (Sennheiser, 2022) and they picked up every participant's contribution in the room. I think these devices will be essential for achieving participation in all future lecture theater sessions.

The specialized microphones will solve a weakness of our use of 360-degree recording in a Socratic discussion. It was noted that the recording's poor sound quality made it difficult to focus on what was being discussed. A key takeaway from the session was to test the audio on the Insta 360-degree Pro before recording the event, and to plug in an additional omni-mic to the AR camera to capture clear dialog.

Case Study Conclusion

The aim of our paper was to review the two learning technology models: (1) the multi-cam and (2) the 360-degree immersive webinar design. We plan further case studies to refine the technical set-up for the Socratic discussion model. However, we now know that a merging of the skills of teaching presentation and media presentation can happen if the attitude to the soft skills of personal performance is recognized as being a key aspect of engagement.

A significant advantage identified is from organizing a single output of information and point of view at one time. By using this method, we avoided the problem of an overload of data that disorientates, confuses and overwhelms the VR experience (Mirzakhani *et al.*, 2010). At the time of this writing VR costs are still prohibitive for widespread use. Set-up of VR for large classes can also be time-consuming. However, the future of immersive learning may be about adaptation and application of the multi-cam model, and the 360-degree webinar model, together to provide engaging learning opportunities.

Case Study 1.5: Using Holographic 3D Representations as Teaching Tools

JULIE A. LESSITER AND HELEN CLARE TAYLOR

In 2018, Louisiana State University in Shreveport (LSUS) received seed funding of $250,000 from an energy company so that we could build a hands-on learning center for teaching and research into various aspects of the field of cyber. Spawning out of this seed money, an academic committee worked with a consultant to develop the LSUS Cyber Collaboratory, a new immersive learning space on campus where students, academics and external partners could come together to play with emerging technologies, and develop their applications to support teaching, learning and research.

The Biotechnology Education Laboratory located within this space houses the latest in molecular biology instruments, including Next-Generation Sequencing (NGS) technology, and an Ultra Performance Liquid Chromatography-Mass Spectrometer (UPLC-MS). In this lab, students can participate in research and development activities such as DNA extraction and the identification of micro-organisms based on their DNA sequences. Students learn how to design experiments and handle instrumentations in common use in biotechnology fields.

In addition to the Biotechnology Lab, the Cyber Collaboratory also houses a Data Visualization Lab where students in our Digital Animation program can learn to create motion graphics and digital paintings, and to apply these to design software such as video games. This contiguity of labs has enabled a creative collaboration between these two disciplines, whereby students in Digital Animation help prepare learning materials for students in Biological Sciences to help the latter understand biological systems on a molecular level.

Description

An academic at LSUS found that students in her advanced biology classes, who were preparing for entry into medical or other professional healthcare careers, often struggled to understand basic concepts such as the relationships between cell structure and function at the molecular level. Much of this content must be mastered before students can apply and understand subsequent advanced concepts.

The academic decided that part of their challenge was the requirement for rote memorization, particularly when it came to understanding the essential functions of DNA and proteins, by looking at 2D images in textbooks. What students needed was a way to explore cell structures in 3D, so that they could see the relationships and function of different parts of a cell. In molecular biology, to understand the mechanisms of how relevant proteins interact with the unique double-helical structure of DNA, especially in the context of genetic diseases, students need to see them in full detail.

Holographic technology is different from 2D or 3D technology, in so much that the image appears to be suspended in space and has a sense of depth and realism to it. Done right, the image can be rotated and shown from various angles, thereby giving a 360-degree view of an image opposed to a flat 2D or 3D image. Software is required to create an image in 3D, and then the hologram is created through a laser, a beam-splitter and a photo-sensitive medium. To view a hologram, a projector, a dark room, and specially designed glasses are needed, as well as software through which the image can be displayed. The price of equipment remains high enough that teaching a class of more than five students can be prohibitive, and there are only a few educational suppliers at the time of writing.

The major challenge when teaching through immersive learning is currently the lack of readily available high-quality open-source content to utilize within the classroom setting. If the content is available, it is usually not created by an expert in the field of study, and so needs additional customization to be appropriate for the level and context of a classroom of students. This can be an expensive and time-consuming endeavor and so is prohibitive when teaching niche science concepts and processes. Although we know students are more engaged when they are able to learn-by-doing, the challenge for the academic is to bring the benefits of immersive learning to the students, while keeping the learning environment affordable.

With a collaborative approach to solving the problem, the science academics and the digital arts academics worked together to ensure that a potential solution could be constructed. The digital arts academics have consistently worked with students on their program to develop capstone course portfolios. Thanks to the growth in motion graphics, as well as VR and AR platforms, talented students in these areas were seeking projects to apply to their capstone course. The academics considered this need, and developed an internship course, so that any senior-level digital arts student could earn credit for working on approved projects with various industry and agency partners.

In one of these internship partnerships, students on the Bachelor of Digital Arts program employed their expertise in software, such as Autodesk Maya and Sketchfab, within the Visualization Lab, to produce appropriate holographic images designed and modified from flat textbook images. Students on the Biology program utilized molecular modeling tools, such as PyMOL, a user-sponsored molecular visualization system on an open-source foundation, as well as databases such as the Protein Data Bank at RCSB.org. Students on the Digital Animation program engaged in project-based learning to apply the technologies of video-game design to refine these holographic images, thereby producing enhanced visualizations and holographic models that could be used to teach cell and molecular biology.

In a continuous feedback loop, the academic and the students on both programs worked together to refine the images so that the nuances of depth and complexity were improved. The problem of customized content for teaching various STEM (Science, Technology, Engineering and Maths) concepts was solved, and the digital arts students were able to graduate from their degree with a portfolio demonstrating how their skills had added value to an industry, in this case teaching.

The academic's students, in turn, could use these images to produce assessment case studies in which the task is to produce a PowerPoint presentation to show pathways and relationships that the students can construct by picking the appropriate images, and showing how they fit together.

Application

The holographic images were enhanced using color and size differentials so that they could be manipulated out of scale for biology students to enable them to understand how the parts of a cell fit together, and how they function both separately and as a whole. The visualizations worked like a puzzle, and students could remove sections to examine relationships, and could then layer the images to understand the complex topics in biology, such as cell signaling pathways. Thus, our students were learning cell biology in a similar pedagogical way to pre-school children being taught about objects using manipulation to understand function. Students could magnify, zoom in and explore the cells until they had mastered the nuances of the structure. This kind of learning is immediate and memorable, offering dynamic hands-on exploration to help students not only comprehend the complexity and relationships of cellular and molecular components within an organism, but to enable them to remember sequences and structures because they have, as it were, traveled through them in a virtual world.

In a further development, the Digital Animation students created 3D printed models of molecular structures and then created holographic images from these. The academic found that these holograms, taken from 3D printed models made in-house, were even more successful in helping students understand the structure and functions of cells. Being able to touch, rotate, dismantle and examine the structure of a cell, compared to just seeing a visual 2D version in a textbook, proved to be pedagogically important, especially when you consider that the majority of students sitting in our classrooms today grew up in a graphically rich environment. In today's Higher Education, there is now an expectation from the learner that concepts can, and will, be explained beyond a traditional textbook and the concept of media-based learning is familiar to them. Immersive learning through video games therefore builds upon students' existing knowledge and experiences.

Impact

The academic surveyed her students about their learning gain using holographic technology, and the majority consistently reported that this active and immersive technique had improved their understanding, and recall, of the content being taught. She has reported higher correct response rates on pre- and post-tests that cover material taught using these holographic visualizations.

Because the manipulation of the holograms is similar to techniques they may have used in videogaming, students reported a comfort level, and ease of use, with the technology, as well as an actual enjoyment of the learning process because it felt to them like a form of entertainment. Students also reported that this form of learning conveys a sense of relevance. The academic did also report that this aspect also had a negative effect for a few students. A small number of students experienced visual issues, and headaches, when they first used the 3D visualizations, and due to this factor, some had to be provided with alternate assignments.

This use of holographic imagery not only helped the learning of biology students. In addition, the Digital Animation students learned to solve problems in a project-based exercise that provided them with a real-world application of their skills in digital illustration and sculpting. They could also see in real time how what they were learning in the classroom could have a direct and significant impact in medical and scientific fields.

Case Study Conclusion

The needs and expectations of the students in our classrooms have changed radically over the past 20 years due to advances in technology, yet our teaching methods have not evolved at the same pace. As a profession, we are slowly integrating more immersive learning into our pedagogy, but there is no rapid adoption in this area as many staff are challenged with either how to utilize the technologies, and/or how to use it to support their teaching. Students of this current generation seek multiple different tools, from which to learn difficult concepts, and supplementing traditional textbooks with graphic imagery is a valuable way to bring learning to life.

As we can see from this case study, students showed positive learning gains from the use of this tool that provided them with an immersive learning environment, yet it was not without problems. Not every student could participate with this technology due to the visual cues causing vertigo and/or motion sickness. As the technology and graphics improve, this issue will reportedly be reduced, but widespread utilization today would alienate students with these visual issues. Additionally, the lack of quality content readily available to academics can create a level of disengagement if the concept, or model, that is needed for a particular lesson is not easily accessible.

Although holographic technology can improve a student's ability to understand a complex process or model, there is still a fundamental problem with the quantity, quality and specificity of the content. Additionally, there is the cost of the purchase of appropriate content and/or image creation. As this technology evolves, it is thought that the number of applications, particularly in the sciences, will become more widespread, thereby driving down costs, and increasing the availability of open-source content.

As with any pedagogical shift, adoption into mainstream teaching and learning will take time, but as we have seen with the evolution of technology in the classroom, it does eventually catch up, and it is clear that holographic technology can provide students with an additional, and perhaps more engaging, method of learning.

Case Study 1.6: Using Immersive Technologies for Professional Practice Learning

LIZ BERRAGAN AND SIMON KERSEY

Simulation and immersive technologies are revolutionizing health and social care education. This change is embraced by UK and global professional, statutory and regulatory bodies (Health Education England, 2020; Health and Care Professions Council, 2021), which reflects the growth in popularity across all sectors and disciplines (Nursing and Midwifery Council, 2023; Social Work England, 2022), as it offers dynamic and contemporary ways for supporting and engaging learners.

The development and use of VR products, to provide immersive learning experiences to support workforce needs, are highlighted as a key work stream within the National Strategic Vision for simulation and immersive technologies in health and social care (Health Education England, 2020). Three hundred sixty-degree video is also increasingly being utilized within health and social care simulation communities (Meese *et al.*, 2021), often being filmed from a static 360-degree camera by simulation academics. This approach may provide a degree of immersion, however such video prohibits any interaction by the viewer.

Virtual Tour software, such as 3DVista Pro (3Dvista.com), may provide an immersive 360-degree experience while facilitating interaction and learning via hotspots, tasks, 3D scans and other links embedded within a scene. This approach is intended to allow the students to control their learning journey and familiarize themselves with the scene at their own pace. This technology may help students to prepare for their practice placements more effectively by virtually placing them in that environment before ever setting foot off campus.

Our work in this area focused upon developing this technology to assist social work students to prepare for practice (Social Work England, 2022), creating a scalable and flexible examination for end-point assessment based on an interaction with a service user, in the practice environment.

This case study describes the student and academic experience of developing and using the VR360 technology. We will explore the experience of social work students, academics and simulation academics in developing, and delivering, learning and assessment through immersive technology. A brief analysis of our use of immersive technology will offer a means of identifying the impact of our work, and of highlighting new and innovative possibilities for professional practice learning. Finally, we will examine the outcomes and impact of simulation and immersive technology and will consider what this might mean for health and social care education, and for wider professional practice learning across Higher Education.

Description

Virtual and Augmented Reality technologies have been increasingly utilized within Health and Social Care education (Blair *et al.*, 2021; Huttar and BrintzenhofeSzoc, 2020). However, they often require the use of costly equipment, for example VR headsets, and sometimes specialist programming knowledge to design and build them. For example, knowledge of Unity or Unreal 5 game engine is often helpful. Such costs are often offset by the developers through expensive licensing agreements for the end user.

The 3DVista Pro software allows the creation of interactive 360-degree virtual tours across many platforms, and can be accessed via personal computers, mobile devices and/or VR headsets. This application has been used within industries as diverse as construction, engineering, fashion and finance, to demonstrate and advertise specific products and places. 3DVista is fully customizable to include "360-degree panoramas and videos, along with hotspots which allow embedded sounds, videos and photos" (3DVista.com).

The software creators encourage users to tell stories that employ multi-functional hotspots, and clickable objects, that the user can discover and engage with when walking through the tour. These hot spots can be introduced at separate times through the scenario, or they can be hidden and then introduced into the environment later, either within a given time, or once a particular task has been accomplished.

Users can explore the simulation at their own pace and decide upon their own information-gathering priorities, and where they want to focus their attention at any point. This is important for learning about the complex and fast-moving health and social care environment.

The 3DVista Pro virtual tour software provides a platform which seeks to enhance the quality of education in health and social work (3DVista.com). It has the potential to create realistic, safe and flexible learning environments, and thus offers a supportive and student-centered approach for students to have meaningful engagement with the complexities of health and social care, and specifically for this case study, social work practice.

The social work course team wanted to create and deliver student assessment and examination that was engaging, authentic and reflective of practice. They were keen to enable students to hear the service user's story and interact with, and understand, the service user's context and environment. The challenges of assessment for social work students in the practice setting have been long rehearsed (Brookfield, 1998; Caffrey and Fruin, 2019).

The complexities of the health and social care practice setting can often be at odds with the requirements for high-stakes student assessments, resulting in a misalignment between assessment activities and professional roles and practices (Ajjawi *et al.*, 2020). Given these challenges, it was envisaged that an interactive immersive environment would enable a multidimensional approach, while also offering authentic and realistic contexts for assessment activities (Huttar and BrintzenhofeSzoc, 2020).

The 3DVista Pro virtual tour software was used to create scenarios that would prepare and assess undergraduate students for the end-point assessment on their social work apprenticeship degree program. Scenarios were designed to draw out knowledge and understanding of course content, and readiness for practice, including critical application of policy and the law, human development, decision-making and professional judgment and ethical care. These scenarios were co-constructed by academics, practitioners and learning technologists, guided by students' feedback from previous cohorts. Scenarios were used as formative preparation for students, enabling students to feedback on their experience of using the technology, and of engaging with the scenarios.

Detailed instructions were provided for students to support familiarization. These instructions explained how the scenario exercise would unfold during the end-point assessment examination. Designed to be taken in-class, with the same timings as the final end-point examination, students were able to engage with untimed practice scenarios to trial navigation of the software, and self-timing through the scenario thus supporting formative preparation for their summative assessment.

While video had previously been used within the curriculum, 3DVista Pro moved a step closer to real-life practice experience including documents, and visual cues, to draw out professional practice knowledge and understanding.

Impact

The impact, benefits and lessons learned in the use of 3DVista Pro were manifold for students and for academic staff. 3DVista Pro provided immersive virtual environments that mimicked real-life social work cases. The software simulated a wide range of scenarios, from client interviews and assessments to crisis interventions, enabling students to consider and be prepared for a variety of situations and contexts that they had encountered, or would encounter, in the field of social work practice (Huttar and BrintzenhofeSzoc, 2020). Working through the scenarios provided heightened realism for learning, fostered experiential learning and facilitated opportunities for students to demonstrate their competence and capability in professional practice skills (Lanzieri *et al.*, 2021), and their empathy for their clients (Rambaree *et al.*, 2023).

The practice of social work often involves sensitive and emotionally charged situations. 3DVista Pro provided a safe space for students to demonstrate their skills without real-world consequences (Bailey-McHale *et al.*, 2019). While this was an examination and end-point assessment for the course, prior formative experience gained through immersion in the scenarios helped establish familiarity with the technology, thereby enabling students to subsequently demonstrate their enhanced levels of professional confidence, and capabilities, in their subsequent examination performance (Berragan, 2014; Minguela-Recover *et al.*, 2022).

Students could access the virtual simulations at their own pace, making this an agile and responsive tool for self-directed learning, formative assessment and familiarization with the examination. This experience provided excellent opportunities for enhancing learning through self-assessment (Boud, 2016) and preparation for high-stakes assessment (Health Education England, 2020). 3DVista Pro accommodated diverse learning approaches, and schedules, enabling students to engage with learning that encouraged self-awareness and self-efficacy. These virtual simulations also reduced the need for physical props, locations or human actors for role-playing, offering a cost-effective and efficient learning approach.

In health and social care, interdisciplinary collaboration is an essential feature of all curricula. Furthermore, these virtual simulations had the potential to include a wider range of healthcare professionals, creating opportunities for enhanced collaboration and teamwork. Opportunities for referral to other health and care services were of value in the various scenarios used by social work students.

For academics, the ability to track students' performance, and provide feedback in real time, facilitated improved learning outcomes. Assessments within the virtual environment were helpful to measuring each student's competence and readiness for social work practice. Improvements in assessment grades of up to 20% were recorded, particularly for students who had previously struggled with written assignment work. Additionally, student engagement was improved for most students.

The 3DVista Pro software allowed for data collection, enabling academics to analyze students' performance and results. This supported students' feedback and enabled academics to modify, and continuously improve, their social work program based on the performance of, and interactions with, students.

While we have indicated that there were some impressive benefits in the use of 3DVista Pro, and significant improvements to student performance, it is important to also highlight lessons learned from this experience.

The initial set-up and design involved a team of academics and learning technology staff. Clarity was key here as the social work team drew upon extensive practice experience to define the requirement for non-social work colleagues. Consideration of the hosting platform was also important, requiring excellent accessibility. Use of the university VLE provided some initial challenges. Stress-testing of the system ensured that multiple users could have a high-quality experience. Once achieved, this was seen as a strength of the system noting that, for some VR systems, headsets are a requirement which can limit availability and accessibility.

There were additional accessibility challenges which included keeping the assessment confidential ahead of the exam. The design needed to ensure that the scenario could be released at an appropriate time, and specific information could be released as students progressed. This was resolved through communication and collaboration within the design team.

Induction to the use of VR for students, and academics, was important, and opportunities and planned time for familiarization needed to be considered. This included awareness of any additional requirements for students to ensure an inclusive experience. Student feedback, and user experience, was particularly important, and resulted in the modification of scenarios to ensure that navigation through the scenarios and instructions for assessment activities were clear for everyone.

While this was very much a collaborative and co-constructed development involving students, academics, social work partners and learning technologists, there is always more that can be done. It is our intention to seek further and future service user, student and practitioner perspectives, to assure and support further adaptation and development for an authentic and realistic experience.

Case Study Conclusion

This case study has explored the use of 3DVista Pro virtual tour software, and its potential to provide a powerful platform to enhance the quality of education in health and social work. We have highlighted its capacity to create realistic, safe and flexible learning environments which prepare students for the complex challenges of the social work profession.

In the ever-evolving landscape of Higher Education, innovation is the key to unlocking new and engaging learning opportunities for students. Use of 3DVista Pro is one such innovation that could deliver a profound impact for health and social care education. Professional practice learning must be engaging and offer an authentic and immersive experience. Our experience of using 3DVista Pro offers some evidence toward this. Future research and evaluation of this, and similar software, as part of education innovation across the professions, will determine its future relevance. With hotspots, tasks, 3D scans and embedded links, learners gained unprecedented control over their educational journey, stepping into the shoes of real-world practitioners, and seeing scenarios through their eyes.

The impact for our social work students was tangible. Student performance and engagement showed marked improvement. The key lessons learned in this journey include the significance of clarity in set-up, accessibility considerations and the need for rigorous system stress-testing.

There is considerable potential for use in formative and summative assessment activities. Social work students face a unique challenge, i.e., they need to be prepared for real-world practice which involves situations which are complex and sensitive. 3DVista Pro assisted us in crafting authentic student assessments and examinations. While not immediate real-life experiences, scenarios were co-constructed in partnership with academics, practitioners, service users and learning technologists, all so were each shaped by prior real-life experiences. The software offered a virtual environment that mirrored realistic social work cases as much as possible, offering a safe space for students to hone their skills, and demonstrate capability and competence without the fear of consequences. This experience has therefore highlighted the potential for this, and similar software, to offer an authentic and immersive future for assessment and learning.

References

Ajjawi, R., Taia, J., Le Huu Nghia, T., Boud, D., Johnson, L. and Patrick, C., 2020. Aligning assessment with the needs of work-integrated learning: The challenges of authentic assessment in a complex context. *Assessment and Evaluation in Higher Education*, 45(2), 304–316.

Andriessen, J. and Sandberg, J., 1999. Where is education heading and how about AI? *Artificial Intelligence in Education*, 10, 130–150.

Armstrong, E., 2019. Maximising motivators for technology-enhanced learning for further education teachers: Moving beyond the early adopters in a time of austerity. *Research in Learning Technology*, 27, 1–23.

Bailey-McHale, J., Bailey-McHale, R., Caffrey, B., MacLean, S. and Ridgeway, V., 2019. Using visual methodology: Social work student's perceptions of practice and the impact on practice educators. *Practice*, 31(1), 57–74.

Basiel, A. and Howarth, M., 2022. Session 3D | Paper 1 – Immersive Web Video for Learning Engagement – Post COVID. *12th Learning at City Conference: Opportunities to Transform the Future of Higher Education*. City University, London. 29th June 2022.

Benner, P., Hughes, R. and Sutphen, M., 2008. Clinical reasoning, decision making, and action: Thinking critically and clinically. *In*: Hughes, R. (ed.), *Patient Safety and Quality: An Evidence-Based Handbook for Nurses*. Rockville, MD: Agency for Health Research and Quality Available from: https://www.ncbi.nlm.nih.gov/books/NBK2643/

Berragan, E., 2014. Learning nursing through simulation: A case study approach towards an expansive model of learning. *Nurse Education Today*, 34(8), 1143–1148.

Blair, C., Walsh, C. and Best, P., 2021. Immersive 360° videos in health and social care education: A scoping review. *BMC Medical Education*, 21(590), 1–28.

Bloch-Schulman, S., 2012. The Socratic Method: Teaching and writing about philosophy's signature pedagogy. *In*: Chick, N., Haynie, A., Gurung, R. and Regan, A. (eds.), *Exploring More Signature Pedagogies: Approaches to Teaching Disciplinary Habits of Mind*. Sterling, VA: Stylus, 15–26

Boud, D., 2016. *Enhancing Learning Through Self-Assessment*. Abingdon: Routledge.

Boyle, A., Maguire, S., Martin, A., Milsom, C., Nash, R., Rawlinson, S., Turner, A., Wurthmann, S. and Conchie, S., 2007. Fieldwork is good: The student perception and the affective domain. *Journal of Geography in Higher Education*, 31(2), 299–317.

Brookfield, S., 1998. Critically reflective practice. *Continuing Education in the Health Professions*, 18(4), 197–205.

Caffrey, B. and Fruin, H., 2019. An exploration of issues affecting the assessment of social work students on practice placement in England. *Practice Teaching and Learning*, 16(1–2), 68–82.

Chiarella, D. and Vurro, G., 2020. *Fieldwork and Disability: An Overview for an Inclusive Experience*. Cambridge: Cambridge University Press.

Das, D. and Chatterjea, K., 2018. Learning in the field—A conceptual approach to field-based learning in geography. *In*: Chang, C., Wu, B., Seow, T. and Irvine, K. (eds.), *Learning Geography Beyond the Traditional Classroom*. Singapore: Springer, 11–33.

Emin, V. and Ney, M., 2013. Supporting teachers in the process of adoption of game based learning pedagogy. *ECGBL Conference 2013*, ACPI, Porto, Portugal, October 2013.

Gold, J., Jenkins, A., Lee, R., Monk, J., Riley, J., Shepherd, I. and Unwin, D., 1991. *Teaching Geography in Higher Education. A Manual of Good Practice*. Oxford: Blackwell.

Health and Care Professions Council, 2021. *Using Simulation to Support Practice-Based Learning*. London: Health and Care Professions Council.

Health Education England, 2020. *Enhancing Education, Clinical Practice and Staff Wellbeing. A National Vision for the Role of Simulation and Immersive Learning Technologies in Health and Care Technology Enhanced Learning (TEL)*. London: Health Education England.

Henderson, M., Selwyn, N. and Aston, R., 2015. What works and why? Student perceptions of 'useful' digital technology in university teaching and learning. *Studies in Higher Education*, 42(8), 1567–1579.

Hockings, C., Brett, P. and Terentjevs, M., 2012. Making a difference—Inclusive learning and teaching in higher education through open educational resources. *Distance Education*, 33(2), 237–252.

Hoolohan, C., McLachlan, C., Jones, C., Larkin, A., Birch, C., Mander, S. and Broderick, J., 2021. Responding to the climate emergency: How are UK universities establishing sustainable workplace routines for flying and food? *Climate Policy*, 21(7), 1–15.

Howarth, M., 2022. Becoming a learning magician: An alternative to head to head online teaching. *In*: Dattolla, A. (ed.), *Remote Learning Practices for Early Childhood and Elementary School Classrooms*. Hershey: IGI Global, 39–64.

Hurst, S., 1998. Use of 'virtual' field trips in teaching introductory geology. *Computers and Geosciences*, 24(7), 653–658.

Huttar, C. and BrintzenhofeSzoc, K., 2020. Virtual reality and computer simulation in social work education: A systematic review. *Social Work Education*, 56(1), 131–141.

King, D., Tee, S., Falconer, F., Angell, C., Holley, D. and Mills, A., 2018. Virtual health education: Scaling practice to transform student learning: Using virtual reality learning environments in healthcare education to bridge the theory/practice gap and improve patient safety. *Nurse Education Today*, 71, 7–9.

Lanzieri, N., McAlpin, E., Shilane, D. and Samelson, H., 2021. Virtual reality: An immersive tool for social work students to interact with community environments. *Clinical Social Work*, 49(2), 207–219.

Leyland, J., Geoghegan, H., Hall, S., Latham, A. and Souch, C., 2022. Classics revisited: 'Muddy glee' – What geography fieldwork means in the current moment. *Area*, 54(4), 522–524.

Martinez-Maldonado, R., Schulte, J., Echeverria, V., Gopalan, Y. and Buckingham Shum, S., 2020. Where is the teacher? Digital analytics for classroom proxemics. *Computer Assisted Learning*, 36(5), 741–762.

Maxwell, M., 2019. *Introduction to the Socratic Method and its Effect on Critical Thinking*, http://www.socraticmethod.net/about.htm

McDougall, D., 2019. VR glaciers and glaciated landscapes. *Geography*, 104(3), 148–153.

Meese, M., O'Hagan, E. and Chang, T., 2021. Healthcare provider stress and virtual reality simulation: A scoping review. *Simulation in Healthcare: The Journal of the Society for Simulation in Healthcare*, 16(4), 268–274.

Mercer, T., Kythreotis, A., Harwood, J., Robinson, Z., George, S., Sands, D., Brown, J. and Sims, T., 2022. The benefits of virtual fieldtrips for future-proofing geography teaching and learning. *Geography in Higher Education*, 47(2), 330–338.

Minguela-Recover, M., Munuera, P., Baena-Perez, R. and Mota-Macias, J., 2022. The role of 360° virtual reality in social intervention: A further contribution to the theory-practice relationship of social work studies. *Social Work Education*, 43(1), 203–223.

Mirzakhani M., Ashrafzadeh H. and Ashrafzadeh A., 2010. The virtual university: Advantages and disadvantages. *4th International Conference on Distance Learning and Education*, 3–5 October 2010, San Juan, USA.

Nursing and Midwifery Council, 2023. *Simulated Practice Learning*. London: Nursing and Midwifery Council.

Petterson, R., Burmeister, K., Atchison, C., Skinner, S., Dean Jones, A., Finley, J and Chin, D., 2021. *Virtual Field Trips as a Tool for Reducing Anxieties and Refocusing Cognitive Loads During In-Person Field Activities*. Washington: American Geophysical Union.

Pringle, J., 2013. Educational environmental geoscience e-gaming to provide stimulating and effective learning. *Planet*, 27(1), 21–28.

Quality Assurance Agency (QAA), 2022. *Subject Benchmark Statement, Earth sciences, Environmental Sciences and Environmental Studies*. Gloucester: QAA.

Rambaree K., Nässén N., Holmberg J. and Fransson G., 2023. Enhancing cultural empathy in international social work education through virtual reality. *Education Sciences*, 13(5), 507.

Rogers, P., 2000. Barriers to adopting emerging technologies in education. *Educational Computing Research*, 22(4), 455–472.

Sennheiser, 2022. *Ceiling Microphone. The Teamconnect Ceiling 2*. Article No. 509161. Wedemark, Germany: Sennheiser

Social Work England, 2022. *Guidance on Practice Placements*. Sheffield: Social Work England.

Stainfield, J., Fisher, P., Ford, B. and Solem, M., 2000. International virtual field trips: A new direction? *Geography in Higher Education*, 24(2), 255–262.

Sternberg, R. and Zhang, L., 2001. *Perspectives on Thinking, Learning, and Cognitive Styles*, 1st edition. Abingdon: Routledge.

Taylor, S. and Hsueh, Y., 2005. Implementing a constructivist approach in Higher Education through technology. *Early Childhood Teacher Education*, 26(2), 127–132.

Whitton, N. and Moseley, A., 2012. *Using Games to Enhance Learning and Teaching: A Beginner's Guide*, 1st edition. Abingdon: Routledge.

Innovative Applications of Technology to Support Online Teaching

2

The following five case studies describe innovative applications of digital technologies to support online and blended teaching. Each case study presents the personal perspectives of those involved.

Case Study 2.1: Applying Active Digital Education for the Design of Online Learning

HELEN CALDWELL, DAVID MEECHAN AND EMMA WHEWELL

Active Digital Education (ADE) places a strong emphasis on 'learning by doing' in a digital environment. Learners actively engage with content, make sense of ideas, represent them explicitly and build knowledge through dialog. The approach outlined in this case study also draws upon the Universal Design for Learning (UDL) framework, as defined by CAST (2018), for making ADE inclusive. It demonstrates how the digital environment can add pace, collaboration and engagement to online learning, with a focus on supporting English as an Additional Language (EAL) students.

Previous thinkers have paved the way for the concept that learners actively build knowledge by assimilating new ideas into their existing understanding. Vygotsky's (1978) insights into the links between social interaction and

DOI: 10.4324/9781032635248-3

learning, along with Wenger's (1998) concept of communities of practice, provide a robust foundation for the use of digitally supported online learning communities. Papert and Harel's (1991) constructionist theories further accentuate the role of digital environments in fostering meaningful knowledge construction. Similarly, connectivist models acknowledge the social context as a fertile ground for learning and underscore the interconnectedness of the virtual and physical worlds (Siemens, 2017).

ADE is therefore rooted in contemporary learning theories such as constructivism, constructionism and connectivism. It emphasizes the active role of learners in constructing knowledge through technology-enabled exchanges and social interactions. In many instances, learners interact with content dynamically, generating shareable products for others to engage with.

The ADE examples we explore in this case study exemplify how engaged communities of learners can drive the re-discussion and re-mixing of content. We look at how the affordances of a learning management system, combined with online collaborative spaces and live documents, can provide a structured yet flexible environment for online learning, by adding pace, and varying methods of engagement. In line with UDL (CAST, 2018) we highlight the importance of providing multiple avenues for students to engage with, represent and act upon their learning. This is of relevance to EAL students who are learning how to learn in an additional language and may also be learning about a different culture. The case study looks at how to structure online sessions to facilitate experiences that happen naturally in an in-person environment and considers the advantages of providing session content in advance. Our conclusion highlights the lessons learned from applying ADE and UDL principles, to create inclusive and engaging online learning environments that enable students to become active co-creators, who expand the original session content through their shared online experiences.

Description

NILE is the University of Northampton's digital campus. It is a collection of online tools provided to support teaching, learning and assessment. NILE is built on the Learning Management System (LMS) Blackboard Learn and it acts as a one-stop shop for students in terms of the information they need access to progress in their studies. Students are enrolled on various module sites within NILE that together form their program of study. Each module site will contain uniform information specific to that module:

- *About Your Module* contains learning outcomes, session schedule, teaching team contacts and a reading list;
- *Module Assessment and Submission* contains assessment information, assignment briefs and assessment submission points;
- *Week by Week* content folders contain learning outcomes for the session, a question to think about before the session, in-session content, in-session tasks and post-session tasks.

Ensuring consistency of format between module sites aims to minimize the cognitive load needed for students with EAL to navigate and retrieve the required information provided on NILE. Creating such familiarity aids in developing the confidence of a student with EAL so that they are able to engage in independent learning and asynchronous tasks.

NILE also hosts Blackboard Collaborate, which is the virtual classroom within which online synchronous sessions can be delivered. Using Blackboard Collaborate consistently aids in developing familiarity with the platform's functions and the expectations of students when engaging with it. Students are introduced to attendee functions which provide multiple options for interaction within the virtual classroom. For example, students can use the 'raise hand' function to get the lecturer's attention, use their microphone to speak or use the chat function to type. Within Blackboard Collaborate, there are also different functions the lecturer can use to support online activities. For example, there is a whiteboard function that students can contribute to anonymously and there is a breakout room function that allows for smaller group interactions.

In addition, the virtual classroom allows for links to external tools. Ensuring consistency across a program in terms of the external tools that are used enables students to develop familiarity with the tool itself, and with the expectations around its use. Padlet and Miro are examples of external tools that can be used to promote collaborative learning. This is important for online students as a visual aid that allows for content depository relating to tasks set in sessions. Online collaboration spaces such as Padlet and Miro encourage the recording of information through text and images, which can then aid a student with EAL when providing feedback to their group or cohort.

Application

NILE presents a structured, but flexible, learning environment that enables students to engage through asynchronous and synchronous activities. The

Week by Week content folders provide a structured learning pathway for students. The inclusion of a *Question to Think About* provides students with a direct indicator of the content that will be covered in the session. Providing such information and insight, prior to a session, allows for students with EAL to prepare and research the upcoming session. By having this structure each week, students with EAL become familiarized with the approach, and can spend more time exploring and understanding the content.

The virtual classroom also provides some familiarity for students with EAL more used to previous learning environments. For example, the *raise-hand* and *breakout room* functions allow for group activities and discussions to take place in an orderly manner, replicating a common approach in traditional face-to-face environments. Informal opportunities for peers to become familiar with one another in an online environment are less common as groups do not have the opportunities for small talk before and after sessions, or between tasks. Allowing students to work in the same breakout groups for several sessions aims to increase students' familiarity with each other. Further structuring of feedback for students with EAL from group activities ensures that all students are being encouraged to speak English. For example, each week a different student feeds back to the rest of the cohort on behalf of the breakout group. This structures the expectations, and supports the development of teamwork, through familiarity.

The use of external tools, such as Padlet and Miro, supports further collaboration and co-construction among students with EAL. Working in familiar groups, breakout tasks encourage students to cooperate and produce responses in the tools via text, images, audio and video. For example, a Miro board was used to capture and facilitate students' understanding in relation to the prompt of what 'good teaching' was by drawing on examples from their own experience, and beliefs, and making links to relevant literature. Within Miro, each group was assigned a space to map out and discuss their responses. When the task was completed, each group presented to the whole cohort to discuss their journey in relation to the prompt, and the sharing of links to relevant literature. This Miro board further served as a resource for all students in the group as they all then had access to each other's mapping and response exercises. The curation and collation of such a resource, in a collective and intuitive way, is an advantage of using Miro.

Using the same breakout groups for several sessions, and hosting activities on Miro or Padlet within the virtual classroom, promotes a sense of community that would not be established if students always worked in random breakout groups without the requirement to produce and feedback. The shared collectivism and ownership over what they produce, and the feedback then received, serves to further enhance the co-creation process and make learning more engaging and effective. The visual and interactive nature of these combined tools minimizes language barriers and supports understanding.

Impact

The integration of the NILE learning platform and associated external tools has bolstered the process of co-creation among students. Using the defining principles of play (Play England, 2020) our learning activities have supported learners' agency, facilitated social interaction and allowed new skills to develop. Central to this enhancement has been the facilitation of collaborative learning experiences through the consistent use of breakout groups, and the employment of online collaborative spaces such as Padlet and Miro. Such tools have provided a rich environment for co-creation, and have enabled students to collaborate, share ideas and construct knowledge reciprocally. As this becomes the familiar approach when teaching students with EAL, it encourages routine and habit when learning.

Case Study Conclusion

This case study has introduced the concept of ADE. We have explored some theoretical foundations, and provided examples of how ADE can be applied in practice to enhance learning, with an emphasis on supporting EAL students.

The examples demonstrate ADE values and the benefits of experiential learning in a digital environment. By engaging with metacognition, and sharing ideas together, learners have been supported to make sense of the knowledge and tasks presented. This collaborative and constructivist approach to tasks builds collective knowledge, and supports learning behaviors. Collective knowledge building is a powerful tool for building agency and valuing the student voice.

ADE facilitates rhizomatic learning, which evolves as the learners interact, respond, build and share their learning in an evolutionary way. Dialog is central to effective ADE teaching and learning practices. By sharing, constructing and exchanging knowledge through technology-enabled activities, EAL learners can develop not only their understanding, but also their confidence to engage. Tutor-mediated breakout groups enable EAL learners to develop language skills, develop specialist terminology and build vocabulary. Multimodal ways of engaging, actioning and representing understanding, in line with the UDL philosophy (CAST, 2018), provide learners with the autonomy to choose how, and when, they interact and respond.

There is much to learn from our work with EAL students that can be applied in other online settings. The interplay between learners and tutors in facilitating engagement, gradually building autonomy, modeling effective learning behaviors and embedding cultural norms is vital in an online space that seeks to support learners to feel safe and engaged. Future practices, both online and offline, can utilize digital collaboration tools to facilitate knowledge construction, and offer means to represent learning as digital artifacts that can support independent study.

This case study recommends that, when planning or reflecting on ADE activities for EAL learners in a digital environment, we should consider the following:

- Value the process as well as the product, i.e., place an emphasis on an active, dialog-rich and creative learning environment that values collective knowledge building;
- Embrace technologies that offer EAL learners a multimodal means of responding to tasks that are inclusive;
- Promote effective learning habits for EAL learners that are rooted in low-stakes and enjoyable activities that build confidence and agency.

Case Study 2.2: Microsoft Teams as a Tool for Student Empowerment and Engagement

STERLING RAUSEO AND RALUCA MARINCIU

The COVID-19 pandemic caused widespread disruption across Higher Education delivery in the UK, and the world, and encouraged innovation (Zhang *et al.*, 2022). In the scramble that resulted from social distancing rules, Higher Education was forced behind screens, to deliver what was previously an intimate personal interaction between student and tutor. Online technologies, such as Microsoft Teams, became the only medium for student-tutor interaction. In the face of such a potentially distancing medium, Higher Education was very concerned about how this might affect engagement between the tutors and students, students' own feelings of belongingness to the institution and ultimately student success (Sobaih *et al.*, 2021). For a UK post-1992 Higher Education institution, there were trials of strategies that sought to increase tutor-student contact. These included combining the roles of dissertation supervisor with personal tutor, and encouraging personal tutors to use the ease of contact offered by Microsoft Teams to increase their outreach to their tutees (Mealey, 2022). The reflections that follow are from two academics, one using Microsoft Teams to deliver the dissertation supervisor role, and the other employing Microsoft Teams to deliver personal tutoring.

My supervision role incorporated all the personal tutoring activities defined by Lochtie *et al.* (2018, pp. 13–14):

> academic feedback and support, personal welfare support, referral to further information and support, embodiment and representative of the university, information about Higher Education processes, procedures and expectations, engendering a sense of belonging, goal/target setting and monitoring of achievements, and solution-focused coaching.

With the combination of dissertation supervision and personal tutoring, some of these activities, for example welfare support, monitoring of achievements and coaching, increased in intensity and regularity. Microsoft Teams eliminated the need to travel to physical meetings and so enabled more conversations. Some students increasingly initiated conversations rather than the other way around, which had previously been the norm. This reduced the pressure on me as the dissertation tutor to be constantly chasing students, and allowed them to take more ownership of their own progress in the dissertation process. The regularity and ease of having meetings also generated stronger and deeper bonds. Students were able to share more well-being issues and concerns, which often were affecting their engagement with delivering the dissertation tasks, and other academic work. It is at this point that solution-focused coaching was employed to assist students in time management, goal setting and goal differentiation. Another benefit of the Microsoft Teams dissertation meetings was that we met our students in areas where their lives took them. The flexibility of Microsoft Teams, combined with the need for several of our students to work in employment to fund their studies, often in gig work, meant that meetings were held in their vehicles during their rest breaks. Students could use the flexibility of Microsoft Teams to engage with their learning.

However, the experiences and impact of these delivery strategies did not always produce results and came with a strain on my time and well-being. For students not engaged, the ease of accessibility of Microsoft Teams was seen as a license to cancel meetings or just not turn up. In several instances, when students apologized for missed meetings, they would sometimes indicate that since the meeting was online and not physical, i.e., not requiring me to travel to a room, they felt it would not be a big inconvenience if they missed meetings. However, conversely some students would use Microsoft Teams to ask for more meetings than had been planned. In both cases the impact on me from their misuse of technology was negative.

Description

COVID-19 produced challenges and strains in students' mental health, and the result of this was often felt by me when students interacted on Microsoft Teams. Often supervision conversations turned into counseling conversations, and then back to focus on supervision. With the added element that I was speaking to students in their homes, and most often in their bedrooms, the need to listen to their personal challenges would overtake any feelings of drawing clear boundaries. While mixing counseling with supervision was common before COVID-19 in on-campus contact, Microsoft Teams, and the ease of online technology use, seemed to increase and magnify both scenarios.

For those accessing meetings, the evident strain of working more hours than they should to support themselves and their families meant that they would have to snatch time during work to have supervision meetings. It was also during such times that pockets of counseling and coaching conversations would occur as the strain of this pressured life overwhelmed them.

Another aspect of the psychological strain experienced was in terms of the instances of meeting students where they were facing, and in some cases I was seeing, the realities of their home lives and the challenges they were experiencing. These challenges included homes with sometimes cramped living spaces, where they were sharing space and IT equipment with other members of the household. Meetings were sometimes interrupted by siblings and parents, and it revealed the constraints that students faced in terms of having appropriate study spaces and equipment to do well in the dissertation module. Overall, Microsoft Teams shone a light on the varied and complex lived experiences of students, a perspective that many Higher Education tutors would not have previously experienced themselves, and which often left an indelible impact on them.

When it came to pure personal tutoring, Microsoft Teams assisted with the development of an environment that promoted availability and accessibility, two essential elements of effective pastoral care. In response to the COVID-19 pandemic, universities around the world were forced to adopt this strategy and provide a virtual provision at the last minute (Howard, 2020). Microsoft Teams became a powerful tool for pastoral care in the context of online and hybrid Higher Education delivery, improving my ability as a personal tutor to relate to, and assist, students on a personal level.

Application

As a personal tutor, one issue that stands out from the others, and illustrates a compelling benefit that Microsoft Teams brought to personal tutoring, is that in the face of the national lockdown, and at a time in which social distancing measures were instituted by the Government, technology was particularly helpful to international students.

In the first instance, the onset of the COVID-19 pandemic posed unprecedented obstacles, particularly for students living abroad and separated from their families. With the closure of our campus, and the impossibility of in-person meetings, Microsoft Teams emerged as a vital means of maintaining an avenue of communication to assuage students' feelings of isolation and loneliness.

Through Microsoft Teams, I established a schedule of regular 'coffee catchups' with all my students. Not only did these virtual meetings provide the students with a familiar face, but they also ensured that each student remained on track with their studies. The international students gained much from these catchups because they were usually feeling homesick, worried and isolated, which was different from the support that home students had in their own environments when they were often living with family or friends.

The important pastoral care norms of privacy, and confidentiality, were safeguarded through Microsoft Teams. Students were reassured that they could express their challenges without worrying that their friends, or other staff members, would overhear them, because conversations on the platform were private, and the staff member would often take the calls from their home. The protection of privacy played a key role in encouraging students to talk openly about their struggles, and in creating an atmosphere of trust and confidence.

Microsoft Teams also addressed the issue of space capacity. It is difficult to locate a suitable, confidential room for one-on-one pastoral care appointments at universities in London, where space is especially scarce. Before the Microsoft Teams platform was set up, finding an appropriate space was a challenge, and students often felt uncomfortable talking openly when in a tutor's office, as they worried that other staff present may overhear their very private concerns. Microsoft Teams went a long way in resolving this issue by introducing a sense of privacy and trust, as staff members were scheduling pastoral care meetings to occur when they themselves were at their homes and so away from offices full of other staff.

Impact

Microsoft Teams was especially useful in organizing pastoral care support sessions, which have been commended for their contribution to community building and student integration (Broadbent *et al.*, 2021). I was able to schedule meetings using the platform's scheduling tool at times that worked for the students' availability and convenience. This flexibility was especially helpful for students who were often juggling several obligations around work, university and home life. In addition, online delivery reduced the burden of logistical issues, typical of on-campus meetings, and made pastoral care support available when required.

Before the introduction of Microsoft Teams, extensive time was often wasted waiting in communal meeting places for late students. On numerous occasions after spending time and money traveling to a café that was convenient for a student, I would find that the student failed to appear. With the new online meeting delivery, if a student did not show up for an online meeting, even though I would still be frustrated, I could easily resume my other tasks for the day without interruption.

The capability of Microsoft Teams to monitor, and record, pastoral care contacts was another significant benefit. Monitoring students' progress and well-being in a virtual environment can be a difficult undertaking. Microsoft Teams, by providing a platform to record our chats, record our worries and keep track of our actions, was able to lessen this problem. This methodical technique made follow-ups more efficient and ensured that no student 'slipped through the cracks'. The Microsoft Teams platform made filling out our personal tutoring monitoring forms much simpler than in the past. It also introduced the facility of having a digital record of my interactions with each student that could be utilized later in the cases when there were appeals initiated by students relating to academic matters.

One important advantage of Microsoft Teams, which proved enormously helpful and transformative, was the ability to easily organize and deliver group pastoral care sessions, which supplemented the individual encounters. These group meetings provided an opportunity for students dealing with comparable issues to connect, exchange experiences and work through their issues as a group. The group meetings were also a way to address the isolation that resulted when students could no longer meet their peers on campus.

In summarizing the two experiences, the positive and negative lessons learned from using Microsoft Teams in purely dissertation supervision/ personal tutoring/pastoral contexts are important to consider, as we continue to utilize it in the post-COVID-19 era. Recognizing the potential for digital fatigue (Maloney *et al.*, 2023) among students using Microsoft Teams is a problem that needs to be addressed in any online delivery of personal tutoring. Constant online interactions, particularly during a period of remote learning, can be mentally taxing (Juntunen *et al.*, 2022). For the benefit of their students' well-being, tutors must establish a balance between virtual and in-person engagement to prevent screen burnout.

Another challenge of using Microsoft Teams, as an online facility, is the need to consider the issue of inclusiveness. Not every student has access to the necessary technology or has the same level of comfort with virtual interactions (Reisdorf *et al.*, 2020). Some individuals may find it challenging to express their concerns, or partake in meaningful conversations, via a screen (Butcher and George, 2022). As educators, we must remain vigilant in identifying and addressing these disparities, and, if necessary, provide alternative supervisory and pastoral support avenues. In addition, technical issues, or the absence of appropriate equipment, can disrupt the flow of any online session, resulting in frustration among tutors and students. It is essential to find a method for integrating Microsoft Teams into the current teaching environment to enhance accessibility, inclusivity and engagement. Simultaneously, we should ensure that students feel comfortable using the platform in the long term as we move forward (Baker and Spencely, 2021).

Case Study Conclusion

When considering tutors, and their engagement with using Microsoft Teams, strategies and support interventions are required as university management have a duty of care to safeguard and protect the mental health and well-being of tutors. The taken-for-granted view that online is simply an extension of on-campus teaching, and personal tutoring, needs to be challenged and resisted. While there have been studies exploring the mental health, and well-being impact, of online delivery during the COVID-19 pandemic on Higher Education tutors (Mosleh *et al.*, 2022), and on distance learning in general (Jelfs *et al.*, 2009), there may be a need for more studies to explore the implications of increased use of online support now that we are in the on-campus setting again post-COVID-19.

In conclusion, Microsoft Teams proved to be a potent tool for strengthening and enhancing dissertation supervision, and pastoral care connections, for both of us during the transition to online and hybrid education. What cannot be denied is that Microsoft Teams, the platform of choice for many in the UK Higher Education providers, rose to the challenge of the crisis created by the COVID-19 national lockdowns, and in doing so it advanced accessibility, protected privacy, adapted communication preferences, planned support sessions, monitored interactions and facilitated group support.

As a crucial supporter of student performance and well-being in these transformational times, Microsoft Teams evolved as a technology instrument that epitomizes effective dissertation supervision delivery, and pastoral care, in the digital era. The legacy of this period is that many of the approaches and strategies that were started in response to the crisis caused by national lockdowns continue now in the post COVID-19 period. Microsoft Teams has become more than a tool as it is now integral to key aspects of our pedagogical delivery.

Case Study 2.3: Developing an Online Learning Ecosystem

TOM RITCHIE

Learning ecosystems are essential for student success in academic modules as they provide students with access to the resources and support that they need to develop their personal, learning and career-skills development (Blau *et al.*, 2020). Whether in-person in the library or with personal tutors, or online using shared resources and/or student support channels, these learning ecosystems help students to develop a sense of belonging within a community of learners, which is equally important for student engagement, motivation and success (Peacock *et al.*, 2020). The benefits of such learning ecosystems for students include improved academic performance, increased self-confidence and better preparation for the workplace.

The COVID-19 pandemic necessitated the rapid transfer of modules from in-person to online, which often resulted in underdeveloped student support elements within these learning ecosystems. This differs from the systemic approach to student support required when developing conventional online modules (Moore and Kearsley, 2011; Moore and Piety, 2022). The development of online learning ecosystems during the pandemic resulted in widespread dissatisfaction among students, despite research demonstrating that it can be as effective, or slightly more effective, than in-person learning when delivered right (Bernard *et al.*, 2004; Means *et al.*, 2014).

In this case study, I will discuss how I used Microsoft Teams to develop an innovative online learning ecosystem in the Chemistry Department at the University of Warwick. The approach improved the learning experience, integrated tools that supported student success and addressed the inherent dissatisfaction with online modules.

The module in this case study, Innovation 101, teaches students about innovation, creativity and design thinking to develop a growth mindset. This optional 15-CATS module is available to Level 6 (final-year undergraduate degree) and Level 7 (Master's) students in the Chemistry Department. When I took over the module in April 2022, it was planned that it would become a hybrid module as part of the return to in-person teaching after COVID-19. However, based on feedback and co-creation work relating to how the module could be improved, I decided to use Microsoft Teams, and integrate other student support tools, to develop a new online learning ecosystem.

From a pedagogical perspective, Microsoft Teams' features enabled me to develop an active learning environment. This involved developing communities of practice and inquiry and enabling students to engage with each other to critically reflect and grow their understanding. This approach also allowed me to provide quicker formative feedback. Beyond these, Microsoft Teams also helped me to seamlessly integrate asynchronous mental health and pastoral care support channels into the module.

Description

Microsoft Teams is a collaborative, cloud-based communication platform that incorporates chat, groups and shared working spaces, online meetings and file sharing. Additionally, it can integrate a wide range of third-party educational apps. Within online education, Microsoft Teams improves communication by providing asynchronous spaces where educators can engage with students, and students can engage with each other, to discuss module content, assessments and other related elements.

While many of us are familiar with Microsoft Teams, as a necessity and constant of learning environments and work-life during the COVID-19 pandemic, it also has several features that align with an active learning approach in module design. For example, it supports active learning by using features such as personalized announcements, @mentions for direct communication between students and educators, the use of emojis for both initial engagement and acknowledgment of module changes and the creation of specialized channels for curated content, academic guidance and pastoral care.

Within these specialized channels, Microsoft Teams allows the formation of smaller learning group spaces, where students can be supported to engage and refine their knowledge of content and learn from each other. These smaller groups deepen their understanding of ideas, which increases their confidence and reduces their fear of failure, encouraging greater contribution to the wider group. The Microsoft Teams infrastructure not only facilitates diverse pedagogical approaches, but also provides practical tools that can be used to support critical reflection, assignment submissions and academic support via prompt acknowledgment and formative feedback on a student's progress through a module. The ability to quickly host, and record, online sessions through Microsoft Teams also increases responsiveness to student feedback and in-module redevelopment.

When applied in this way, Microsoft Teams can transform an online learning environment into a community of active and critical learners by bridging the gaps between learning and support. This helps educators to create a learning ecosystem that facilitates student success, engagement with content and a sense of belonging comparable with in-person teaching.

Application

Unlike traditional approaches to online module design, I did not simply redesign the Innovation 101 module and then taught it via Microsoft Teams. Instead, I used the functionality of Microsoft Teams to inform the design of the module. I did this by first gathering feedback from previous students, and discussing expectations with students who were joining the module in the following academic year. We co-designed various aspects of the module design and delivery, including assessment feedback, teaching methods and module support. Using Microsoft Teams allowed me to be innovative and explore how the platform could best be used to incorporate these co-designed ideas into the online learning ecosystem.

The first thing the students told me was that feedback on their weekly content tasks and summative assessments needed to be quicker, to allow them to incorporate feedback into subsequent assessments. Since Microsoft Teams allows instant feedback, I redesigned the weighting structure of assessments to allow me to single-mark four out of five assessments. This meant I could mark and respond to students' work within 1–2 days, rather than 20 working days as part of the University policy. This is an example of how taking a technology-driven approach to module design led to a small change that can have a big impact on the student learning experience.

Students also mentioned that it took a few weeks to understand how to navigate the module and what was expected of them. I used the Microsoft Teams video recording capabilities to create an Onboarding video, and made it required viewing by replacing the first week of content with it. This allowed me to discuss the weekly content and assessment structure, emphasize how to use the different support channels available through the module and reduce students' Microsoft Teams skills gaps. I continued to use short recordings to provide clarifications in response to comments that the students posted, which further removed 'hidden curriculum' elements.

I used Microsoft Teams to organize and make all elements of course material, and module support, more accessible by creating separate Microsoft Teams channels. The list below details some of these channels, which were linked to either the learning experience or student support aspects of the online learning ecosystem. By using separate channels, I created waypoints in the learning journey so that students could instantly find what they were looking for when they needed it. This approach also helped to remove traditional barriers between the learning experience and student support, equating their importance to students' success on the module. The channels included:

- General channel – this provided a central hub for content updates, announcements and weekly checklists. It ensured students had access to the latest information, could receive ongoing cohort feedback and had an overview of the module's progression;
- Collaboration space channel – this provided a space for students to engage with all other members of the cohort and share their resources and ideas in response to the weekly content. The ability to post and respond to different online resources helped create a sense of ownership and community, with students posting and commenting over 1,000 times across the ten weeks of the module;
- Critical reflection channel – this established a clear set of expectations for how students should engage with the weekly content;
- Assessments channel – this provided extensive descriptions, detailed marking criteria, to-do lists and 'top tips' for the five assessments. It also provided clarity and guidance, ensuring students understood expectations and could effectively prepare for assessments;

- 'Fill up your cup' channel – this space provided specific pastoral advice and student support resources linked to different phases of the module, including settling in, completing weekly tasks, overcoming procrastination, and how to apply skills to a CV and cover letter. I encouraged students to share well-being tips, songs, memes and quotes to foster a supportive and positive online learning community.

I also integrated our Virtual Learning Environment Moodle and scheduling tool Calendly to enhance the learning ecosystem. These third-party apps simplified where module content was located and provided students access to my calendar, allowing them to book 15-minute catchups with me when they needed, rather than relying on a weekly office hour. Through the integration of these third-party apps, Microsoft Teams increased the depth of feedback I could offer, provided me with greater insights into how students were experiencing the module and also allowed me to incorporate elements of professional coaching into the support I could offer students.

Impact

My Microsoft Teams-centered learning ecosystem approach to module design and delivery received positive feedback from my students. All respondents agreed that "The module is well organized", with 75% strongly agreeing. Similarly, all respondents agreed that "Appropriate support is available to me throughout the module," with 83.3% strongly agreeing.

Student feedback comments further exemplified the impact of this approach, reflecting the positive outcomes that the online learning ecosystem approach had on creating a supportive, engaging and empowering learning experience. The shift in assessment and feedback design, and the use of Microsoft Teams to provide student support, were also positively received:

> I was skeptical about it being online, however, it's been one of the most engaging courses.
>
> Anonymous Student

> The best organized module by a landslide, and by far the most engaging. Really felt like there was a large amount of support available at all times, and the content was high quality.
>
> Anonymous Student

Really loved the weekly checklist, and the fact that all information was readily accessible either on Moodle or Teams, both of which were crystal clear and very user-friendly. The coaching call was a really good idea as well - an excellent way to break the ice and encourage students to look for, and give, feedback.

Anonymous Student

Support and feedback throughout the entire module have been fantastic. He is very clear and honest with what you have to do and with how important things are. He has really helped me throughout the module. I've enjoyed the content and have learned a lot from it. The content in the module is something that will help me this year, but also in the years to come.

Anonymous Student

The constant feedback throughout the module is very helpful.

Anonymous Student

Despite negative perceptions of online modules, using Microsoft Teams to redesign the online learning ecosystem within Innovation 101 resulted in a highly rated module experience for my students. This student feedback led the module to be nominated for a Warwick Award for Teaching Excellence by over 20% of its students, and was highly commended as a result. The success and student feedback from the module also informed my approach to our departmental curriculum review. I have subsequently co-designed and convened a new year one module called 'Beyond Science', which builds on the same Microsoft Teams-based online learning ecosystem design.

Case Study Conclusion

What is clear from the experience of teaching Innovation 101 in Microsoft Teams is that using technology in this way does not guarantee a good student experience. Instead, it provides the foundation on which you can build a learning ecosystem that supports all parts of the student experience. A related lesson is that the ecosystem must be tailored to meet the needs of all students. This includes those with different learning preferences and access requirements.

Inclusive co-design is essential to ensure the approach addresses all students' needs. It is worth noting that developing and implementing this approach require significant time and effort. Microsoft Teams cannot respond to student comments, questions or feedback on its own. The effort required to effectively use Microsoft Teams may impact the scalability, and sustainability, of this approach to module design. However, Artificial Intelligence (AI) could potentially help in the future.

Applying a Microsoft Teams-centered learning ecosystem approach to module design and delivery is an effective way to improve the student learning and support experience, as well as module satisfaction and feedback. Moving forward, I believe that we will see a continued shift toward more personalized and engaging learning experiences in Higher Education. This Microsoft Teams-centered learning ecosystem approach is well-suited to respond to this shift which may include the further development and use of plug-ins, and existing functionality will allow educators to create customized learning environments for each student, which respond to their learning styles, preferences and access requirements.

I am also excited about the potential for AI to support the development of future online learning ecosystems. I am currently investigating how AI can be used to provide students with real-time feedback on their assessments and learning journey. Used with Microsoft Teams, this technology could be used to develop online learning ecosystems that can adapt module content and support individual students based upon their needs. It could also highlight those who are struggling with a particular concept, or need additional help, to develop their knowledge and succeed, revolutionizing the learning experience.

Case Study 2.4: A Pedagogical Model for Engaging Postgraduate Researchers Online

KELLY LOUISE PREECE

From 2015 to 2022 I led the Researcher Development Program (RDP) for Postgraduate Researchers (PGRs) at the University of Exeter. When I took over the program in 2015, it was largely delivered face-to-face, but also included ten asynchronous or 'static' online courses on our Moodle site 'ELE', and a program of eight online sessions for our part-time and distance PGRs. Under my leadership, the RDP for PGRs underwent a significant redesign, including the introduction of a pedagogical model for Researcher Development that drew on what I called 'multiple ways of doing' (Preece, 2023) and the practice of authentic teaching (Johnson and LaBelle, 2017).

Due to increasing numbers of part-time and distance students, and the need to work flexibly, particularly for our disabled students, I identified the need to update our online courses, and to expand our webinar program. I wanted this to be part of an online provision, rather than just an online duplication of our face-to-face offer, and so I needed to consider the various online interaction and engagement methods I had with the PGR community. While building a thriving learning community was undoubtedly important, I was also aware of my role as a Researcher Developer in creating space for peer learning and interaction, given how isolating the PGR experience can be (Meschitti, 2018).

Description

I developed a pedagogical model that combined these methods of online engagement into an innovative learning experience, utilizing multiple technologies to create an engaging, cross-campus and international PGR community. The model consists of a triad of live events, static resources and social media to create a sense of a community for the PGRs.

The 'live' element of the model consisted of synchronous, interactive learning events, for example webinars, Q&A panels and writing retreats. Over my seven-year tenure running the RDP for PGRs, we used a range of video conferencing technologies to facilitate these learning events, such as Adobe Connect, Skype for Business and Microsoft Teams. The learning experience was constructed to introduce 'multiple ways of doing' through presenter delivery, which is the formal sharing of and speaking to visual aids, and to provide an opportunity for informal, peer learning through group discussions in the chat boxes, breakout rooms and/or on virtual whiteboards.

The 'static' element of the model consisted of asynchronous online resources, for example recordings of live events, curated links and multimedia resources. These were used to provide training on demand, with greater flexibility and accessibility for our part-time and distance PGRs. This was initially delivered through the University's Moodle platform 'ELE' using SCORM packages that ran on Flash and the Moodle Book function, but later became two websites. This was to ensure that the resources were available to our PGRs both before they formally started their research degree and after they had finished, as well as being of benefit to the rest of the sector. The resources on these websites are multimedia, built with accessibility in mind, with resources available in multiple formats. These were created using a wide variety of software and digital tools including

Adobe Acrobat, Microsoft PowerPoint, Microsoft Teams, Zoom, Canva, Panopto and Microsoft Stream.

Finally, the 'social' element of the model consisted of sharing resources and facilitating discussion through different social media, such as X (formerly Twitter) blogs, and podcasts. This created a space more directly focused on discussion and dialog, but also one that was more embedded in researcher's daily lives. The technologies used to create the podcasts and transcripts were Zoom, Audacity and Otter.ai.

Applications

Considering the 'Live' element, while now online training is ubiquitous, in 2015–2020 the idea was still relatively unusual, with only a handful of institutions offering a version of their RDP provision online. The aim was therefore to provide a comparable learning experience, with similar learning objectives and teaching strategies, as we would use when face-to-face, but translated into an online environment rather than simply reproducing class materials and/or recordings online (García-Cabrero *et al.*, 2018, p. 814). This included informal learning and community building that are central to the workshop program, where a significant proportion of student feedback referenced the benefits of meeting and sharing experiences with other PGRs.

Interactive tools were key to creating these opportunities, for example using virtual whiteboards or Mural in the same way that we would use flip chart paper in person, enabling us to collate experiences and ideas in much the same way as in a face-to-face environment. But having started delivering webinars in Adobe Connect, with only slides and a chat box, I still found the opportunity to create a sense of community, building rapport through interaction with comments in the chat box, always taking note of and responding to student comments and questions. For me, the emphasis has always been not on the 'flashiness' of the tool, but how you use it to facilitate learning (Preece, 2015).

Turning to the 'Static' elements, the RDP resource website is designed to facilitate the navigation of students between different asynchronous resources according to their personal training and developmental needs (https://researcher-development.co.uk/). It is structured into sections based on the strands of the RDP at Exeter: (1) essentials; (2) careers; (3) data; (4) sharing your research; and (5) writing. Each section led to a series of subsections, themed around the workshops and webinars on the RDP. For example, the 'Sharing your Research' section contains subsections on making the most of conferences, designing research posters, presentation skills, writing journal articles, digital research communication and engaging with the public, policy and media. Each of these subsections can be worked through as a stand-alone course. PGRs could therefore work through each section chronologically to cover all facets of a topic. Alternatively, if they want to address specific training needs, they could go straight to specific resources that addressed that need. Although I led the project, I only developed a small proportion of the resources myself. Instead, I secured funding to pay some of our PGRs as Postgraduate Teaching Assistants (PTAs) to develop these resources. As a result, the materials were by PGRs, and for PGRs, building on informal interactions with peers as a source of learning and development (Elliot *et al.*, 2020, pp. 77–84).

Moving to the 'Social' element, X has played a key role in academic life as a tool for digital scholarship, providing a space for academics to publicize their work, build their network, engage with the public and manage information (Carrigan, 2015). But as Budge *et al.* (2016, pp. 218–219) argue, X is also increasingly a space for open dialog, and for the pushing of boundaries in which we challenge norms of academic ways of being and behavior.

While I used our team's X account to share resources, I used my personal X account to interact with our PGRs, engage in discussions and share my experience of being an academic and researcher in a way that mirrored my practice of authentic teaching in webinars (Preece, 2023). For example, I used my personal X account to embark on a yearlong well-being and self-care project (Preece, 2021) which led to discussions with PGRs about their mental health.

Impact

This triad of live events, static resources and social media developed a thriving online community of learners. This impact was a product not of the technologies themselves, but instead was related to how I used them to create an experience of community and belonging. Impact can be measured in many ways, such as engagement data, qualitative feedback and/or longitudinal data on progression and completion rates. Given the model's central focus on community building, in this case study I have prioritized the student voice through qualitative feedback.

The 'live' webinar program grew from 8 sessions in 2014/2015 to 116 in 2020/2021, which not only meant a more comprehensive training offer, but also created a sense of community and connection. This was particularly meaningful for distance students, for whom community building is often seen as the result of initial in-person contact (Melián *et al.*, 2023, p. 148).

> As a distance-learning part-time student who was living and working overseas I can honestly say that the expansion of the offer from RDP to use of Webinars was instrumental in the increased level of support provided to those students who were hard to reach. This use of a Webinar provided me with opportunities to feel connected to a PGR community, and that I was not alone.
>
> Academic

Student feedback confirmed that it was vital for presenters to build rapport by interacting with comments in the chat box, always taking note of, and responding to, student comments and questions. These live events also transformed the learning experience of our campus-based students.

In feedback on our webinars, campus-based students noted that they liked the convenience of learning from home and appreciated the 'bite-sized' nature of these one-hour online training sessions. We had previously struggled to bring together our distance and campus-based PGR communities as whole, but the webinar program built this shared learning community for us.

The engagement of our campus-based students with the webinar program meant that the community of learners encompassed both our campus and distance students, thereby creating a cross-campus, international learning community, which was something we had always struggled to achieve through other means.

The 'live' webinars worked in tandem with the 'static' asynchronous resources as a source of training and development. Although webinar recordings were always made available after the live events, these static resources were designed for an online environment. Static resources introduce another dimension of flexibility into the learning experience. For example, they are easier to access for some international students due to time differences and data access.

The resources developed were multimedia and included practical tasks but were not interactive or dialogic. The community-building element of these resources was linked to PGRs creating the content. Students were therefore connected with their peers through the asynchronous resources they had developed, and so they were able to learn from each other's experiences, and from taking each other's perspective (Wilson *et al.*, 2023).

It's like having a front row seat to all these different experiences, and ways of doing things. It's improved my game and given me fresh ideas for my own research journey. It is like a global coffee shop experience that promotes collective growth and encourages learning from one another.

Postgraduate Researcher

Conversely, my use of X was inherently dialogic and focused on me becoming a part of the PGR and wider academic community as a peer.

Kelly-Louise's use of her personal [X] account to share the ups and downs of her own work, gave us all a sense of perspective. In doing so, she welcomed us into the PGR community, as an integral part of it.

Postdoctoral Researcher

Although each element of the model contributes to, and results in, community building, it is the interrelatedness of these approaches that leads to a combined sense of community for PGRs. There are obvious ways in which the approaches are interrelated in practice. For example, I shared booking links to live webinars, and static asynchronous resources, from the Doctoral College X account, enabling a flow of information and communication through the different elements of the model. But it is the presence of multiple methods of learning, dialog and engagement through the different elements of the model that creates space for all PGRs to engage, whether they are based on or off campus, located in the UK or internationally, and whether their training needs are research skills or navigating the neoliberal university. Furthermore, it enabled us to support students whether their learning preferences or needs are visual, auditory, written or multimodal.

Case Study Conclusion

My reflections on this case study, and my application of the model, are on the benefits of being flexible and adaptable as an educator. Throughout my time in Higher Education, I have employed new pedagogical tools such as authentic teaching, and new technical skills including video editing, to meet students both metaphorically in terms of their learning preferences and training and development needs and literally in terms of their geographical location. With a group as diverse and complex as PGRs, this required multiple pedagogies, multiple approaches and multiple technologies to come under one umbrella which was my triadic model. Through this approach,

I have managed to engage some of the most hard-to-reach parts of the PGR community, and to make them feel like they were a part of it.

I am now the Head of Educator Development at the University of Exeter, and I am working to bring our online provision into this more structured and coherent model for online delivery. While we currently deliver many of the individual components of the model, including webinars, writing spaces, static online resources, social media and podcasts, we are not fully leveraging their interconnectedness to create a community of educators. The PGR community is diverse, including educators ranging from PTAs to Professors, and Professional Services to Academics. Viewed together, this community presents quite different and emerging sets of circumstances. The challenge is in some senses greater here because of this, but it is a unique opportunity to test the applicability of the model with different groups and communities, and with different approaches and technologies.

Case Study 2.5: Ensuring Effective Asynchronous Curriculum Delivery

CLAIRE STOCKS, DAWNE IRVING-BELL, DAVID WOOFF AND SCOTT FARROW

In response to the COVID-19 global pandemic, there are numerous examples of technology being used to enhance learning and teaching practices across Higher Education, many continuing in the post-pandemic era. Here the authors share their lived experience of using technology on a teaching development program for new academics, and the impact it has had on the resulting student learning experience.

BPP University is a specialist Higher Education provider which focuses on 'building careers through education' in the areas of law, business, technology and nursing. BPP uses dispersed teaching centers across the UK for delivery. In this context, we deliver a Postgraduate Certificate in Learning and Teaching (PGCLT), to support our new teachers who are often recruited directly from industry or practice, and to establish and develop their teaching practice. To facilitate engagement with the program across staff from a range of centers, the program is delivered online and asynchronously. We use a range of Microsoft applications including Microsoft Teams, which is our primary way to deliver the program. We also use Microsoft Sway, and OneNote, which is the focus of this case study.

Asynchronous delivery clearly has benefits for the geographically distributed participants on the PGCLT, but there are also numerous challenges with asynchronous delivery which, arguably, are predominantly the same challenges that affect synchronous, in-person teaching. Ensuring that learners are engaged and making good progress, as well as checking their understanding, are common issues which can be even more difficult to monitor in asynchronous programs. Furthermore, in initial teacher education programs such as the PGCLT, modeling effective approaches and providing tools that participants can adapt for their own practice are essential. The program team has therefore adopted a gamified approach to the early stages of learning, by utilizing OneNote to create an asynchronous digital escape room. At the time of writing, the escape room has been used with 3 cohorts comprising of around 100 learners in total.

Description

OneNote is essentially a digital notebook, often described as a virtual equivalent to the lever-arch-style files with cardboard dividers that many lecturers, and former university students, are likely to be familiar with. OneNote integrates with Microsoft Teams where the tutor can create a 'Class Notebook' – essentially a digital folder of resources that can be distributed, as individual copies, to each learner in a class.

The tutor sets up various sections within the notebook and can distribute 'pages' to the sections, and then learners can work in them, creating new sections and pages. The teaching team can access the notebook to offer feedback, check progress and even mark assignments. Importantly for this case study, the teacher can lock sections, and then release them to learners at appropriate points in the course. Users can use OneNote notebooks to curate a range of different types of resource, including typed and written text, pictures, audio recordings, web links and videos, and this flexibility means that it can be used to create interactive, engaging and dynamic learning spaces.

In educational settings, OneNote has been used across a range of disciplines, to create digital laboratory books (Guerrero et al. 2019) and ePortfolios (Cavana, 2019), and to support the gathering of research data (Blair et al., 2018). Others have also used OneNote to create escape rooms (Thirkell, 2019), although there seem to be fewer published accounts of this application of the platform. In her reflection on using OneNote to create an escape room on a Business program, Thirkell (2019) notes three aims: (1) to test students' understanding of the material; (2) to equip learners with digital employability skills; and (3) to 'enrich' their learning. We had the same basic aims in mind but argue that our context of supporting teachers to develop their practice, particularly in terms of using technology to support learning, is more complex and multifaceted.

Application

On the PGCLT, we intended our digital escape room to introduce learners to the program in an appealing and flexible way, as well as allowing learners to experience how technology can be used to support learning, and how gamification can increase learners' interest and engagement. O'Brien and Farrow emphasize the experiential learning potential of escape rooms, which:

> Put the player directly into the game, thus being truly experiential. This has added benefits where education is involved, [since] as well as reducing barriers between the player and the experience, it brings them closer to the learning.
>
> (O'Brien *et al.*, 2020, p. 81)

For us, this is an essential feature of the escape room as we want our new teachers to experience the technology, and its benefits, as learners. This enhanced understanding can then be used in their practice to develop their own students' learning. Our learners are asked to reflect on the experience, to consider the curriculum design and pedagogical decisions that are likely to have underpinned the approach and to think about ways in which some of the learning or strategies could be used in their own contexts.

During the escape room activity, participants are required to introduce themselves to their peers on the program, using the space created in Microsoft Teams. This initial task is designed to build a sense of cohort among the dispersed participants. Once they have completed the task, they are issued with the first unlock code to progress to section two of the OneNote activity. They then familiarize themselves with the PGCLT curriculum through a pre-recorded presentation in Panopto, review guidance on how to reference literature using the Harvard system, which is the system they are asked to use on the program, use ThingLink to explore a virtual classroom and then further prepare for their teaching philosophy by engaging with a task to help them to start to understand and apply Advance HE's Professional Standards Framework to their teaching practice. Finally, they need to review a pre-recorded presentation to understand the assessment requirements for the module. Each unlock code is hidden in the materials for each section, and so by paying close attention to the content, participants can identify or generate codes which facilitate their progression through the sections.

The reasons that OneNote was specifically selected as the host for the escape room included:

- The ability to lock sections provides a logical way to create a series of 'rooms' for learners to explore and escape from;
- The range of media that OneNote can house means that we are also able to use it to expose learners to other technologies to illustrate how the tools can be used;
- Creating individual copies of the escape room for each learner means that they can progress at their own pace, and they can also add notes and materials to their own notebook if they wish to;
- OneNote allowed the team to create a structured escape room experience where success depended on learners engaging with the materials in the order intended by the program team. Sections of the notebook are numbered, and unlock codes will allow learners only to progress to the next section that they are required to complete;
- All staff at BPP have access to OneNote through the institution's Office365 package, meaning that they are free to use it in their own daily and/or teaching practice;
- Integration with Microsoft Teams offered a seamless experience, with no need to log in and out of different systems.

Impact

The way the PGCLT curriculum was designed has allowed us to evaluate the escape room experience via responses to reflective questions that participants were asked to complete after each taught unit. Feedback on the escape room has been overwhelmingly positive, and although we designed the experience in an evidence-based way with clear pedagogical aims in mind, we were surprised by how effective our approach has been. For example, we anticipated that some participants may find the approach 'gimmicky' or become frustrated if they struggled to identify one or more of the codes to escape the sections. However, although some participants have reported getting stuck, their reflections also reveal that they understood how becoming stuck encouraged them to revisit the material to be successful.

Several participants in each cohort also revealed that they felt nervous about the escape room, generally because they were not confident in their use of technology, particularly in educational settings. However, the structure that the program team provided through OneNote's sections and pages helped to guide participants through, and the team was able to access each individual student's OneNote record to help if participants became stuck, thereby providing a safety net that increased their confidence. Each participant was provided with clear instructions prior to engaging with their escape room, even if they had used OneNote before.

A few participants across all the cohorts used OneNote in their own teaching, but even then, we did not see anyone who had seen it as an escape room before. They therefore reported that they appreciated being exposed to a potential new use of technology, and the idea of gamifying teaching in this way.

The main criticisms of the approach are that the escape room requires learners to engage with a lot of information, and that the codes must be entered in a very specific format to be effective. For example, codes are case-sensitive. Nevertheless, participants do recognize that their OneNote remains available for them to revisit at any time throughout the program, and the clear instructions provided by the program team helped.

Participants can become confused by the different versions of OneNote because the online and desktop versions look slightly different in terms of where the sections appear. Again, clear instructions overcame this, although some participants did still need a quick Microsoft Teams call to diagnose and resolve issue(s), and this relies on them reaching out to the program team to ask for help. Participants reported a range of benefits for their learning and practice as educators. In particular, increased confidence in the use of technology to support learning was a common theme, as was an appreciation of the value of 'gentle competition' to increase learners' motivation.

From the perspective of the program team, there are several main challenges of using OneNote for this purpose which are:

1. The time invested to set up the escape room, for example checking that it worked as intended and distributing it to learners. However, once the initial OneNote was set up, subsequent iterations required only updating and redistribution.
2. In our experience, OneNote is less intuitive to use than many other Microsoft products, which means that participants can sometimes find it a little challenging to use.
3. If the program team loses the codes, everyone will, in theory, be locked out of the OneNote escape room permanently. However, this particular

notebook was set up so that following the first code, which was provided to participants, all of the subsequent codes were discoverable within the materials. Therefore, as long as the first code is kept safe, the others should be easy for the program team to discern.

4. Taking such a gamified and digitally enhanced approach, right at the start of the program, sets learner expectations high, and that can be difficult to maintain throughout the program. To address this final point, the program team has been gradually reviewing all units to identify other places where innovative and creative approaches can be used to maintain the engagement established by the escape room.

Case Study Conclusion

Our use of OneNote to create a digital escape room has been very successful in engaging our learners, and particularly effective in supporting their reflections about the use of technology in education. Building on this success, future developments aim to explore features of OneNote that we have not yet exploited on this program. For instance, the potential to use the OneNote Class Notebook as a collaborative space to facilitate the sharing of resources, and for peer learning, is one potential area for development. This would allow participants to experience an additional approach to asynchronous collaborative learning, and so gain a broader understanding of the features and benefits of OneNote.

Our experience suggests that OneNote can be a powerful tool to support learning, especially in asynchronous settings. Our sense is that it is underutilized, perhaps because asynchronous online delivery is still relatively uncommon in Higher Education. We hope that our case study will encourage others to explore the potential of OneNote within their own settings.

References

Baker, L. and Spencely, C. 2021. Blending Microsoft Teams with existing teaching environments to increase access, inclusivity and engagement. *Foundation Year Network*, 3, 3–20.

Bernard, R., Abrami, P., Lou, Y., Borokhovski, E., Wade, A., Wozney, L., Wallet, P., Fiset, M. and Huang, B., 2004. How does distance education compare with classroom instruction? A meta-analysis of the empirical literature. *Review of Educational Research*, 74(3), 379–439.

Blair, J., Luo, Y., Ma, N., Lee, S. and Choe, E.K., 2018. OneNote meal: A photo-based diary study for reflective meal tracking. *AMIA Annual Symposium Proceedings Archive*, 5 Dec 2018, 252–261.

Blau, I., Shamir-Inbal, T. and Avdiel, O., 2020. How does the pedagogical design of a technology-enhanced collaborative academic course promote digital literacies, self-regulation, and perceived learning of students? *Internet and Higher Education*, 45, 100722.

Broadbent, R., Patten, A. and Campbell, D., 2021. Building virtual communities of learning via Online Group Tutoring Sessions. *Foundation Year Network*, 4, 5–11.

Budge, K., Lemon, N. and McPherson, M., 2016. Academics who tweet: "Messy" identities in academia. *Applied Research in Higher Education*, 8(2), 210–221.

Butcher, J. and George, C., 2022. Digital poverty as a barrier to access. *Widening Participation and Lifelong Learning*, 24(15), 180–194.

Carrigan, M. 2015. *Social Media for Academics*. London: SAGE

CAST, 2018. *Universal Design for Learning UDL: The UDL Guidelines*. Lynnfield: CAST.

Cavana, M., 2019. Using OneNote as an ePortfolio: Promoting experiential learning and self-regulation. *Proceedings of the 18th European Conference on e-Learning*. 7–8 Nov 2019, Reading, UK.

Elliot, D.L., Bengtsen, S.S., Guccione, K. and Kobayashi, S., 2020. *The Hidden Curriculum in Doctoral Education*. Cham, Switzerland: Palgrave Pivot.

García-Cabrero, B., Hoover, M., Lajoie, S., Andrade-Santoyo, N., Quevedo-Rodríguez L. and Wong, J., 2018. Design of a learning-centered online environment: A cognitive apprenticeship approach. *Educational Technology Research and Development*, 66, 813–835.

Guerrero, S., López-Cortés, A., García-Cárdenas, J., Saa, P., Indacochea, A., Armendáriz-Castillo, I., Zambrano, A., Yumiceba, V., Pérez-Villa, A., Guevara-Ramírez, P., Moscoso-Zea, O., Parede, J., Leone, P. and Paz-Y-Miño, C., 2019. A quick guide for using Microsoft OneNote as an electronic laboratory notebook. *PLoS Computational Biology*, 15(5), e1006918.

Howard, J., 2020. Meeting the students where they go: Creating remote tutoring at a multi-campus university. *Learning Assistance Review*, 25(2), 361–370.

Jelfs, A., Richardson, J. and Price, L. (2009) Student and tutor perceptions of effective tutoring in distance education. *Distance Education*, 30(3), 419–441.

Johnson, Z. and LaBelle, S., 2017. An examination of teacher authenticity in the college classroom. *Communication Education*, 66(4), 423–439.

Juntunen, H., Tuominen, H., Viljaranta, J., Hirvonen, R., Toom, A. and Niemivirta, M., 2022. Feeling exhausted and isolated? The connections between university students' remote teaching and learning experiences, motivation, and psychological well-being during the COVID-19 pandemic. *Educational Psychology*, 42(10), 1241–1262.

Lochtie, D., McIntosh, E., Stork, A. and Walker, B., 2018. *Effective Personal Tutoring in Higher Education*. St Albans, UK: Critical Publishing.

Maloney, S., Axelsen, M., Stone, C., Galligan, L., Redmond, P., Brown, A., Turner, J. and Lawrence, J., 2023. Defining and exploring online engagement fatigue in a university context. *Computers and Education Open*, 4, 100–139.

Mealey, A., 2022. Locked down but not locked out: Personal tutoring for philosophy, ethics and religion students and the wider community at Leeds Trinity University during COVID-19. *In:* Jamil, M.G. and Morley, D.A. (eds.), *Agile Learning Environments amid Disruption: Evaluating Academic Innovations in Higher Education during COVID-19.* Cham, Switzerland: Palgrave Macmillan, 675–689.

Means, B., Bakia, M. and Murphy, R., 2014. *Learning Online: What Research Tells us about Whether, When and How.* Abingdon: Routledge.

Melián, E., Reyes, J. and Meneses, J., 2023. The online PhD experience: A qualitative systematic review. *Review of Research in Open and Distributed Learning*, 24(1), 137–158.

Meschitti, V. 2018. Can peer learning support doctoral education? *Studies in Higher Education*, 44(7), 1209–1221.

Moore, M. and Kearsley, G., 2011. *Distance Education: A Systems View of Online Learning.* Boston, MA: Cengage Learning.

Moore, S. and Piety, P., 2022. Online learning ecosystems: Comprehensive planning and support for distance learners. *Distance Education*, 43(2), 179–203.

Mosleh, S., Kasasbeha, M., Aljawarneh, Y., Alrimawi, I. and Saifan, A., 2022. The impact of online teaching on stress and burnout of academics during the transition to remote teaching from home. *BMC Medical Education*, 22(1), 475.

O'Brien, R., Farrow, E. and Farrow, S., 2020. Escaping the inactive classroom: Escape rooms for teaching technology. *Social Media for Learning*, 1(1), 78–93.

Papert, S. and Harel, I., 1991. Situating constructionism. *Constructionism*, 36(2), 1–11.

Peacock, S., Cowan, J., Irvine, L. and Williams, J., 2020. An exploration into the importance of a sense of belonging for online learners. *International Review of Research in Open and Distributed Learning*, 21(2), 18–35.

Play England, 2020. *Charter for Play.* Bristol: Play England

Preece, K., 2015. Social media platforms as educational interfaces. *Enhancing the Learner Experience in Higher Education*, 7(1), 15–28.

Preece, K., 2021. A year in self-care. *In:* Lemon, N. (ed.), *Creating A Place for Self-care and Wellbeing in Higher Education.* Abingdon: Routledge, 13–34.

Preece, K., 2023. The dance of authenticity and multiple ways of doing. *In:* Elliot, D., Bengtsen, S., and Guccione, K. (eds.), *Developing Researcher Independence Through the Hidden Curriculum.* Cham, Switzerland: Palgrave Macmillan, 127–136.

Reisdorf, B., Triwibowo, W. and Yankelevich, A., 2020. Laptop or bust: How lack of technology affects student achievement. *American Behavioral Scientist*, 64(7), 927–949.

Siemens, G., 2017. A learning theory for the digital age. *In:* West, R. (ed.), *Foundations of Learning and Instructional Design Technology.* Montreal, Canada: Pressbooks. https://pressbooks.pub/lidtfoundations/chapter/connectivism-a-learning-theory-for-the-digital-age/

Sobaih, A., Salem, A., Hasanein, A. and Elnasr, A., 2021. Responses to COVID-19 in Higher Education: Students' learning experience using Microsoft Teams versus social network sites. *Sustainability*, 13(18), 10036.

Thirkell, E., 2019. *'Escaping' Traditional Technologies Through A Onenote Escape Room.* York: Advance HE.

Vygotsky, L.S., 1978. *Mind in Society: The Development of Higher Psychological Processes.* Cambridge, MA: Harvard University Press.

Wenger, E., 1998. Communities of practice: Learning as a social system. *Systems Thinker*, 9(5), 2–3.

Wilson, C., Arshad, R., Sapouna, M., McGillivray, D. and Zihms, S., 2023. 'PGR Connections': Using an online peer-learning pedagogy to support doctoral researchers. *Innovations in Education and Teaching International*, 60(3) 390–400.

Zhang, L., Carter Jr, R., Qian, X., Yang, S., Rujimora, J. and Wen, S. 2022. Academia's responses to crisis: A bibliometric analysis of literature on online learning in Higher Education during COVID-19. *British Journal of Educational Technology*, 53(3), 620–646.

Innovative Applications of Technology to Support Student Engagement and Inclusivity

3

The following six case studies describe innovative applications of technology to support student engagement and inclusivity. Each case study presents the personal perspectives of those involved.

Case Study 3.1: Creating Microsystems to Improve Student Engagement

ANGELINE DHARMARAJ-SAVICKS

According to the Office for Students, and the UK Student Engagement Survey, a key goal of education is to influence student engagement as this can have a direct impact on their learning (Bretts, 2018; Challen, 2016). 'Engagement' is a fuzzy construct, but the nature, conceptualization and measurement of this have gained recent attraction and widespread discussion (Bergdahl, 2022; Bond *et al.*, 2020). In this case study, I consider the influence of educational technology for engagement, both behavioral and affective (Hollister and Lee, 2022), within the post COVID-19 environment of the master's level course that I lead. For this context, I define engagement as being a two-dimensional phenomenon:

DOI: 10.4324/9781032635248-4

1. An active response in which students participate regularly in both online and face-to-face learning, and maintain positive conduct;
2. Evidence of students' emotional investment, i.e., reacting positively to their learning environment, colleagues and academics, and so indicating a strong sense of belonging (Bond *et al.*, 2020).

I highlight how the change to synchronous education has led to a shift in students' learning, but within the UK Higher Education context, this has not been sufficiently understood from a sociological position. This I find is problematic as it has allowed a widening of participation (WP) for key student groups, such as international students, students with special educational needs and disabilities, other minoritized students and those from lower socio-economic households with reduced educational opportunities (Hulene *et al.*, 2023).

This case study adapts Bronfenbrenner's (1979) Bioecological Model of Human Development, and Skinner et al.'s (2022) Bioecological Student Engagement Framework (BSEF), which together helped me understand the complex systems related to how students interact. This has shaped my own pedagogic practice as a result and has helped me to see how I can increase student engagement within a synchronous learning environment.

My practice of providing various platforms to hear the voice of students has enabled me to evaluate my own pedagogy, to influence the systems and processes being used at my university and thus mitigate issues surrounding students' engagement in synchronous learning (both curricular and social). It has also enabled me to consider social mobility and student experience. Most importantly, it has helped me as a practitioner to see, and hear, those students who would otherwise be left without legitimate consideration and support.

Description

With a lack of a clear definition in place, most academics have adopted their own understanding of what 'engagement' is (Ashwin and McVitty, 2015). There is often confusion about 'student engagement' and 'student attendance', which is also evident from the arguments discussed by a number of researchers who see the use of the term 'engagement' critically, whereas others see the term as being vague and uncritical.

Engagement is an influential element for stakeholders, policymakers and educational leaders, as it holds the power to mitigate and/or drive inequity (Trowler *et al.*, 2022). The attendance and engagement policy at my institution measures students' participation in terms of attendance at scheduled and timetabled events, both virtually and on campus, and the frequent use of content captured on the Virtual Learning Environment (VLE) platform. This is mirrored in the school- and course-level policies for student engagement. This engagement data alone does not provide the information necessary for academics to develop an understanding of behavioral and affective engagement of students, as their interactions between the various complex systems can cause WP students to fall through the invisible gaps.

The BSEF exemplifies the complex reciprocal interactions between students and the systems that shape their engagement (Bronfenbrenner, 1979; Bond et al., 2020). With Higher Education impacted by a number of social, political and historic decisions and practices, such as pedagogies, discourses, values and policies, the quality control within courses is often dealt with through changes to the VLE, curriculum and modular design and the introduction of further active learning. However, barriers faced by students that limit their engagement, such as those associated with synchronous learning, have not been considered from a holistic perspective (Carroll *et al.*, 2021; Skinner *et al.*, 2022). Often a reductionist approach is taken by blaming the recruitment process for admitting students below prescribed academic standards, but this oversimplifies a student's competency, and any resulting low attainment and engagement that may occur (Mulisa, 2019).

Several microsystems have been created within my institution to support student engagement. Examples include:

- Student engagement officers to support those with non-academic challenges;
- Learning development tutors to provide academic support;
- Personal tutor frameworks to provide individualized support;
- IT training and support for synchronous learning and digital assessments;
- Diversity in assessments provides opportunities to succeed for diverse kinds of learners;
- Project-based learning opportunities.

These have all proven to be successful initiatives, and ones which I fully support and appreciate. However, these initiatives do not completely address the underlying issues. The remaining gaps I have identified are:

1. Little focus to inculcate a strong and confident culture of engagement with the VLE beyond baseline expectations, i.e., digital assessments;
2. Current microsystems mostly operate independently rather than in concert.

These gaps have created inequity for WP students who do not gain holistic support. The lack of a conduit to integrate the present microsystems so that they inform each other enables several students to fall into the gaps, and consequently, this will impact their ultimate attainment and opportunities for social mobility. For example, this will include student characteristics such as being away from their family and familiarizing themselves with a new culture and/or education system, belonging and digital literacy. These characteristics, when not considered and supported, will impact upon students' behavioral and affective engagement. This example demonstrates that academic engagement is not determined by intelligence itself, but also allows room for the preconceptions of some academics who may attempt to label students, which is a colonialist perspective, and needs to be addressed.

Personally, I adopt a postmodernist approach to questioning this reductionist perspective, and so I try to show how I use the BSEF to understand the complex ecologies that can shape a student's academic interest and confidence. This helps me understand issues surrounding behavioral and affective engagement in relation to synchronous learning within the course. With the majority of the cohort being international students, and a significant number having special educational needs, this understanding is important.

I focus on the current ecosystems within the university, including student feedback at module and course level, and feedback from the Student Voice Committee, to reflect on my own practices. I use this understanding to contribute to the development of the current ecosystems so that we can influence and nurture a strong and confident culture of engagement with the VLE which falls behind baseline expectations. Furthermore, I highlight the methods that can be adopted to allow microsystems to inform each other when helping students, in order to optimize student support, and strengthen their confidence, which in turn will feed their motivation to engage more fully.

Application

With students being the focus of development through proximal processes that interact, and influence, or even sometimes hamper their development (Skinner et al., 2022), I focused on ensuring there was open and free communication between the students and myself. This provided the students with the ability to voice their struggles and views directly, or indirectly, and thus exercise and develop their own agency. Context and time being elements of the theory (Bond, 2020), I used all the feedback from students as a lens to view the five components of the BSEF as detailed below:

1. Microsystem – within this component of the framework, a variety of activities within lectures were designed using simple online platforms such as Kahoot, Google Classroom and even QR codes to access relevant material. Personal tutor time was offered via Google Meet. A focus on interpersonal interaction with tutors and peers was fostered in virtual sessions to encourage sharing via online platforms. The course team were encouraged to follow similar methods regularly to help students develop familiarity and comfort with online platforms. The UK's Teaching Excellence Framework (TEF) considers that using digital resources actively, and consistently, in this manner enhances learning and is an example of outstanding practice (Department of Education, 2017);

2. Mesosystem – developed the social ecology by reviewing barriers emerging at course level (decisions and systems) to foster positive interactions with, and between, microsystems. Regular feedback was provided during timetabled sessions, in tutorials and via student representatives, about issues faced with VLE engagement. Examples of feedback included access to electronic devices, facilitating the use of appropriate platforms and the support for special educational needs. These factors were collated, and decisions and systems rethought, modified and/or changed to ensure the needs of students were met. WP student feedback suggested that they received the needed support and training, and as a result settle better into the Higher Education learning environment and synchronous learning. The attendance of students in sessions, and their increased interaction, suggested their comfort at being present. This resulted in increased levels of contribution and co-creation in both virtual and on-campus environments. Department of Education (2017) indicated that such personalized provision for students, from all backgrounds, helps to secure their engagement and active commitment toward their own learning, which is another example of outstanding practice;

3. Ecosystem – developing teaching and learning systems and having a raised sensitiveness to WP student needs and expectations, and with improved conditions including session time and space, guest talks and external links, together created time for participation in other campus activities, and exposure to links beyond just campus resources. This was a focus that was collectively decided upon by the course team. I was personally able to contribute to developing a conduit within the VLE

platform where support systems, including personal tutors, student engagement officers and learning development tutors, could update their input and advice about academic progress and engagement, as long as it was non-sensitive and used with the permission of the student. This approach ensured that key information was also visible to others who were involved in supporting the corresponding student. This provided a comprehensive approach to student support and follow-up;

4. Macrosystem – we used each student's prior knowledge and experience to shape their new experience, by providing a platform to use this prior experience as the basis to reflect and become a part of their learning. Prevailing microsystems were used to input data within lecture time, working in concert with each other to address barriers linked to using the selected technologies to support teaching and learning;

5. Exosystem – overall contextual beliefs were used to influence the entire system including the principles of British democracy, global citizenship and meritocratic notions. Interestingly, some of these theories were created before the true advent of the web, but they nevertheless remain useful in understanding it.

Thus, using the methods discussed above, the implementation of a constant feedback, and feedforward, system has proven to me that engagement can be consciously facilitated for students, and that such engagement impacts on leadership and decision-making for the course upon which the students are centered, and that developing an appropriate culture can empower students to be effective learners within a synchronous model.

Impact

As an academic and an educational leader, the benefits and impact of BSEF on teaching and learning are numerous. With the shift to synchronous learning since the pandemic, I have recognized that without constantly adapting pedagogy, and with careful planning in the way technology is introduced and used, tutors can cause unintentional disengagement among students (Logan-Goyette et al., 2021). Listening to the voice of the students is essential to develop a transformational change in my pedagogy and leadership that is needed to drive engagement within a synchronous model. It further highlighted the struggles students experience in having their voice heard, which therefore made me rethink representation, to ensure all students are included. To achieve this, we needed to introduce different avenues for hearing the student voice.

It was clear that students were not fully benefiting from the collective effects of the complex ecosystems offered by faculty, school and wider university. For example, the lack of communication between the learning development tutors, student engagement officers and personal tutors meant that each ecosystem was working independently from each other, and so the students did not have the required strong collective effort to support them.

The conduit is now being reviewed to develop a stronger mesosystem in which a WP student's personal struggles are considered alongside any decisions made by academics, and by other ecosystems that a student may interact with and/or be affected by. Similarly, efforts are continuously being made to including campus-wide facilities within timetabled activities, such as the immersive learning offered by other schools, which enhances interest and motivation to engage with curriculum, facilities outside the school and technology-based teaching and learning. Such opportunities have supported my own students' ability to draw from, and reflect upon, their prior and current experiences (mesosystem), and so shape their new experiences as Higher Education students. Thus, through this approach, efforts to help students cope with the changes they face are now being successfully managed.

Digital literacy of students, and staff, has the potential to drive engagement and confidence (Anthonysamy *et al.*, 2020). My focus as a leader was to ensure that the quality of teaching and learning was enhanced, with decisions around the use of digital platforms uniformly taken to ensure that training opportunities were both advertised and provided, within and outside the course, and that there was sufficient scaffolding in place to support the use of digital tools for assessment and evaluation purposes.

Identifying the person(s), and the different components, of the BSEF dispelled the views of the reductionist approach to conceiving low engagement and attainment. This enabled me to enrich my understanding of engagement in the context of the current educational practices that are often digitally driven and synchronous. The impact of this is evident in the development of my own pedagogy, and the influence that I have had on the decisions made to improve student 'engagement'.

Case Study Conclusion

The ability to create microsystems that combine digital and traditional face-to-face interactions, and lead to the creation of bidirectional relationships for students with resources in the whole university, has been a slow process. The BSEF has helped me understand the impact inclusive digital technology can have on student development, and this needs to be clearly conceptualized within the framework. As we look to the future, the framework will be formally presented to the course team, and the case study extended into a larger study, to draw upon these results, and so impact on the formal structures of my organization.

Case Study 3.2: Using Technology to Support Online Presence and Student Engagement

ROSEMARY PEARCE, RACHEL BANCROFT AND RACHEL CHALLEN

The pandemic exponentially increased the conversation about presence, and how to evolve a face-to-face community online, and keep students present and engaged. In our various roles in learning and teaching in a School of Arts and Humanities, engagement was a constant focus for us as we navigated concerns from colleagues, and students, about online attendance, disabled webcams and an ongoing sense of disconnectedness.

Description

David White (2021) talks powerfully about this time in the pandemic which "ripped away our opportunities to be physically co-present." He notes that "we immediately turned to our technology in an attempt to repair this loss. We wanted to 'see' each other and feel connected in meaningful ways" (https://daveowhite.com/). This was certainly our experience too, and our case study does not solely locate presence as a sense of an instructor's presence for students, but also as a sense of presence between students. Within this case study we will use three examples of how academic staff we supported used technology in innovative ways to create this sense of presence. Innovation in this sense does not involve cutting-edge technology, but instead is about finding innovative ways to rethinking and adapting how common, and accessible tools, can be used when a rapid change of delivery style is required.

Additionally, innovations that were developed during remote learning, and that allowed us to adapt to these changing circumstances, potentially hold future value for us as a sector. As we move forward, we are exploring flexible learning opportunities, and different learning pathways, for students who increasingly balance jobs and other responsibilities with their studies. Engagement and presence continue to be of high importance here, as we strive to nurture a sense of belonging and connectedness, whatever the method of delivery.

In our context, while in many cases teaching has returned to on-campus delivery, many of the innovations developed during the COVID-19 pandemic continue to be used, albeit often in an adjusted and refined form. Since on-campus learning has resumed, teaching has not returned to our pre-pandemic 'norm'. Instead, new pedagogy is emerging, including new approaches that encourage student presence, whether online or on campus.

Application

Our examples will visit three separate approaches focusing on online presence that have been implemented during, and since, the COVID-19 pandemic lockdowns: (1) the use of news items to engage students; (2) self-interview recordings; and (3) community building in large-group online sessions. Together, these innovations tell a story within our Arts and Humanities context, moving beyond established practice to find new ways to help students succeed in a digital learning environment.

Example 1: Considered use of the module newsfeed

The newsfeed, a common but often overlooked tool within VLEs, is not generally considered cutting-edge or innovative. It is often used to remind students of upcoming deadlines, or changes to schedules. However, the approach of one academic, Dan, went far beyond this, engaging students, creating a connection and providing a regular sense of his presence in between timetabled sessions on his 'Nuclear Literature' module.

This approach simply used three different categories for module news items:

- 'Nuclear news' items – these picked out the themes of the module across different contemporary media and cultural artifacts, demonstrating his active interest in the subject and the broad reach of the subject content;
- 'Nuclear literature scholarship' items – these picked out scholars from the resource list who were not covered in the core module activities, to encourage students to read further;
- General announcements – these were about practical aspects of the course, including when he released formative feedback and the results of polls students had undertaken.

Through providing consistent titling, and an icon for each, students could easily differentiate between the types of news.

Impact

Dan's approach to his module newsfeed provided an extra sense of his presence for his students and encouraged them to engage more deeply with the topic. He received feedback suggesting that the care he put into the online learning environment, demonstrated by the regular and considered news items, was noticed by the students. In evaluation survey feedback students noted that the online learning environment for his module was kept up-to-date, and new things were frequently added. This study considers how online communications from instructors influence student motivation and behavior. This model is supported by Leners and Sitzman (2006, p. 317) who argue that demonstrating 'care' can be a 'significant motivator' to students. Sharing results of polls also created an opportunity for students to feel each other's presence as their responses were collected and discussed together.

Example 2: Making students visible to each other in large-group online sessions

Despite sometimes having over 100 students attend his voluntary online Academic English sessions, another academic we support, Dave, managed to create a learning environment with an engaged cohort of students who were present for one another without being literally visible. Using webcams is not feasible for such large groups, even if students did feel comfortable turning them on. However, as frequently observed by students and instructors alike, online sessions where no one can see one another can feel isolated, and this is supported throughout the literature (Rasheed *et al.*, 2020; Kaufmann and Vallade, 2022). Instead, he built up the sense of a present learning community through multiple routes of interaction to garner student responses, including an audience response tool.

Interaction for students began right from the start of the sessions. They were greeted on microphone as they arrived, and immediately asked to select and post a reaction GIF in the chat on a particular theme. This created an informal moment that built rapport. While there was information to impart during the sessions, much like a lecture, there were still opportunities for students to interact with the material, with opportunities to check knowledge and understanding using polls embedded throughout. Regular pauses invited students to submit specific reaction icons that were displayed on the slides, to indicate whether they had understood what is being discussed, or whether they were still unclear.

Impact

This example demonstrated that large cohorts of students could be present for each other without being visible. The immediacy and anonymity of this approach offered insight into when something needed more explanation, and this helped students feel comfortable contributing despite the size of the group. They were also able to see that they were not alone in needing more clarification, creating a sense of connectedness and presence. Furthermore, this approach did not rely upon students turning on their webcams, and instead it provided a sense of connection in a way that was more comfortable for them to engage with.

Dave also observed an emerging learning community forming within his online sessions which was illustrated by emoji reactions from students to each other's comments and questions, thereby providing positive feedback in the moment. This was another way that students could make themselves visible to one another. Additionally, where this positive reinforcement from peers happened in sessions, it appeared to lead to students asking more questions, which was vital for their own learning. The feedback from students about Dave's continually evolving approach to his online sessions made clear that students recognized, and appreciated, the different opportunities for interaction that he put into place in his sessions.

Example 3: Rethinking language speaking practice for remote delivery

Not all innovation during the remote teaching period was focused on replicating an in-person sense of presence with an online equivalent. Sometimes it involved identifying barriers to learning that the lack of presence presented, and exploring how these barriers could be overcome in a different way. When teaching online sessions during the pandemic for the 'University Language Programme', and for both enrolled and external students, an academic named Shialing found that students were less likely to speak up and practice vital speaking skills.

With the move to remote sessions, eye contact and a sense of physical and social presence had been lost, and students were less inclined to speak to each other during sessions. This led the academic to develop a formative assessment opportunity which encouraged students to practice their speaking, and so allowed her to provide students with even more detailed feedback than time allowed for during the face-to-face sessions. Students were given the opportunity to record themselves in a 'self-interview', responding to a series of prompt questions provided by the academic. To ensure an inclusive approach that allowed all students to participate, activities were embedded directly into the module learning materials, and this provided students with a simple recording tool and / or the option to use their own device.

Impact

Shialing was able to gather feedback from her students to understand their experience of the activity, a vital part of introducing a new digital approach, and feedback was positive. All respondents agreed that they found the activity helpful for improving their Spanish speaking and would want to participate again in future. While some of the 'realistic' experience of a synchronous conversation could not be replicated in the move to remote teaching, feedback suggested that students identified some additional benefits of the activity, such as more focus upon details and pronunciation. So, while this activity was not a like for like replacement for in-class discussion, it did allow students to gain vital speaking practice in pursuit of their learning outcomes. The flexible method of delivery allowed students to pick a route that worked best for them, while ensuring that no students were excluded due to a lack of equipment or technical ability.

Case Study Conclusion

'Presence' looks different in all three examples. Perhaps this is to be expected for three different teaching scenarios, with different students and across different disciplines. Throughout though, the constant focus was upon what the students needed as they made the transition from campus to online teaching.

For Dan, presence meant cultivating a sense of connectedness in between contact time, and for Dave it represented visibility as being key, thereby allowing students to feel each other's presence while not being able to see one another. Shialing focused on tackling the issues arising when replicating a sense of presence online proved difficult, and instead tried rethinking and designing new ways for her students to learn.

While these case studies are diverse in terms of discipline, approach and pedagogy, there are also similarities in what makes these approaches innovative. When discussing 'innovation' there is sometimes a focus on specialist tools, state-of-the-art equipment or perhaps even the creation of bespoke engineered technical solutions. However, one observation we make here is that these teaching approaches do not necessarily require bespoke equipment, nor advanced specialist technical knowledge – instead, the innovation is to be found in how we adjust our teaching in response to changing situations.

With a clear focus on student needs, including both academic and pastoral aspects, the innovations in these case studies have made a positive impact on the student experience. They achieved this by developing a sense of connectedness at a time when disconnection was felt due to the lack of physical delivery, but these changes have continued to influence our teaching approaches since.

Case Study 3.3: Using Technology to Direct Student Learning Behavior

LYNN GRIBBLE AND JANIS WARDROP

Teaching large courses is a significantly complex process in terms of time and administration. Students can easily become 'lost in the crowd'. While there is an obvious need for consistency of messaging, it is important that students feel supported as much as possible so that they have a personalized experience rather than being just a 'number'.

Large classes inherently carry a greater administrative burden meaning teachers are often time-poor, making elements of care pedagogy and personalization difficult to implement. Considering this, the ability to support students' individual learning needs can be reduced. Individualized support can be difficult even in small classes, however, at scale, ensuring students understand the necessary actions that underpin learning success can become even more difficult. As students most commonly encounter large courses early in their studies, their experiences of being lost and overloaded are manifold. When commencing their studies, students have an increased cognitive load beyond grappling with the requirements of any specific course. Students are also learning how to navigate university systems, while seeking to engage with new concepts, and potentially new ways of learning.

Contextually, in universities, technology constraints such as the Learning Management System (LMS) must be noted. By using tools that are 'hidden in plain sight', data from the LMS can transform teaching and learning. Our case study shows how we deployed such technology to ensure that every student had a personal experience despite being a part of a very large compulsory core course on business ethics delivered within a postgraduate business program. The course is taught three times a year, with enrollments of over 1,000 students each term. The student cohort is comprised of mainly international students studying in a second (occasionally third or fourth) language, with many of them planning to specialize in finance, business analytics or accounting. As a result, students are often less than engaged in this course. A very large cohort of 'conscripts' means that they may treat the course as a hurdle to overcome, rather than engaging with it deeply. The content and subject matter is often not of their choosing. Given they are likely to have a strong preference for quantitative content, as evidenced by their choice of major subject area, the students may lack the efficacy required to undertake the written and oral assessment items (Wang *et al.*, 2018) embedded in the course. Yet these aspects of the teaching are required to fulfill the broader program learning outcomes.

Through the innovative use of technology, the student learning experience can be personalized at scale, reducing the cognitive load of managing course requirements for both educators and students. This enables students to focus upon the task at hand, i.e., learning. In this case study we have implemented a pedagogically driven use of learning management technology as detailed by Sankey (2020). Our pedagogical approach was underpinned by care, as described by Nakkula and Ravitch (1998), in which mutual transformation occurs. This is the result of teachers providing care, and students being in the 'care receiving mode'.

While most teachers self-report caring, it is the visible fostering and maintenance of bonds that matter. This applies from listening, to empathy, and having high expectations in work and behavior, along with showing active concerns (Mercer and Dörnyei, 2020), that teaching at scale risks losing all of this. As a result, personalization through technology is required which enables this pedagogy to be supported. By focusing on methods to engender authentic dialog, we wanted to support students to engage in transformative learning behaviors (Fleck-Henderson and Melendez, 2009). Care pedagogy also shows the need for compassion, and affirms action, which are both important for building student confidence and a sense of belonging.

The use of such technology was originally deployed during the COVID-19 pandemic when students were globally dispersed and isolated. This fundamental shift in learning environment, for many the first time that they had engaged in online learning, witnessed an exponential rise in student communications, as they sought guidance and reassurance from course authorities. Once this information would have been sought on the way into classrooms, and then clarified during the class itself. During the pandemic, even if they were 'present' during an online class, the dislocation and disassociation many students experienced meant that they were less likely to seek advice or assistance, feeling that they were 'on show' to the whole class if they did so.

The result was that some students would reach out via email to seek advice and clarification. For others, they would try and work it out themselves, or worse, to retreat and disengage completely. We needed to find a level of individualized communication to reach all students that was also sustainable. With our success during the pandemic to support students, and keep them engaged, we have continued to use these tools and approaches now that classes have largely returned to campus. This case study explores how the Personalized Learning Designer (PLD) was deployed based on the mapped student journey. Through the analysis of student actions, we were able to increase engagement, and support learning behaviors, by using personalized 'push and pull' communications.

Description

PLD is a tool within the Moodle LMS. Using the data stored in the LMS, including logons, and by tracking student engagement with documents and activities within the platform, the PLD can be used to send 'in platform' messages, and direct emails and reminders on the basis of predetermined rules. It can also draw data from the grade center to target student behaviors linked to attainment or assessment outcomes. Once the process is set up, and rules are encoded, the process is automated and occurs (largely) without further human intervention by the instructor.

Application

We initially introduced the use of the PLD to create 'personalization at scale' in a large compulsory core course, when students were learning online, and suffering from increased sense of dislocation and disengagement. Hence our goals were to:

1. Ensure no student felt lost or alone;
2. Free up cognitive load, and so reposition the students from managing the learning, to engaging with the content of the learning;
3. Ensure consistent messaging about expectations and requirements in a timely fashion;
4. Support appropriate learning behaviors, such as proactive engagement with course resources, and with the feedback being provided to students;
5. Reduce academic administration.

With the return to face-to-face teaching, we have continued to observe that students are still struggling with understanding the necessary behaviors to support a positive learning experience, and thus we continue to use the PLD.

While we know that timeliness in learning activities supports success, both in online learning and in the classroom, in terms of completion and outcomes (Dvorak and Jia, 2016), we also recognize that, beyond cognitive load, a lack of planning, procrastination and/or just simple lack of technical skills to use the LMS may lead students to miss core information or to not be able to complete the tasks required.

To achieve the most impact through the use of the PLD, it is important to create a process map of the learning journey. Through defining learner behaviors, course milestones and deadlines, as well as points of regular communication, we have been able to direct each student to the support available, and to drive their learning behaviors within certain timelines incorporating the touch points that would be expected by the course authority/educator. The data points informed the PLD 'rules'. These rules can be based on specific dates (for example, one week from an assessment deadline we could send a reminder email to all students of the due date), grades (for example, all students that received a High Distinction grade would receive a congratulatory email) and expected activity or action in the LMS (for example, one week from an assessment deadline, where a student has not accessed the assessment information, we could take students to this information immediately on their next login to the LMS).

The PLD rules can be set up significantly in advance or 'just in time' as needed. Importantly, once created, these rules can be easily 'rolled over' from term to term, reducing the time involved for the set-up and implementation for future cohorts. By mapping the student journey, and by analyzing student engagement and behaviors, we generate personalized push and pull communications that both supported and directed students to undertake good learning behaviors. The interventions used a variety of means to engage the students, such as pop-ups when logging on, and directing students to a specific activity (such as immediately opening of the assessment booklet/outline rather than merely reminding students to do so). These interventions encouraged every student to 'find their way', even the ones who were struggling get to where they needed to go.

We also generated emails as a more personalized way of one-on-one communication with students, even though this was computer-generated. A focused email enabled personalized follow-up after each assessment to drive engagement with the feedback provided. This had a motivating effect for our most disengaged and engaged students, where students performing well were acknowledged for their results, and those doing poorly were directed to resources. Most, if not all, LMSs include similar systems, and hence the applications discussed are applicable regardless of the platform in use.

Impact

Moodle data was collated through a Learning Analytics Insights (LAI) program which provided more granular information related to student interaction on Moodle, thereby enabling analysis of student academic performance. While acknowledging the reasons for failing a course is complex, 'starting a course well', attending and being attentive, as well as understanding what is expected of them, are all important aspects that need to be considered (Linnenbrink and Pintrich, 2003). Hence nudging students to engage with the platform, and the materials, means that, at the most fundamental level, students know both how they will be assessed and how to engage with the learning materials for those assessment items (Gribble and Huber 2022).

When we considered data for student Moodle activity across the term for students who passed the course, and those that failed the course, it revealed that students who passed the course were overall more active on the LMS platform across the whole term than those students who ultimately failed the course. We isolated the Moodle activity for the group of students who had no Moodle activity in Week 1 (irrespective of their final grade). From this we could see the impact of the early PLD reminders on this cohort, with a marked increase in platform activity by this subgroup across Weeks 2 and 3, which was then maintained across the remainder of the term. This was unlike the 'general course population' where the Moodle activity declined across the term. Course results for this subgroup of students revealed that 77% of students who received a nudge in Week 1 ultimately went on to pass the course. Clearly there were benefits to students receiving targeted and personalized reminders when the course commenced.

There are clear benefits for teaching staff of automating the processes for reminders and support. We know, anecdotally, that delivering care pedagogy at scale through an automated targeted process reduces the administrative burden of seeking out individual students to check on welfare and / or address their anxious inquiries about what they need to do. These automated nudges generally lead to action, and subsequent completion of the activity, by three out of four students. As a compulsory core course, supporting students to successful completion is very important. Given this, the PLD is now well embedded into the course providing a reminder for all students to undertake desired learning behaviors and activities in a timely manner. Further, by utilizing data captured by the LMS, students who were at risk of failing are identified earlier, enabling early intervention to support their efforts, or to support their withdrawal / change of courses with no financial penalty.

Discussion

There was a distinct learning curve to map the desired learning behaviors, and to consider the possibilities and constraints within the tool. To deploy such technology required support from educational technologists who could work in a problem-solving manner. Rather than focusing on the technology alone, working in a partnership in a problem-based learning manner enabled the tool to be deployed based upon pedagogical concerns over technology benefits alone.

After completing some basic training to understand the potential of the PLD, approximately two hours were required for each week of the ten-week course to map the expected learning behaviors of students, and to identify both their and our 'pain points', as well as assessment details deadlines to develop the PLD 'rules'. The time invested to map student learning behaviors, and set up the rules, ensured that the data was properly aligned, which meant a positive outcome in terms of time reduction could be achieved for any subsequent teaching sessions using these same rules.

For each subsequent term, it was important to check the PLD rules against any changes in the course. Our experience showed that, in the subsequent terms, it took approximately 30 minutes per assignment to update the associated PLD rules, when all other elements of the course remained the same. This was a total of no more than 2 hours and was a considerably smaller investment in time than the original set-up cost of 20 hours.

The student response also taught us that they appreciated the interventions. While the data itself does not provide us with the 'why' behind the student behavior, or the lack thereof, it often nudges students to reach out personally so that we learn more about their own unique situation, thereby allowing us to provide further individualized support when and where required. Our message to the students has been clear: our intention is to 'catch' the student at risk of failing due to a lack of engagement. Our job is to ensure they do not 'fall through the cracks', which can happen in large courses. From the student responses, many of them reported that they found the emails to be highly motivating in terms of continuing their efforts.

While the PLD was initially a COVID-19 response and implementation, it has been maintained with the return of face-to-face teaching. Now in place, the PLD facilitates a positive and supportive learning environment with little to no cost.

Case Study Conclusion

Large courses will continue to be a fact of life at many institutions. Technology increasingly can reduce the quantity of work without reducing the quality. Automated personalization has enabled us to enact a care pedagogy at scale, with reduced administration burden and email traffic. Our students clearly wanted and needed this type of support. Through this approach, we provided directed and individual support at scale by using the PLD technology.

The initial time invested to deploy this technology has reaped many efficiency and effectiveness rewards. After the initial set-up time, the incremental changes required for each iteration of the course provide further efficiency gains.

Nudging students to proactively undertake their studies, seek support or maintain their involvement has supported this large cohort of compulsory core students to be successful. For such gains to be achieved, it requires us to consider what tasks could be automated, or programmed, yet still have the human touch and oversight to ensure they remain unique and genuine, and also aligning with the pedagogical design of the course.

Case Study 3.4: Effects of Learning Technologies on the Critical Reflection of Equity and Social Justice

UMA PATEL

This case study considers the effects of mobilizing learning technologies for staff development workshops that focus on inclusive education practice. The learners in this context are staff across all four faculties in a post-1992 university, and practicing educators enrolled on the Postgraduate Certificate in Education Practice course. Building on research using the Equity Compass (Archer *et al.*, 2022) which has been adapted for Higher Education (Patel, 2022), the workshop comprised of self-guided, self-access online content, and a series of synchronous video conferencing, and hybrid mode workshops, augmented by established tools such as Mentimeter and Padlet, alongside emerging Artificial Intelligence (AI) Avatar presenter tools.

The discourses of inclusivity, equality, equity and social justice are grounded in feminist and critical race theory, sociology of education and social justice research (Archer *et al.*, 2022). Academic research and debates in these fields involve technical language and concepts that can feel like niche academic navel gazing to uninitiated outsiders. The policy discourse of equality, diversity and inclusion in Higher Education, and beyond, is driven by the Public Sector Equality Duty enshrined in the UK Equality Act (www.gov.uk/guidance/equality-act-2010-guidance). The entrenched inequalities in Higher Education have previously been well evidenced (Bolton and Lewis, 2023). In this climate, staff development has emerged as one institutional strategy to tackle inequalities, including unequal access to opportunities, tools and resources.

In this case study the inclusivity focus is on ethically minoritized communities, and the historical and cultural systemic challenges embedded in Higher Education curricula and pedagogies, that seek to maintain the status quo. Equity approaches to inclusivity advocate for recognizing and valuing differences, while social justice approaches set out to change the structure and practice that maintain inequalities, including confronting the colonial past of education and research funding (Blake *et al.*, 2022).

The aim of the workshops was for educators to contextualize and enhance practice in their discipline or field, toward more equitable and socially just education outcomes for their students. Going beyond training, or generic enhancing of teaching and learning, staff development was conceived as being a generative process that involves change in which educators are supported in contextualizing how equitable education is realized in their own education practice (Lovett *et al.*, 2023).

Covering a period of 18 months, the case study reflects on three rounds of staff development workshops. Observations and experiences from each round informed the design of the next set of workshops. Insights at each stage suggested the affordances and limitations of digital tools for different learning types (Laurillard, 2012), and how these are entangled with engagement, learner motivation and efficacy.

Description

The first set of workshops introduced the Equity Compass Tool (Archer *et al.*, 2022). Evaluation of the tool in schools, and informal science education sectors, has shown that the academic grounding of the tool provided a level of credibility and rigor that attracted both practitioners and institutional leaders. Archer *et al.*'s (2022) Equity Compass consists of eight dimensions organized into four areas. Educators are invited to reflect on where they are along each of the dimensions in the context of their practice:

1. *Challenging the Status Quo from:*
   i   Prioritizing minoritized communities *or* prioritizing the dominant;
   ii Transforming power relations *or* reproducing power;
   iii Redistributing resources *or* reinforcing privilege.
2. *Working with and Valuing Minoritized Communities:*
   iv Participatory working-with *or* not participatory by doing-to the participants;
   v   Asset-based approach *or* deficit-based.
3. *Embedding Equality:*
   vi Equity is mainstreamed *or* equity is tokenistic.
4. *Extending Equity:*
   vii Community/society reorientation *or* only the individual/individualistic;
   viii Long-term action *or* short-term tick boxing.

Each dimension is accompanied by questions to prompt critical reflection adapted for the Higher Education setting (Patel 2022). An accompanying visual representation works as a conceptual heuristic. Often described pictorially as being three concentric circles, toward the center of the visual representation of the equity compass the practices are less equitable, for example tokenistic and short term. The outer circles indicate more equitable practices, for example asset-based approaches. The compass scaffolds generative thinking in three ways: (1) dimensions and questions focus critical reflection upon current practice; (2) discussion and questions are a guide to planning change toward more equitable outcomes; and (3) decision-making considers appropriate indicators of equitable outcomes.

The second set of workshops responded to the lack of language consensus around inclusivity and social justice. Drawing on my own personal research, an archival study into Technology-Enhanced Learning research, the workshops adapted the Foucauldian technique of framing foundational questions such as What is it? Where does it come from? (Patel, 2015). This is the Foucauldian notion of 'history of the now' and the 'disciplining power of disciplines'.

The third set of workshops tackled the uncomfortable dynamics of belonging, and the other effects of identity within the education setting. Stories or vignettes are short descriptive narratives from the educator's point of view (Lovett et al., 2023). The stories are located where teaching takes place, e.g., in the lecture theatre, online or lab, and importantly are specific to context of teaching. While the account is realistic, it is not necessarily real as they are experiential composites from the point of view of the educator.

The focus on critical incidents and conflict can be uncomfortable for the person leading the workshop and sometimes for people in the room, even if it is an account of lived experiences within an educational setting. To tackle this, I experimented with AI-generated Avatars to invoke experiences that are tied to visible identity. As a distancing device, to take the heat out of the discussions, AI-generated Avatars populated the dimensions of the compass with stories from the field, and strategies for inclusive practices attached to the stories.

Application

The first round of workshops (six in total) were voluntary, and each was scheduled for one hour using Zoom. Participation ranged from 10 to 20 people. I started the workshop by presenting the Equity Compass Tool using shared screen and PowerPoint. Next, I invited participants to critically reflect in smaller breakout groups. I asked them to (1) select a dimension and (2) share examples of their current position and ideas for moving their position toward more equitable approaches. On return, the participants were invited to share their thoughts in the Chat Panel, relating to what they would take away from the workshop, and also what they would like to see more of in the future.

The second series of workshops (five in total) were requested by Heads of Department as part of annual planning. Each of these workshops was scheduled for two hours. The departments represented ranged from Business, Marketing and Finance, to Media, Design Engineering and Humanities. Following institutional priorities, the focus was on inclusive assessment and group-work. The workshops were hybrid, and participation ranged from 10 to 15 in the room and up to 15 online. For this series of workshops, I sought to bring to the surface the historical context of language, and academic work, thereby allowing open discussion before introducing the Equity Compass.

I started the session by invoking an emotional response via Mentimeter by posing two questions: (1) 'Express in five words the feelings of not belonging, feeling accepted or fitting in' and (2) 'Describe in five words the sensation of being valued when your contributions are sought and appreciated'. Next, I employed the concept of the 'history of the now' to stimulate a discussion on evolving language constructions related to inclusivity and decolonization. This journey traversed terms like 'black' and 'persons of color' to modern concepts such as 'minoritized' and 'global south majority'. Discussions encompassed shifts from political and military colonization to decolonization in the UK academic curriculum. Participants then collaborated in small subject groups to devise pertinent questions, focusing on strategies for inclusive group-work and assessment within the 'working with and valuing minoritized communities' dimension of the Equity Compass.

These questions were then refined collectively as headers for a Padlet share board, which served as a collaborative resource post-workshop. Posts on the Padlet were sorted into categories to identify practice that work well and challenges. Example categories used included:

- Preparing learners for group-work assessment;
- Challenges to setting up groups;
- Managing groups;
- Damaging group behaviors;
- Benefits of group-work;
- Group-work good practice.

The third series of workshops included substantive content from earlier workshops. However, rather than the traditional recorded lecture delivered by me, I wrote scripts for each segment and replaced myself with an AI Avatar. In addition, as examples, I scripted two AI Avatars who told two-minute stories. Using an Avatar means that the animation can invoke the identity characteristics of the speaker, for example mediterranean, male, athletic with an accent and specific gestures, in other words an identity placeholder. The title of the story invoked a critical juncture to be discussed, for example 'there is no fixing the damage everybody was angry'. The next stage involved critical analysis of the story by using the Equity Compass to make sense of the underlying issues. This was a way to develop strategies, not least for self-awareness, and to discuss the hidden curriculum of Higher Education with the participants with specific relevance to their own education practice.

Impact

The first round of workshops was characterized by the affordance and limitations of synchronous technologies. While critical reflective practice is embodied in the Equity Compass, the process involves effort and time and those involved being open to change. Participants joined online because it was easy to drop-in.

The workshops were time limited and voluntary, and there was no meaningful way of knowing how the participants would use the Equity Compass. I found the participants to be engaged, for example in sharing examples of co-constructing group-work. At the same time what emerged was 'fear of causing offense' (perhaps because of my own ethnicity). I had assumed readiness and needed to revisit efficacy in terms of creating a safe space for more authentic discussions. For this, I turned to the idea 'history of the now'.

The second round of workshops evidenced hybrid participation effects, robust adversarial debate and asynchronous affordances for rich collective resource generation. Participants attended both in person and online. For example, in response to the question about not belonging, feeling accepted or fitting in, one person amusingly expressed, "I have never felt like that". This was a form of challenge which was juxtaposed by a word cloud generated from input by others in the room that acknowledged their own experiences of isolation and feeling alone.

The Foucauldian challenge that all fields have a 'history of the now,' and the 'disciplines are disciplining' sparked amicable yet provocative debate. Despite my comfort with rebuttal, around half of the participants, including some from minoritized communities, remained silent. While defiance is a form of engagement, silence can signal internally rejection, evasion, feeling of defeat or simple processing. This dynamic was possibly accentuated because of the hybrid mode, and the faculty requirement that staff attend.

I had assumed that the learners uniformly accepted that my question about the history of their field/discipline would invite reflection on positionality going beyond opinion and identity performance. It was a provocation to engage with critical thinking and evidence embodied in the literature including the Equity Compass. A positive outcome was that, from each workshop, champions did come forward (eventually) to form a network of inquiry.

The third round of workshops provoked conversation, but initially this was about the use of AI Avatars. While some people found the Avatar annoying at first, it quickly became a representational device, and the conversation moved on to the production possibilities of representing different stories. Moving forward there is potential to work with the inclusivity champions in producing context-specific stories for each of the dimensions of the Equity Compass.

Discussion

The ambition for the workshops in this case study was to design generative processes in which the learners contextualized the challenges of equitable practice in their teaching, and so built on research undertaken to change practice toward more socially just outcomes for all their students. Building on this prior research and scholarship, the workshops provoked critical reflective practice for intentional planning.

Following Laurillard's model of learning types (2012), the first stage was a case of *ready-or-not* and primarily involved knowledge acquisition through video and PowerPoint, with minimal collaboration in breakout groups. The introduction of the Equity Compass, along with associated questions, successfully disseminated knowledge encompassing equity, social justice, power dynamics, privilege and cultural contexts within education. Given the time limit of the exercise, the Equity Compass was experienced by the participants in an abstract and reified form.

The second stage shifted to more active learning methods, such as collaboration through Mentimeter, discussions and sharing contextualized practice using Padlet. This phase encouraged critical self-analysis, prompting participants to acknowledge their beliefs, practices and emotional responses related to power and privilege as a form of *history-of-the-now* in their teaching practice.

The ongoing final stage introduced both AI Avatars and stories. This showed promise as a generative and detached medium for *disrupting-identity*. It offered a novel avenue for empathetic analysis of personal stances, including aggression, withdrawal and evasion, revealing affective inner worlds and beliefs regarding power, privilege, emotional belonging and agency.

Case Study Conclusion

Turning the staff development workshop into this case study has highlighted the effects of Learning Technologies for promoting generative engagement. There has been an intentional focus on equity and social justice. It transpired that the staff development wrapper was inherently flawed in terms of the time constraints, and the unknown motivations of the participants, and in framing efficacy. However, promising outcomes included the emergence of a community of champions, and the possibility of adding generative AI Avatars to the Equity Compass in the future.

Case Study 3.5: Developing Solutions to Re-Engage Students with Low Attainment

BARRY AVERY, REBECCA LEES AND DANIEL RUSSELL

Kingston Business School is part of Kingston University which is a medium-sized, and mid-ranked, institution near to London in the UK. The student demographic has a diverse ethnicity, with many students who are the first entrants into Higher Education. Students are recruited with middle-level grades, and experience frontloaded contact time in their first year. Our teaching has a focus on authentic assessments, which link with employment, to situate learning within realistic settings. Blended learning (Garrison and Kanuka, 2004; Martyn, 2003; Singh, 2003) has been embedded across the curriculum in the Canvas LMS to support face-to-face delivery, which is still the priority of our student experience.

Attendance for most classes in the Business School is typically 50–60%, indicating a high 'churn' rate for physical presence, with many students not attending every session, and variable usage of the LMS. This is a common characteristic of our student base with 60% of students commuting across the Greater London area, and travel times ranging from 30 minutes to two hours. Previous analysis has shown 59% of the first-year students (n = 155) reported they were working alongside their studies, with 24% working 14 hours or more a week (Avery and Lees, 2019).

Numerous studies suggest that engagement correlates with attainment (Finn and Zimmer, 2012). Analysis over the academic year of attendance, online participation and assessment submission reveals a correlation between students who gradually attend less frequently, and have a declining engagement with online activities and materials, and those who fail to submit one or more assessment elements. Data from previous cohorts reveals the correlation between non-attendance and low online engagement, with consequential effects on outcomes.

Description

This initiative details our attempt at intervening early to recover students identified as poor engagers and reinforce good practice for those identified as stronger engagers. Based around the idea of *Linear-on-the-Fly* (LOTF) testing (Luecht, 2005), students were asked to participate in online activities, and differentiated formative tasks, which had been tailored for them based on their levels of in-class and online engagement. Data presented in this case study has been gathered from attendance statistics, analytic information from the LMS and commentary derived from anonymized early module reviews and in-class interactions.

We were guided by the importance of active learning, which encourages belonging and engagement, and the philosophy of assessment for learning with regular formative feedback (Wiliam, 2021). Both are considered essential for retention and success in Higher Education. Tinto tells us that student involvement (engagement) is required for them to be successful. If we can encourage students to be more socially involved then they are more likely to graduate as a result (Tinto, 2012). Central to this idea is a focus on creating a structured learning environment that empowers students to 'need' to learn within a 'web of consistency', and that keeps students engaged and on track in their learning (Biggs, 2012). These principles underpinned the approach we have taken to design an early intervention program of reinforcement activities, to re-engage students with low engagement and to 'recover' them back to a trajectory for module success.

This study tracked participants from two modules over the first five weeks of an academic year when studying (1) a first-year module covering IT and analytics on an undergraduate Business Management program and (2) a specialized option module covering more technical IT subjects for final-year Business, Marketing and Accounting students. Both modules were delivered in a lab, in an interactive style, with the first-year students attending two two-hour sessions per week, and the final-year students attending a specialized option delivered as a one three-hour lab session each week.

For these two modules, we gathered analytic information from two sources to form an aggregate measure of module engagement. Attendance information was collated from a student tap-to-check-in system, and LMS participation activity was collated from the system-reported analytics. These analytics were used to report page views, downloads, forum activity and quiz completion.

Attendance data was collated on a lesson-by-lesson basis as students had to tap during entry to their class. The reports generated from the system provided the count data of how many face-to-face classes a particular student had been registered as attending during a week. The data was then available to be exported in raw comma-separated value (CSV) files.

The LMS participation metric comprised of statistics generated from student interactions within the online Canvas module, including viewing a page, downloading a file, completing a quiz or participating in an online discussion. As with the attendance data, the LMS reports provided the raw count data available for export. The institutional LMS templates were important here, as they explicitly standardized the structure of modules, ordering materials into clear successive weeks. This enabled the participation statistics to suggest when students were interacting with subjects, and over which weeks and days this occurred.

Aggregate Measure of Module Engagement (AMME)

Defining student engagement is problematic due to its complexity and multi-faceted nature. In her comprehensive literature review, Trowler notes that "engagement is more than involvement or participation – it requires feelings and sense-making as well as activity" (Trowler, 2010, p. 5). Therefore, student engagement had two uses here. First, we identified a simplified metric called the Aggregate Measure of Module Engagement (AMME) which classified students' engagement level using attendance and participation metrics. The data from these sources were readily available to the teaching team. Second, to promote re-engagement among low-engagement students. We were cognizant of the broader spectrum of engagement incorporating sensemaking and feeling. Students were sent targeted feedback, activities and expectations to help them in making sense of their own progress. These interventions were supported with content targeted for their specific profile to create buy-in and a feeling of personalization.

For this project, customized Python scripts were used to merge the data sets, and to present engagement activity each week. Combining these data sets revealed an AMME, making visible each student's pattern of activity on both a weekly and a daily basis.

Because of the pandemic response, the teaching team had curated a wealth of asynchronous module content including pre-recorded lecture overviews (typically 7–10 minutes each), online activities and formative assessments such as Multiple-Choice Questions (MCQs) designed using the ABC toolkit (Avery and Wason, 2022). An appropriate selection of material oriented around the AMME engagement level of the students were placed on weekly topic pages inside the LMS. This mirrored the class content. The pages also included extra MCQs which served as a supplementary engagement indicator. Access to these was via class notifications and targeted individualized emails.

Application

By combining the two data sets, each week we classified students into low-, medium- or high-engagement categories:

- *Low:* students with no attendance for that week and less than half of the average activity for a student in the LMS;
- *Medium:* 50–100% attendance and between one and two-thirds of the average activity for a student in the LMS;
- *High:* 100% attendance and in the top third of activity in the LMS.

Online participation as a measure of engagement was not as clear as attendance, due to the variable nature of the measure. A week with more online activities would automatically generate higher participation as students navigated around the module looking at pages and downloading materials. To account for this, the participation measure for students was calculated weekly and then scaled to the maximum participation for that week. Care was taken to ensure that the occasional outlier student, with an extremely high level of activity, did not skew the calculated boundaries.

Activity based on AMME level

Low-engagement students were emailed links to full sets of videos covering all the materials, along with MCQs, framed as catch-up activities. We made clear that these were not to be taken as a replacement for attendance, using phrasing to suggest that completing the MCQs was mandatory, for example: "after working your way through the materials in Canvas, you should attempt the online quiz".

Medium-engagement students were offered videos that highlighted subjects which were regarded as more complex, or those that require extra "effort" to learn. The MCQs in this context were framed as recap, or revision tests, to encourage participation, with questions assuming a degree of familiarity with the subject areas. The phrasing in this instance suggested that completion of the MCQs would be a useful reflective exercise to see how they were progressing, for example: "the MCQ is available for you to try to reinforce your learning".

As this case study was situated at the start of an academic year, high-engagement students were given the same tasks as the medium category described above. Adding extra content at the beginning of the module was deemed appropriate due to the complexities inherent in transitioning into Higher Education, and/or between levels. Students in this category were however sent additional messages of encouragement acknowledging their efforts to facilitate sustained higher levels of engagement.

Impact

The engagement for many modules followed a common pattern of higher levels of LMS activity on days of physical attendance, decreasing between the points of on-campus presence. Levels of engagement also surged around summative assessment, but this fell outside the period of this project which was oriented around the first five weeks of the academic year.

For the first-year module in this study, students attended twice a week, with 20–31 of the cohort active on the LMS on the attendance days over the five-week period (n = 37). Between, and outside, of these days, 3–9 students used the LMS, but this increased to 11–14 on the day where students were emailed, or notified, of the outside class activities. Overall, 14–17 of the students completed the formative MCQs each week, with 5–9 students in the low group, and between 2 and 8 students in each of the medium and high groups. For at least a third of the cohort, our notifications created a subsequent peak of activity, with students accessing pages, videos and the MCQs outside of the common patterns seen.

For students in their final year, 20–23 students engaged with the LMS materials on the attendance day before, during and after class (n = 25). For days of non-attendance, 0–6 students accessed the module online, and following the email notification of additional activities, this rose to 6–11 students. This tends to be a lower percentage than the first-year students, but an additional peak of activity was created with 5–15 students completing the formative MCQs over the five-week period, and with 2–7 students in the low-engagement group, and 3–9 in the medium and high categories. For both groups, those with medium levels of engagement were marginally less likely to complete formative MCQs compared to those in the lower and higher groups.

Comments collated from the early module reviews suggested that clarity was required on the formative nature of the MCQs, particularly where part of the assessment strategy was portfolio-based. No negative comments were associated with the process, and students acknowledged that the activities provided reinforcement opportunities: "I am doing the extra-curricular work to better understand" (final-year student).

Students who were classified as highly engaged regularly asked for more activities, or requested that the pace be increased: "in addition to the quizzes can we have extra tasks?" (first-year student).

Case Study Conclusion

This case study has shown that regular weekly interventions, with customized activities outside of the class, can increase participation and engagement. The quantitative results, while based on relatively small samples, suggest that targeted emails and activities supported additional interactions between students and the module materials. The qualitative feedback also indicated that there are elements of sensemaking which may generate a desire to learn, and while our initial approach was to target low-engaging students, there are benefits of communication with participants at all levels of engagement.

Throughout, it was made very clear to students that online materials would not form a replacement for in-class attendance. Although we acknowledge the complexity involved in the use of the scripting technologies in the study, this could be achieved by any module that has some form of attendance and online activity data available. Extra costs could be involved in creating content and reflective activities, although many institutions have a repository of materials created for the pandemic response that could be available for reuse. It is also conceivable that AI engines could assist in processing the analytics and even to generate draft MCQ questions. As a next step, this approach could be used to provide stretch activities for high-engagement students, as indicated by requests in the early module review feedback.

The level of categorization here is admittedly broad, grouping students into low, medium, and high engagement, but it is as far as the analytics can go with the data that is available at the current time. Further personalization in true LOFT style will be possible if content is presented inside the LMS in smaller chunks, coupled with reflective activities. This would then become visible in the analytics so that more targeted activities could be suggested. Such automation is not built into most LMSs, but this study shows that similar outcomes could be achieved through scripting languages sitting alongside the LMS to collate and align learning activities to enhance engagement and achievement.

Case Study 3.6: Enabling Students to Evaluate Their Academic Writing

SONYA MCCHRISTIE

Studiosity is a support service that provides students with personalized feedback on the quality of their academic writing. The University of Sunderland added the service to our support offering as a pilot in the academic year 2021/2022. It targeted both new undergraduate students and also those entering their integrated foundation year at our Sunderland and London campuses. In this case study, I will discuss what Studiosity is, and where it fits into the university, how we deployed the service from a technical point of view, how we drove adoption using the innovative 'Write it Right' activity and the exciting outcomes of the pilot.

The University of Sunderland is strongly committed to the WP agenda and is proud of its reputation as an 'anchor' institution in the region, recruiting a high proportion of students from the local area. This presents challenges, as the Northeast of England is one of the country's most deprived areas, and our students are therefore more likely to have experienced poverty, and to be the first in their family to access tertiary education. For example, Sunderland is the 23rd most income-deprived local authority in England (Office for National Statistics, 2021). This problem is reflected in the data in our Action and Participation Plan as the university recruits 55.9% of students from the POLAR 1–2 groups, over double the sector rate of 27.7%. Progression to employment or further study is 61.7% for this group, compared with 69.9% for the wider sector (University of Sunderland, 2022).

The Action and Participation Plan outlines a number of strategies to address these issues, including a project on Personal Academic Tutoring that seeks to align our tutoring provision with UKAT's Framework for Advising and Tutoring (UK Advising and Tutoring Association, 2023). This project began in the academic year 2020/2021, and in its second year, we started our pilot with Studiosity with the specific goal of improving our retention, progression and attainment rates. Studiosity was aligned with this goal as there was a plan from its inception for an early intervention activity using Studiosity that would be set and run by tutors to cultivate these benefits.

Description

Studiosity is an Australian company founded in 2003 to provide students with detailed and personalized feedback on the quality of their academic writing, covering areas including structure, language and use of academic conventions. Importantly, they do not provide feedback on the academic content of submissions, which remains the purview of students' tutors. Another significant value-added aspect of Studiosity is that, by having their specialists located globally, their service is available 24/7, 365 days a year, which is a level of service that would be prohibitively expensive to provide in-house. They have a service-level agreement that feedback will be provided within 24 hours, 90% of the time, but in our pilot year, the median return time was impressively under 3 hours, and no case exceeded 24 hours.

Studiosity provides two related services: (1) *Writing Feedback* which allows students to submit written work for feedback asynchronously and (2) *Connect Live* which provides students with a direct connection with Studiosity's specialists. A third service that will connect students with each other for peer feedback is in development. At the University of Sunderland, our pilot has focused on the Writing Feedback service, which is the only area that will be discussed and evaluated in this case study.

All student interactions with Studiosity are with real people who are subject specialists recruited from "universities ranked in the top 10% globally" (Studiosity, 2023). There is no use of AI, chatbots or simple automated checkers, as is found in applications like Microsoft Office or services such as Grammarly. At Sunderland, Studiosity was introduced as a means of supporting and complementing our existing internally provided student support services, such as our Study Skills team.

Functionally, the Writing Feedback service looks much like any assignment submission point that is familiar from LMSs, but with some additional options for students to indicate what stage their writing is at, the type of document being submitted and which areas they would like feedback to be concentrated on. Once feedback is available, students are presented with a 'Disclaimer' reiterating the nature of Studiosity's feedback. This Disclaimer also contains links to some of our other key student support services, including our Wellbeing service. We recognize that assignment submission points are often periods of high stress and anxiety. Once the Disclaimer has been acknowledged, the feedback interface is again reminiscent of other such screens in tools such as Turnitin and Canvas' SpeedGrader, i.e., the assignment appears on the left, annotated with areas where specific feedback has been provided. In line with Studiosity's ethos of providing help, not answers, feedback is given in a form "based around scaffolding, empowering and building capacity within students" (Studiosity, 2022a).

Finally, Studiosity links back into our in-house services via a system of 'Referrals' and 'Interventions'. Referrals are signposts for students toward our in-house support services. By far the most common type of referral is for 'study skills', which happens when the Studiosity specialist considers that the student would benefit from a more in-depth discussion to improve their writing. The early intervention monitoring system is for more serious issues, and these are received by a dedicated support team within the university. Studiosity specialists use this type of referral when they feel that a student has more extensive issues with their writing which may require direct intervention from their tutors. These referrals are far rarer, and the university team who monitors them will carefully consider the referral before passing it on to the students' individual personal academic tutor if they deem this to be necessary. Our pilot year saw us receive a total of 29 such referrals, and one additional referral on well-being grounds rather than academic. This final category is reserved for cases where the Studiosity specialist has expressed concern for the immediate health and well-being of a student.

Application

Studiosity is a service, but it is made available to students via technology. Specifically, access is controlled via the university's Canvas LMS. The University of Sunderland was the first institution to deploy Studiosity through Canvas which presented challenges and learning opportunities. The Studiosity app uses the industry Learning Tools Interoperability (LTI) standard, which was installed into Canvas via an XML configuration file.

This was a breath of fresh air for me. I have installed many Learning Technology Integrations (LTIs) over the years, and they usually involve a lot of manual input and configuration. However, while the XML file made the process quick and easy, it also caused some issues as, by default, the Studiosity app was configured to appear within Canvas everywhere it could, which would have resulted in students who were not eligible for the Studiosity pilot seeing and accessing the service. From my experiments with our Business Analyst partner at Studiosity (in our Beta Canvas environment), we discovered a solution to this problem by installing the Studiosity app directly into a single dedicated Canvas course, and only eligible students were enrolled onto this course. The course was then built to include information about Studiosity and how to use it, with a detailed FAQ and video guide showing the entire process, from setting up your account to accessing and understanding feedback.

Turning now from technological considerations of deployment to pedagogical, the rationale for limiting the pilot to the selected cohorts was that, as identified in our Action and Participation Plan, these were the students with the greatest need for the service, who were most likely to withdraw from their course during the year, or to not progress into their next year. To familiarize students with Studiosity, and proactively identify any issues with their level of writing at an early stage, we planned an activity that would be conducted during their first three weeks at the university. This structured activity would become known as 'Write it Right', and we asked students to submit a short piece of writing, c. 500 words, on a topic set by the students' personal academic tutors.

Impact

Early indications of success came in the form of weekly activity reports received on a Monday morning. In addition to usage data, this report also collected student feedback. At the end of every interaction with Studiosity, students were presented with a short form to rate their experience and leave comments. In the last available report for the pilot year, cumulative satisfaction with the Writing Feedback service stood at 95% of students being 'Somewhat' or 'Extremely' satisfied (Studiosity, 2022b).

A quality monitoring process is available with Studiosity. The process flags any negative feedback received which is then checked by a second specialist. I could also access and check these interactions myself via an admin panel. Indeed, this is something I did routinely during the pilot phase until I was satisfied that there were no systemic issues that we needed to be concerned about.

On access and uptake, across the two student intakes at the Sunderland campus in September and January, and the four intakes at our London campus throughout the year, over 5,000 students were eligible to access Studiosity during the pilot, of which 1,206 went on to use the Writing Feedback service at least once. This represents a conversion rate of over 24% compared to a typical first-year uptake rate of c. 15% at other institutions according to Studiosity themselves.

The impact of 'Write it Right' is also apparent from looking at the usage throughout the year. Peaks were visible in November and April–May, coinciding with the main formative and summative assignment submission periods. While this could be expected for a system that is designed and marketed as an aid for improving academic writing, the largest peak occurs in late September which coincides with Week 3 of the semester, and right at the point at which the 'Write it Right' activity was being pushed. Other intakes in semester 2, and at the London campus at different points of the year, do not have sufficient student volume to show clear peaks.

Discussion

I began this case study by stating that the reason for implementing Studiosity was to improve the retention and progression of our students, and their overall attainment, and we now have data on this following the pilot. Space here does not allow for a detailed breakdown by campus, Faculty and School, and therefore, I shall share the overall figures only.

First, in terms of average module marks, for International Foundation Year (IFY) students in Academic Year (AY) 2021/2022, those who did not use Studiosity scored 48.5%, whereas for those who did use Studiosity this rose to 60.8%, which provides a variance of +12.3%. The like cohort from AY 2020/21 scored 54.9%, which demonstrates a variance of +5.8% in AY 2021/2022.

The performance of new undergraduates was similarly impressive. The average module mark in AY 2021/2022 for those who did not use Studiosity was 50.8%, while for those who did use Studiosity, they scored 57.8%, which indicates a variance of +7%. The like for like cohort from the previous year scored 53.05%, which means there was a +4.7% increase in AY 2021/2022.

Statistics on retention and progression also showed marked improvements. For IFY students, comparing the cohort from AY 2020/2021 to AY 2021/2022, the percentage of students who were retained increased by 5%, while those who returned and progressed to the next level increased by 13%. For new undergraduates, the percentage of students retained increased by 8% in AY 2021/2022, while the percentage of those who returned and progressed was 11% higher.

These statistics demonstrate a clear correlation between students who used Studiosity, and improvements in both average module marks, and retention and progression. However, limitations must be acknowledged. Correlation does not equal causation, and Studiosity is only one part of the activity which the university is engaged with to improve performance levels, and it is therefore not possible to attribute this success solely to Studiosity.

It is also possible that the students who engaged with Studiosity were more likely to be engaged and motivated, and therefore more likely to utilize any other interventions which could have been made. However, our experience at Sunderland has been evidenced at other institutions. A meta-analysis by Liz Thomas Associates found a "positive correlation between using Studiosity and higher attainment" in two representative case studies (Thomas, 2023).

Case Study Conclusion

The University of Sunderland ran a pilot of Studiosity in AY 2021/2022 to help improve our progression, retention and attainment rates, and the outcomes strongly point to success. We have therefore continued to provide the service to cohorts that need it the most, and at the time of writing are exploring options for expanding our use of Studiosity. One area which has consistently been in high demand has been new students entering at the postgraduate level, as these students at Sunderland are often returning to study after a long break.

We have learned that staff buy-in is key to successful adoption. One aspect not explored here is the disparity in uptake between our Sunderland and London campuses, and one reason we are attributing to this is the level of awareness of the service among academic staff at London campus as our messaging just does not seem to have penetrated there to the same extent.

Our early intervention activity appears to have been highly successful in driving adoption and I would be pleased to see this idea tried elsewhere. For more about this, my colleague wrote a useful case study about how this was applied in Psychology in which he shares his approach of tying the 'Write it Right' exercise to an early formative submission (Rees, 2022).

Writing this in 2023, I cannot help but consider the impact of generative AI on Higher Education over the past six months. Our Studiosity awareness campaign at the start of this year included marketing around getting help from valid, authorized sources, rather than needing to turn to illegitimate ones. Studiosity themselves have been researching the possibilities of generative AI, and exciting product announcements may be coming.

References

Anthonysamy, L., Koo, A.C. and Hew, S.H., 2020. Self-regulated learning strategies in Higher Education: Fostering digital literacy for sustainable lifelong learning. *Education and Information Technologies*, 25, 2393–2414.

Archer, L., Godec, S., Patel, U., Dawson, E. and Calabrese Barton, A., 2022. 'It really has made me think': Exploring how informal STEM learning practitioners developed critical reflective practice for social justice using the Equity Compass tool. *Pedagogy, Culture and Society*, 32(5), 1243–1265.

Ashwin, P. and McVitty, D., 2015. The meanings of student engagement: Implications for policies and practices. In: Curaj, A., Matei, L., Pricopie, R., Salmi, J. and Scott, P. (eds.), *The European Higher Education Area*. Cham, Switzerland: Springer, 343–359.

Avery, B. and Lees, R., 2019. Commuter students: Are you local? *Society for Research into Higher Education (SRHE) Annual Research Conference 2019: Creativity, Criticality and Conformity in Higher Education*, Newport, December 2019.

Avery, B. and Wason, H., 2022. Pivoting a business schools teaching online. In: Jamil, M.G. and Morley, D.A. (eds.), *Agile Learning Environments Amid Disruption:*

Evaluating Academic Innovations in Higher Education During COVID-19. Cham, Switzerland: Palgrave Macmillan, 311–328.

Bergdahl, N., 2022. Engagement and disengagement in online learning. *Computers & Education*, 188, 104561.

Biggs, J., 2012. What the student does: Teaching for enhanced learning. *Higher Education Research & Development*, 31(1), 39–55.

Blake, S., Capper, G. and Jackson, A., 2022. *Building Belonging in Higher Education*. London: Pearson/WONKE.

Bolton, P. and Lewis, J., 2023. *Equality of Access and Outcomes in Higher Education in England. No 9195*. London: House of Commons Library.

Bond, M., Buntins, K., Bedenlier, S., Zawacki-Richter, O. and Kerres, M., 2020. Mapping research in student engagement and educational technology in Higher Education: A systematic evidence map. *Educational Technology in Higher Education*, 17(1), 1–30.

Bretts, J., 2018. *Building a Culture of Student Engagement: Our Priorities for 2022–23*. Bristol: Office for Students.

Bronfenbrenner, U., 1979. *The Ecology of Human Development: Experiments by Nature and Design*. Cambridge, MA: Harvard University Press.

Carroll, M., Lindsey, S., Chaparro, M. and Winslow, B., 2021. An applied model of learner engagement and strategies for increasing learner engagement in the modern educational environment. *Interactive Learning Environments*, 29(5), 757–771.

Challen, C., 2016. *Engagement in Teaching and Learning is it Enhanced by the F-factors?* London: British Educational Research Association (BERA).

Department of Education, 2017. *Teaching Excellence and Student Outcomes Framework Specification*. London: Department for Education.

Dvorak, T. and Jia, M., 2016. Do the timeliness, regularity, and intensity of online work habits predict academic performance. *Journal of Learning Analytics*, 3(3), 318–330.

Finn, J.D. and Zimmer, K.S., 2012. Student engagement: What is it? Why does it matter? In: Christenson, S., Reschly, A. and Wylie, C. (eds.), *Handbook of Research on Student Engagement*. New York: Springer, 97–131.

Fleck-Henderson, A. and Melendez, M., 2009. Conversation and conflict: Supporting authentic dialogue in the classroom. *Teaching In Social Work*, 29(1). 32–46.

Garrison, D.R. and Kanuka, H., 2004. Blended learning: Uncovering its transformative potential in Higher Education. *The Internet and Higher Education*, 7(2): 95–105.

Gribble, L. and Huber, E., 2022. In the business of connecting: Nudging students. In: Wilson, S., Arthars, N., Wardak, D., Yeoman, P., Kalman, E. and Liu, D. (eds.), *Reconnecting Relationships Through Technology*. Amsterdam, Netherlands: Elsevier, e22222.

Hollister, J. and Lee, J., 2022. An exploratory study on virtual reality and related technologies in terminal LIS degree programs in the United States and South Korea. *Knowledge Content Development & Technology*, 12, 85–106.

Hulene, G., Cronshaw, S., Davies, E., de Main, L., Holmes, H., Hope, A., Odindo, C., Page-Tickell, R., Rawal, A., Roberts, S. and Talbot, D., 2023. *Student Engagement Guidelines: Learning from Innovative Practices Introduced in Response to COVID-19.* Gloucester: Quality Assurance Agency for Higher Education (QAA).

Kaufmann, R. and Vallade, J., 2022. Exploring connections in the online learning environment: Student perceptions of rapport, climate, and loneliness. *Interactive Learning Environments*, 30(10), 1794–1808.

Laurillard, D. 2012. *Teaching as a Design Science: Building Pedagogical Patterns for Learning and Technology.* Abingdon: Routledge.

Leners, D. and Sitzman, K., 2006. Graduate student perceptions: Feeling the passion of CARING online. *Nursing Education Perspectives*, 27(6), 315–319.

Linnenbrink, E.A. and Pintrich, P.R., 2003. The role of self-efficacy beliefs in student engagement and learning in the classroom. *Reading Writing Quarterly*. 19(2), 119–137.

Logan-Goyette, R., Huston, L., Smith, R. and Chien, J., 2021. *Teaching to Engage Asynchronous Online Learners.* Victoria, Canada: University of Victoria.

Lovett, C., Bridges, M.W., DiPietro, M., Ambrose, S.A. and Norman, M.K., 2023. *How Learning Works 8 Research-based Principles for Smart Teaching.* 3rd edition. New Jersey: Jossey-Bass.

Luecht, R.M., 2005. Some useful cost-benefit criteria for evaluating computer-based test delivery models and systems. *Journal of Applied Testing Technology*, 7(2), 1–31.

Martyn, M., 2003. The hybrid online model: Good practice. *Educause Quarterly*, 26(1), 18–23.

Mercer, S. and Dörnyei, Z., 2020. *Engaging Language Learners in Contemporary Classrooms.* Cambridge: Cambridge University Press.

Mulisa, F., 2019. Application of bioecological systems theory to Higher Education: Best evidence review. *Journal of Pedagogical Sociology and Psychology*, 1(2), 104–115.

Nakkula, M.J. and Ravitch, S.M., 1998. *Matters of Interpretation: Reciprocal Transformation in Therapeutic and Developmental Relationships with Youth.* Hoboken, NJ: Jossey-Bass.

Office for National Statistics (ONS), 2021. *Exploring Local Income Deprivation.* Newport: ONS.

Patel, U., 2015. *A Discourse History of Technology Enhanced Learning Research (1945–2012).* PhD Thesis. Sydney, Australia: University of Technology Sydney.

Patel, U., 2022. Adapting the equity compass tool for Higher Education. *In:* Polkinghorne, M. (ed.), *Fusion Learning Colloquium 2022 – Proceedings.* Poole: Bournemouth University, 20.

Rasheed, R., Kamsin, A. and Abdullah, N., 2020. Challenges in the online component of blended learning: A systematic review. *Computers & Education*, 144(2020), 103701.

Rees, J., 2022. *How Studiosity Was Embedded into a Core Psychology Module*. Sunderland: University of Sunderland.

Sankey, M., 2020. Putting the pedagogic horse in front of the technology cart. *Distance Education in China*. 5, 46–53.

Singh, H., 2003. Building effective blended learning programs. *Educational Technology*, 43(6), 51–54.

Skinner, E.A., Rickert, N.P., Vollet, J.W. and Kindermann, T.A., 2022. The complex social ecology of academic development: A bioecological framework and illustration examining the collective effects of parents, teachers, and peers on student engagement. *Educational Psychologist*, 57(2), 87–113.

Studiosity, 2022a. *Academic Integrity Policy*. St Leonards, Australia: Studiosity.

Studiosity, 2022b. *Service Summary Report 22 to 28 August 2022* (unpublished). St Leonards, Australia: Studiosity.

Studiosity, 2023. *Meet Out Online Specialists*. St Leonards, Australia: Studiosity.

Thomas, L., 2023. *Studiosity: Summary Report: A Review of the Experience and Impact of Studiosity in UK Universities, 2017–2022*. York: Liz Thomas Associates Ltd.

Tinto, V., 2012. *Completing College – Rethinking Institutional Action*. Chicago, IL: University of Chicago Press.

Trowler, V., 2010. *Student Engagement Literature Review*. York: Higher Education Academy.

Trowler, V., Allan, R.L., Bryk, J. and Din, R.R., 2022. Pathways to student engagement: Beyond triggers and mechanisms at the engagement interface. *Higher Education*, 84(4), 761–777.

UK Advising and Tutoring Association (UKAT), 2023. *The UKAT Professional Framework for Academic Advising and Tutoring*. York: UKAT.

University of Sunderland, 2022. *Access and Participation Plan 2020–21 to 2024–25*. Sunderland: University of Sunderland.

Wang, C.H., Harrison, J., Cardullo, V. and Lin, X., 2018. Exploring the relationship among international students' English self-efficacy, using English to learn self-efficacy, and academic self-efficacy. *International Students*, 8(1), 233–250.

Wiliam, D., 2021. What is assessment for learning? *Studies in Educational Evaluation*, 37(1), 3–14.

Innovative Applications of Technology within Virtual Learning Environments   **4**

The following five case studies describe innovative applications of technology within Virtual Learning Environments (VLEs). Each case study presents the personal perspectives of those involved.

Case Study 4.1: Using Technology to Enhance the Learning Environment for Postgraduate Researchers (PGRs)

FIONA KNIGHT, JULIA TAYLOR AND LOUISE BRYANT

The case study relates to developing and implementing a bespoke online system for administering and monitoring postgraduate researchers (PGRs) in the context of a Higher Education institution in the UK. There is much focus in the literature on the complexity of PGR supervision, and this is an area of growing research interest (Polkinghorne et al., 2023). However, the intricacies associated with PGR administration have meanwhile received comparatively little attention or scrutiny (Urqhuhart et al., 2016; McGloin, 2021).

The challenges of PGR administration cannot be underestimated as they are complicated, and multilayered. There may be common elements across Higher Education Providers (HEPs), but some of the issues may also

DOI: 10.4324/9781032635248-5

be unique to individual institutions, depending on the size and research maturity of each institution, the nature of the research degree programs offered and the specific policies and procedures in place locally. Furthermore, differences between disciplines, or research areas, can add further complexities, as each HEP will have its own unique requirements and processes. Finally, the individualized nature of PGR learning and progression, and the reliance on specialist supervisory support and expert assessment panels, creates further tensions.

Maintaining an overview of PGR progression is necessary for the HEP for several reasons. Research degree supervision is comparatively resource-intensive, with usually at least two supervisors allocated to each PGR's team (Gunnarsson *et al.*, 2013), and an array of academic regulations, policies and procedures tailored specifically to a research degree context. This means that a significant amount of academic and administrative time is concentrated on supporting this cohort of students, which ultimately impacts upon workload and allocation of labor (Masuku, 2021). HEPs will have specific targets and aspirations around the recruitment of high-caliber applicants, the awarding of associated external funding and the retention of their existing PGRs (Masuku, 2021). Completion rates are often scrutinized as a perceived reflection of quality assurance, and PGRs have an increasingly valuable role to play in both the People, Culture and Environment statement and in the publication metrics applied to the Research Excellence Framework (REF) due to take place in 2029.

The impact on the PGRs themselves of deploying technology which supports their learning environment, and promotes their timely progression, should not be underestimated. Recent research indicates that PGRs experience increased anxiety levels when presented with uncertainties in their research degree progression and administration (Casey *et al.*, 2022). The technology which supports PGRs while undertaking their research is therefore a critical factor for HEPs when endeavoring to provide a healthy and supportive environment.

In addition, there is an increasing need to meet external regulatory reporting requirements such as the Office for Students' Condition of Registration which requires HEPs to demonstrate that the standard of education they provide is consistently high (https://www.officeforstudents. org.uk/advice-and-guidance/regulation/registration-with-the-ofs-a-guide/ conditions-of-registration/). As such, it is imperative that HEPs can track, and monitor, the progression and engagement of individual PGRs. Online monitoring systems provide an excellent mechanism to follow the learning journey of individual PGRs, while ensuring excellent quality, reliable standards and positive outcomes for all.

The monitoring of PGRs is the combined responsibility of PGRs, their supervisors, their departments and the institution at large (Manathunga, 2005). It is important that all stakeholders understand and implement their institution's policies and procedures for supporting and monitoring the progress of PGRs (Gower, 2021). In addition, it is important to recognize that these policies and procedures are the foundations of the support that help PGRs to maintain momentum and progression (Taylor, 2019; Friedrich-Nel and Mac Kinnon, 2019), and reach agreed academic checkpoints within an appropriate timeframe (Bulat, 2018).

An online system that translates policy and process into a structure which supports timely progression and ensures compliance with internal and external regulations and governance is an essential administrative tool. This can only lead to a better PGR understanding of the process. In addition, online systems can streamline administration and simplify these processes. However, due to the complexity of the PGR journey, generic online monitoring and progression systems, or learning platforms, alone do not support the range of PGR needs, particularly regarding the variation in the support that they require throughout the stages of the research life cycle (Abd Wahab, 2016).

In summary, this case study provides an overview of the process through which we developed a bespoke online system, to provide an administrative framework, to support the PGR journey and the PGRs themselves. In doing so, we sought to streamline the process, ensure adherence to policy, increase the monitoring capability and enhance the experience for all stakeholders. However, embedding any new online system or learning platform into a community can be a challenge, and we recognize the importance of operating a continual improvement process, which considers feedback from stakeholders, and recognizes the changing needs of the institution.

Description

This case study focuses on the development and launch of Bournemouth University's (BU) bespoke online administration and monitoring system, ProGRess, which was launched in September 2022. This system supports the process which is defined by the academic regulations, policies and procedures that underpin postgraduate research degree support. These are captured in the university's *Code of Practice for Research Degrees* (Bournemouth University, 2023). This *Code of Practice* is updated annually before the start of the academic year, with all substantive amendments, clarifications and updates being overseen and approved by appropriate university committees.

Prior to the launch of ProGRess, the university operated an online system developed by, and purchased from, an external provider. In its final two years, the system was unsupported by the external provider and therefore posed significant risks to the institution ranging from impact on individual PGR progression, to an inability to comply with statutory external reporting requirements. These issues, combined with other critical ongoing business and technical concerns about the fitness for purpose of that external system, caused the Doctoral College and IT Services (IT) to consider a replacement which offered an alternative solution. In doing so, we recognized that returning to a paper-based and spreadsheet solution would be a retrograde step. We investigated the possibility of developing a solution within the university's existing VLE for undergraduate and postgraduate taught programs, but the required functionality could not be met within the VLE's structure. The university's current student record system also offered a solution through a specific research degree component, but as with the VLE, this bolt-on option would not address the degree of complexity required. As such, we rejected this option too.

Based upon our minimum requirements, there were, at this time, two off-the-shelf solution suppliers available. However, both were ruled out due to the initial purchase cost, and the amount of integration and additional customization which would subsequently be required. There was anxiety regarding the significant development work necessary to integrate them sufficiently within existing systems. We were also concerned about the nature and extent of post-purchase vendor support, and the degree of control which we would wield over developments and enhancements to the system once implemented.

Taking all these factors into consideration, including the significant financial commitment, it was proposed that a solution be developed in-house by the university's IT Services. Adopting an agile approach for the build and launch allowed the deployment of internal resources, and the tailoring of the solution, to meet the specific needs of the Doctoral College and the PGR community. Although this solution meant that the final product took longer to be delivered than an off-the-shelf solution, the functionality, branding and support would remain within the control of the university and could be overseen directly by the Doctoral College.

ProGRess was designed to be a comprehensive and efficient solution for supporting the PGRs and enhancing their learning environment. In parallel, it was designed to support progression monitoring by Supervisors, and other stakeholders, at departmental and institutional level. ProGRess would provide a central repository for information, the streamlining the process of PGR engagement and progression monitoring, and for supporting the administration of assessment and *viva voce* examination. In essence,

ProGRess was designed to be a hub for postgraduate research degree stakeholders.

The functionality of ProGRess is summarized below:

- *PGR Functionality:*
  - Visualize clear timelines;
  - Identify upcoming deadlines;
  - Complete milestone process;
  - Submit change requests;
  - Track progression.
- *Supervisor Functionality:*
  - Record supervisory meetings;
  - Action requests;
  - Comment on progression;
  - Nominate examiners.
- *Faculty Functionality:*
  - Track PGR progression;
  - Monitor cohort performance;
  - Streamline administration;
  - Action requests;
  - Ratify outcomes;
  - Increase efficiency.
- *Institutional Functionality:*
  - Integrate the Student Record System;
  - Action requests;
  - Provide real-time data;
  - Report and analyze data;
  - Report statutory information.

Application

As outlined above, it was agreed that a solution would be developed in-house by IT Services in line with the seven phases of the established System Development Lifecyle (https://www.intellectsoft.net/blog/what-is-system-development-life-cycle):

1. *Project Planning.* As outlined, initial conversations about the development of ProGRess began in 2020. During this phase, we compiled a project brief which identified a proposed solution, and detailed the benefits, risks and issues, and resourcing implications;

2. *Requirement and Data Analysis.* To guarantee the success of the project, it was essential that the new online monitoring system meet postgraduate research degree business requirements. During this phase we articulated the research degree workflow from the perspective of each stakeholder group. This provided an opportunity to streamline processes and encouraged a consistency of approach between faculties. In addition, it was imperative that the workflows aligned with those set out in the *Code of Practice for Research Degrees.* In terms of our requirements for the system, we needed it to support integration with the student record system and enable migration of historic data from the previous system. It also needed to be populated with individual timelines for PGRs, with configuration for pre-defined workflow steps relating to each milestone or checkpoint. Automatic notifications and reminders of actions were required together with a reporting functionality that served operational and strategic needs;

3. *Design.* At this stage, the IT developers took our requirements and began defining the details for the overall system, including specific aspects, such as its user interfaces, system interfaces and underlying databases;

4. *Coding.* The IT development team translated our requirements, and developed the code, which would ultimately allow the tool to be built according to the design documents and outlined specifications. Throughout this process we were in dialog with the IT development team to ensure that the final product met our requirements;

5. *Testing.* During the testing stage, we worked with the IT development team to identify any bugs or defects that need to be tracked, fixed and later retested. Based on the experience of launching a previous system, we understood the importance of rigorous user testing to ensure that the end-user experience would be positive, and that the resulting product would be universally fit for purpose. As such, representatives of each stakeholder group were invited to take part, including PGRs, postgraduate research administrators and supervisors. It was important that the final system met the quality standards defined in the requirements phase;

6. *Deployment.* To ensure positive user engagement from the outset, a detailed communications plan was developed and actioned according to predetermined phases, with information being released to stakeholders in a coordinated approach. We shared information about the system via multiple communication channels, offered group and one-to-one support and developed a suite of user resources. However, the system was incredibly intuitive, and even in the early stage of deployment, feedback was supportive. However, there were some changes which needed

time to be assimilated, including the number of system notifications now being received by users, and the requirement for them to undertake prompt action in response;

7. *Maintenance.* Following deployment of ProGRess, we maintained close contact with the IT development team to ensure that any issues identified by key stakeholders on the live system were reported and addressed as quickly as possible. This included residual bugs and new issues we had not anticipated. Critical bugs or issues continue to be resolved immediately, but there is now a biannual window for the development and deployment of other enhancements considered non-critical. The Doctoral College and IT share an enhancement log to record user improvements, and 'Request a Project' three months before the deployment window. The benefits of the in-house development have already been widely appreciated, whereby maintenance, especially of critical issues, can be quickly addressed.

Impact

As discussed above, ensuring a positive user engagement from the outset was paramount. We developed a detailed communications plan which included dissemination, via formal and informal channels, up to six months prior to the launch. Training, both online and in-person, was provided to all stakeholders and supplemented by user guides including narrative descriptions, screenshots and workflow diagrams.

The embedding of the system was greatly aided by the pre-work that had gone into the development, which meant that it was highly intuitive, closely reflecting the underpinning process, so that from an early stage of deployment, feedback was largely positive. Many PGRs, and supervisors, reported notable improvements to their understanding of the process, while others found that the supervisory meeting functionality enabled additional academic discourse to take place. Specific comments included:

> *I am really liking it in terms of look and feel, functionality and clarity.*
>
> PGR

> *Progress has made the whole process so quick, easy and intuitive.*
>
> PGR

> *The user interface is good, and I like the reminder messages which have already proven to be really helpful.*
>
> PGR

The report feature is fantastic, and it will really improve the way we report, and the accuracy of our data.

Postgraduate Research Administrator

Quick feedback on my first major review using ProGRess ... amazing!

Supervisor

One of the key challenges was communicating the standardization of workflow processes where differences between faculties, and even disciplines, had been accommodated previously. An example of this is where the alignment of approval processes for assessor, or examiners, of key academic review points, and *viva voce* examinations, did not accommodate the different reporting structures at faculty, or even departmental, level.

As one driver for the implementation of a new online administration and monitoring system for PGRs had been to ensure parity of learning experience for all PGRs, the imperative of the system for a consistent approach to the process was a clear benefit.

The implementation of the new system did necessitate a certain degree of culture change. While most users were very positive, there were some pockets of resistance. These tended to be where consistent and regular action was required to maintain the smooth operation of the workflows. Inevitably, some users felt that the previous system was better, and the new system increased the required effort to navigate. However, the PGR environment is rapidly changing as numbers grow, quality standards rise and an increased level of reporting PGR activity is expected across the sector. It is important to articulate to the PGR community that creating new systems which augment the monitoring of PGRs is essential, not only to support timely completion, but also to ensure that we are able to meet rigorous internal and external requirements.

We continue to work with the IT development team to identify and prioritize enhancements, as we acknowledge that there is always room for improvement.

Discussion

This case study has described the process of developing and using technology to enhance the learning environment for PGRs. The implementation of ProGRess was assisted by the fact that the system was intuitive to use, and therefore comparatively quick and easy to navigate, particularly for a community already familiar with the underlying processes.

Undertaking a postgraduate research degree can be challenging (Metcalfe et al., 2018), but providing PGRs with a tool which will assist them to navigate their way through the process can make it a little less daunting. The impact of ProGRess is wider than improving the individual PGR experience, as it also offers an opportunity to improve the overall management of postgraduate research programs, by creating an online environment which increases quality assurance, efficiency, transparency, accessibility and data analytics.

The automation of administrative tasks, such as progression tracking and processing of requests, increases efficiency. It also enables supervisors to focus on the academic aspects of their role, and postgraduate research administrators to focus on the administration of academic progression. Automated reminders help to ensure that important deadlines are not missed, although, as noted, a change of culture is required in some areas to ensure a consistent message of timely action to support the smooth operation of the workflow.

The system can also support those with responsibility for PGRs at faculty, or institutional, level, by providing a transparent view of the progression of PGRs with access to real-time information about milestones, deadlines and program requirements. This can both highlight where there are areas of concern and promote accountability for dealing with these. Linked to this is the increased accessibility to data which allows administrators to analyze trends and patterns in program performance. Again, this data-driven approach can help identify areas requiring quality assurance improvement and is essential to support the growing number of PGRs and changing program requirements.

Case Study Conclusion

This case study describes how the implementation of Bournemouth University's online administration and monitoring system (ProGRess) has played a transformative role in supporting the postgraduate research student journey. ProGRess has increased the clarity of the research degree journey, the timing and process of the key milestones and the record of PGR-supervisor interactions, and has demonstrated how technology can enhance the learning environment for PGRs. In addition, the system has significantly improved institutional reporting, as well as aligning to increased external requirements arising in the evolving landscape of Higher Education within the UK.

Ultimately, this case study underscores the importance of creating an appropriate online environment to facilitate PGR learning and progression.

Implementing such systems can significantly improve the overall quality of postgraduate research programs, and the experience of both PGRs and HEPs. ProGRess has enriched the experience of our PGRs and provided a more streamlined system for our supervisors to follow when undertaking their administrative responsibilities. The system has also improved efficiency, transparency and communication across our postgraduate research administration.

The postgraduate research environment is rapidly evolving and the focus on research degrees is increasing. In September 2023, the UKRI (UK Research and Innovation) recognized the need to improve support for research students, and the importance of having the best possible experience (https://www.ukri.org/what-we-do/developing-people-and-skills/new-deal-for-postgraduate-research/). The UK's Office for Students is aligning the monitoring of PGRs to that in place for undergraduates and postgraduate taught students. As such, it is important that we have a system that enables us to meet the increasingly data-driven, evidence-based, reporting requirements of these external regulatory bodies.

Case Study 4.2: Using Technology to Create a Flexible Learning Pathway

HELEN KEEN-DYER, SHANNON DELPORT AND VIVIAN ROMERO

The Central Queensland University (CQUniversity) Strategic Plan 2024–2028 positions the university as one that 'Changes Lives'. "As an agent of profound social impact" (Central Queensland, 2024, p. 9), CQUniversity embraces the United Nations Sustainable Development Goals while reinforcing the commitment to people, planet and partners. The role of sustainable development can be contextualized in the heightened awareness of climate change and wider disaster management (Kelmen, 2017). Teaching individuals and workforces to adapt to and manage emergencies and disasters is at the heart of CQUniversity's Emergency and Disaster Management (E&DM) offerings.

CQUniversity offers three E&DM online postgraduate offerings: (1) Graduate Certificate; (2) Graduate Diploma; and (3) Master's Degree. These offerings each recognize the changing nature of emergency and disaster management, the important role that research and evidence-based practice play in underpinning contemporary perspectives and approaches and the imperative of preparing individuals and communities to respond to increasingly complex events.

Our CQUniversity offerings are targeted at people working in emergency service agencies, those working in private, government, non-government and community-based organizations who play a role in emergency and disaster management, and those with a personal and/or professional interest in the field. Historically, our students have come from the first group, that is, people working in emergency service agencies. However, we have seen a noteworthy shift in our enrollment patterns. A significant portion of the enrollments in E&DM units now emerge from associated disciplines, including public health, health service management and business, and to a lesser extent engineering.

From these enrollments, we can see the diversity in our cohort emerge. Of particular note to this case study, and representing the highest percentage of enrollments, are the public health students who are predominantly international students. There is also a high proportion of students from the E&DM industry sector, who often come to their online postgraduate course with vocational or technical education and training, but little experience of the university learning environment or online learning. Accommodating the diversity of learners requires us to design an effective yet flexible learning experience. We use technology to help us facilitate an inclusive learning environment (Gunawardena *et al.*, 2018).

Description

The advent of the Learning Management System (LMS) has transformed education technology by revolutionizing the interaction between educators and learners engaged in online course delivery (Turnbull *et al.*, 2020). LMSs are complex applications that offer many tools that aid online course delivery. At CQUniversity, we use a Moodle LMS, which is one of the most popular open-source learning platforms and one of the most versatile and powerful LMSs. It caters to both individual and institutional needs. According to Moodle.org, it has 166,542 registered sites in over 239 countries and hosts 46,359,184 courses with 392,870,584 users (https://stats.moodle.org). It hosts several features and has extensive built-in activities, resources and plugins that can be used to drive a range of learning activities. One of the many features is the Moodle Book, which has received widespread acknowledgment for its innovative approach to seamless learning through online books.

The Moodle Book feature offers flexible navigation options, allowing students to choose between linear and non-linear styles. Linear navigation is ideal for structured course content in which concepts build upon one another, while non-linear navigation allows students to explore with a more self-directed approach. Educators are provided with the flexibility to personalize the appearance of the Moodle Book and tailor it to suit their teaching methodologies by incorporating an array of multimedia elements such as videos, infographics, audio clips and interactive quizzes to strengthen concepts and engage students successfully.

The Moodle Book feature also fosters collaborative learning experiences in which educators can embed discussion forums directly within the online book, thereby enabling students to actively participate in content-situated discussions. This encourages students to contribute their insights, exchange ideas and gain alternative viewpoints from their peers, and so enrich their learning journey. The Moodle Book approach emphasizes personalization, allowing students to choose what activities they would like to engage with that are ultimately aligned with their professional contexts and interests, or to systematically engage with each activity in turn (https://moodle.com/solutions/lms/).

The decision to use the Moodle Book feature in the way we describe it was born from a strategic response to a pressing challenge. At CQUniversity, we pride ourselves on our commitment to diversity and inclusivity, welcoming students from across the globe and across the industry-education nexus into our online learning environment. However, this inclusivity and the diversity of our E&DM cohort presented us with a challenge to better support the unique needs of our student cohort.

Application

To better support the E&DM cohort and fully leverage the available technology, we developed a pedagogical model. Based on the work of Race (2007), the guided flexible learning pathway is an online pedagogical model developed to enhance learning, and to support the specific needs of the E&DM cohort. In action, the pathway consists of a series of facilitated and self-directed learning objects that have been purposefully built and curated into a learning sequence, ensuring the content is unpacked in easily digestible chunks that are scaffolded from one object to the next (Müller, 2022). The pathway is both guided (e.g., specific materials, activities and interactions at specific times) and flexible (e.g., choice of additional materials, activities and interactions if desired or required and a flexible navigation option).

The learning objects are built using a range of technologies, including both synchronous and asynchronous technologies, which is particularly important for ensuring all students can participate (Stone, 2017, 2019).

Critically, though, all learning objects, irrespective of the technology used or the mode of engagement (synchronous or asynchronous), are curated into the Moodle Book pathway. The Moodle Book is, therefore, our one-stop shop for student learning.

Importantly, the learning objects cover three specific areas: (1) the technical content of the unit; (2) broader academic literacies, e.g., academic integrity and library skills; and (3) navigating university life more generally, e.g., systems and structures, including the online learning environment. The explicit focus on the broader academic literacies, university systems and structures recognizes that, while universities may be offering increasingly sophisticated learning environments, students are not necessarily familiar with or sufficiently skilled to navigate them (Brown *et al.*, 2022). The learning objects supporting academic literacies and university life, including the use of technology and university systems, are embedded within the curricula, meaning they are encountered by students at a time and place when they are most needed (Stone, 2017, 2019).

In addition to the specially created pathway of learning objects, for example, interactive infographics, video and audiofiles, collaborative workspaces and formative activities, the guided flexible learning pathway includes specifically timed communications. Communication is timed to align with key dates, for example, assessment due dates and/or course administration dates, and is facilitated through the Moodle LMS. Communication nudges are known to have a positive impact on student learning (Brown *et al.*, 2022).

As a teaching team, we take a proactive and strengths-based stance. We are therefore concerned with building the skills and capability necessary for our students to successfully navigate their coursework. As such, we use a preplanned communication schedule. That said, while we have a preplanned communication schedule, learning analytics data available through the LMS is also used to support term-based needs. Learning analytics can, for example, provide data on the level of activity, timing and frequency of access, which can be used for individual or cohort-level support. While the accessing of materials, e.g., learning objects from the flexible learning pathway and engaging with timed communication, does not guarantee learning, access to materials is a factor that supports student achievement (Brown *et al.*, 2022).

Impact

Prior to the use of the Moodle Book pathway, a review of the available learning analytics and Student Unit Teaching Evaluation (SUTE) data highlighted to our teaching team that there was a range of learning and university system navigation challenges faced by our students. By mining the SUTE qualitative data, we were able to delve deeper into the nuances of these challenges and better understand at what points, and in what ways, our system of Higher Education learning and teaching presented challenges in the learning journey. Navigating the LMS technology platform, issues of academic integrity, such as academic writing and referencing, were raised. The use of other learning systems, including the online eReading list, and making sense of these in relation to the module content also presented challenges to the students. Similarly, the sensemaking information around what needed to be learnt, and by when, was considered confusing, and how the different learning resources fitted together with unit content was not clearly understood.

The guided flexible learning pathway pedagogical model, and its enactment in the Moodle LMS using Moodle Book, addresses many of these identified challenges. Feedback, since its implementation, suggests that this learning pathway affords the level of structure that the SUTE data indicates students craved. The way in which content, learning objects and communication are all purposively organized and scaffolded within a learning sequence that is navigable in a linear way is highly valued by the students.

In one SUTE comment about the approach to learning resources, the student went so far as to recommend that:

> *CQUniversity think about implementing this or all subjects with international students.*
>
> (Student comment on SUTE, 2023)

and went on to comment that:

> *In each country the rules for writing and academics are different, and this subject made it easy to understand.*
>
> (Student comment on SUTE, 2023)

The way that the pathway offers autonomy through supplementary activities, formative learning objects, and the ability to navigate between pages, sections and content in a non-linear way is also greatly valued.

The feedback mechanism afforded through the formative learning objects was singled out by students as a positive aspect of the pathway. As one student noted when providing feedback on the optional and formative objects:

> *The feedback provided was constructive, and I was able to build on this during subsequent assessments.*
>
> (Student comment from SUTE, 2023)

The use of Moodle Book has allowed us to develop a pathway, and all that it consists of is contained within the one navigable interface. This has the advantage of limiting the number of different interfaces needing to be navigated by the student. As one student noted when commenting on the Moodle Book pathway approach:

> *It makes study life so much easier and sets students up for success.*
> (Student comment from CQUSuccess, 2022)

The required learning, supplementary learning opportunities and communication, are all in one place, with the option to navigate as a linear experience, or dip in and out as chosen by the student.

A range of lessons were learnt while building the guided flexible learning pathway in Moodle Book, and during the early days of its enactment. SUTE data, from students who have used the pathway, point to additional lessons. Four lessons in particular stand out:

1. Seamless integration is essential. Learning objects built in other technology interfaces must seamlessly integrate with Moodle Book, and students must be able to engage with the object without exiting the Moodle LMS environment. Switching between systems, or having systems close the Moodle Book page, disrupts the learning journey;
2. Topping and tailing learning objects is important. Sensemaking is enhanced when there are linkages between elements, that is, there is a descriptive narrative that links different content chunks or learning objects together;
3. Keep it simple. Complex learning objects with 'all the bells and whistles' do not guarantee a positive learning outcome. Difficult-to-use learning objects that are not intuitive or user-friendly are less likely to be used, or will not be used, to their full advantage;
4. It takes time. From the perspective of the teaching team, the initial development of the Moodle Book pathway takes time. Subsequent changes and enhancements are less time-intensive, but you need to build time into your teaching schedule to develop and format the Moodle Book.

Case Study Conclusion

The CQUniversity E&DM student cohort is diverse and is increasingly drawn from a range of associated disciplines. This change in student demographics has challenged the E&DM teaching team and made us rethink our historical ways of delivering E&DM Higher Education. Certainly, it made us reconsider the way in which the Moodle LMS was used, and how it could be better leveraged to create an effective student learning experience for our E&DM cohort. Effective learning must be purposefully designed, and the learning environments in which this learning occurs must take into account the strengths of the diverse groups the learning serves (Gunawardena *et al.*, 2018). For CQUniversity E&DM, that meant enacting the guided flexible learning pathway pedagogical model within the Moodle Book.

While the pathway continues to be well-received by students, and receives high student evaluation scores, moving forward, integrating additional tools may enhance our learning pathway and further enable a universal design for learning approach. Universal Design for Learning suggests that there are multiple ways to engage students in the many ways that knowledge can be displayed (Capp, 2017). For example, products that improve reading comprehension may further support our international students, or those for whom English is their second language. Similarly, immersive learning objects that take students into the middle of emergency and disaster events could add additional authenticity.

However, the ultimate lesson for the teaching team is that, whatever these enhancements are, they need to seamlessly integrate with the Moodle Book learning pathway, be connected to existing objects on the pathway, and be user-friendly.

Case Study 4.3: Using a Learning Design Framework to Engage and Support Students

CARINA BUCKLEY AND KAREN HEARD-LAURÉOTE

Latterly, Higher Education has been characterized by disruption that has seen traditional forms of learning and teaching practice challenged by external health crises, internal financial constraints triggered by declining student recruitment, stagnation in the value of the student fee and ever-increasing sector regulation.

Disruption is a variously described notion, but for the purposes of our discussion of altered teaching practices, we consider two key forms. The first is *turbulence* which is intensive and fast and prompts the question 'what now?' It stimulates awareness, innovation and commitment, but equally its impact can be negative for individuals, teams and for the organization. The second is *perturbance* which prompts the question 'what next?' It is reflective, considered, collaborative, problem-solving, slower and social (Jackson, 2023, p. 112).

It is arguably turbulence that best characterizes the disruption experienced in our context, because COVID-19 lockdown triggered extensive learning and teaching innovation, while being an intensely lived experience for the academic community at the teaching 'coal face'. The most significant innovation in the context of the institution, which is the focus of this case study, was the rapid development of an online learning model called the Solent Online Learning (SOL) Standard. This was mediated through the VLE, and applied to all modules, to ensure a consistent and high-quality student experience. The intensity of the experience was manifested in the short practice time, scale and scope of work (c. 200 courses) with previously distant colleagues working together in a matrix environment (Heard-Lauréote and Buckley, 2021, 2022).

In actuality, the evolution was more natural given the existence of a long established and embedded approach to blended learning. Indeed, following the pandemic turbulence, a more settled period of self-reflection led to longer lasting change. The resultant Local Development Framework (LDF) represented the best of what we learnt from the turbulence, building on it further, ratifying insights and formalizing the expectation with course teams of a multimodal blend, while also respecting the nuances of subject areas. Most importantly, it was clear that students enjoy flexibility in terms of where, and when, they do their learning. In this regard we discovered the VLE had much more potential as a learning space than we had previously appreciated.

Description

The LDF brings together Collaborative Learning (CL), Directed Learning (DL) and Guided Learning (GL). The LDF constitutes a framework for the design and practice of learning and teaching across digital and physical learning spaces, which are equally important and have distinct roles to play. While on campus teaching is good for group-work and activity learning (Allsop et al., 2020), peer-to-peer (Assinder, 1991), problem-based learning (Hmelo-Silver, 2004), the VLE is best suited to disseminating inclusive and flexible learning opportunities that students can engage with independently, or together, but without experiencing direct live interaction with educators. The vital role of the LDF is to align these two learning spaces, and the activities that take place within them. CL in the classroom, and DL online, are mutually supportive and create an extension of the classroom into the online space through an active learning community. This can be complemented by GL which adds value to the student experience in terms of developing confidence and the 'whole person'. All three strands are underpinned by a foundation of digital literacies for staff and students.

The LDF brings together online and physical classrooms, the individual with their peers and the academic with professional services. It is based on the principles of inclusive and innovative learning and teaching that is impactful, developed in partnership, and which is enhancement-led and metric-minded. Over the past year, we have optimized the full repertoire of tools available to support the LDF, including developing an underpinning foundation of digital literacies for both staff and students. This has enabled them to take full advantage of the opportunities offered.

Application

There were at least four key drivers to using the LDF to engage students in their studies:

1. The framework completely aligns with the institutional ethos of students first. As such, it prioritizes student belonging and learning communities;
2. Aligning learning and teaching to the LDF across the institution provides a consistent learning experience in which all students benefit from an equal and positive experience whatever the subject of study;
3. The LDF promotes students' value for money in that it highlights the learning hours, and learning opportunities, that occur beyond the formal classroom sessions.
4. It improves clarity for staff around VLE requirements in the post-COVID context. This includes dissuading staff that hybrid teaching, i.e., teaching online and onsite student cohorts simultaneously, does not make for an inclusive learning experience.

The overall development of the approach to embedding a new framework for learning design was underpinned by pedagogical research and then agreed to by the key stakeholders. This process included student consultation and co-creation via student partners who investigated, and quality assured, its inclusivity and accessibility.

We then began the implementation phase. The framework was applied to all Modules via a Moodle template, with built-in guidance for how it should be completed, and which emphasized the interactive and participatory nature of the LDF. We took a whole-course team approach to harmonize the student learning experience and to enable colleagues to better support each other. Alongside the integration of the template to all modules was a menu of staff training and development, to build their confidence and capabilities in digital literacies.

A key aspect of staff development and communication was respect for the diversity of subject areas and their specificities, within the overall framework. Rather than taking a one-size-fits-all approach, we chose to promote a shared ethos of what learning and teaching should look like throughout the institution.

Impact

There are multiple benefits being delivered, and still to be derived, from the implementation of the LDF. Most significantly for students, the LDF has provided greater opportunities to feel part of a learning community that places increased emphasis on employability throughout their course, thereby preparing them better for their future career. It also provides an inclusive and accessible learning environment in which all students can succeed and thrive, and it facilitates enhanced scaffolded autonomy where students increasingly become independent learners as they move through their years of study.

For academic staff, the LDF has encouraged the development of a common language for talking about learning, and about what the classroom is for. Institutional conversations around DL, and CL, clarified for staff how they and their students would ideally spend their time together in a way that had meaning and value. In addition, the LDF frees up time in the classroom to ensure that physical co-location creates high-value learning opportunities that really enhance the overall student experience. This all contributes to increasing the 'stickiness' and relevance of modern university campuses.

Other key stakeholders have also enjoyed sustainable benefits. For academic developers, the LDF makes life easier in that every Module has a consistent look and feel. Moreover, the roll-out of the LDF has enhanced our reputation as pedagogic experts and helped develop trusted relationships with colleagues. For university applicants, the LDF provides a clear picture of how learning and teaching will look at the university, what they can expect and what is expected of them in return. Finally, the LDF has reaped benefits in terms of the institution's external reputation for the quality of our educational provision. This is exemplified by the 2023 National Student Survey (NSS) results which attested that many of our courses achieved very high levels of positive feedback, and that we are placed in the top 30% of UK universities across the majority of the survey's scores. We are also in the UK's top 20% for the key Assessment and Feedback measure (www.officeforstudents.org.uk/data-and-analysis/national-student-survey-data/). Undoubtedly, demonstrating an appetite for transformative change broadly enhances a Higher Education institution's reputation of being a progressive, and innovative, learning organization.

Discussion

There were four key lessons learnt from institution-wide LDF implementation:

1. The first relates to the power of peer networks to trigger and sustain meaningful communities of practice. These peer networks enabled and facilitated a peer-led approach to enhancement, in which colleagues mentored, supported and developed each other through sharing good practice. We found this to be altogether more valuable than any mandated central development program.
2. Many staff were resistant to changing their educational practices or had trouble conceiving of a different way of teaching. To counter this, we developed a range of exemplars and templates to suggest new possibilities, and emphasize the benefits to be gained, such as time saved in preparation. This aligned with one of the other key institutional drivers behind the LDF which was to free up staff time for additional academic citizenship, and research and knowledge exchange activities, as part of a contemporaneous review of university promotions pathways.
3. A key, but not fully anticipated, consideration was the apparent difficulty of fitting the LDF into a timetabling system, especially the work planning element of this. For example, it was seemingly impossible in the early stages to timetable DL so that it could show on student timetables. Moreover, staff were uneasy at the perceived reduction in contact time, and they did not fully appreciate how the LDF multiplied access to learning opportunities, by involving other specialist staff in their learning. Conversely, students were more comfortable with the offer. To address this tension, constant reassurance and detailed, consistent and repeated explanations were required with a view to genuinely developing a common understanding of the underpinning pedagogic approach. The consistent development of live FAQs, which were constantly updated as new questions and solutions emerged, proved to be incredibly useful.
4. Finally, the roll-out of the LDF brought to light an inherent fear of the unknown among some parts of the academic community, for example

a deep-seated mistrust of student engagement with learning content, and a fear of losing their intellectual property rights by posting material on the VLE. DL focuses on the concepts, theories and background material of a subject for students to work through at their own pace, freeing up the classroom time for genuine CL. Many staff argued that their students would not do the work, or that they preferred lectures, and that they themselves would be irrelevant. We recommended setting expectations for students, and to maintain them, to establish these new ways of working.

Case Study Conclusion

Like any new initiative, the LDF has experienced teething problems in terms of both implementation and staff buy-in, and it will inevitably continue to evolve. Notwithstanding its future shape, the framework's continued and long-term success is contingent on further strengthening of the foundation of digital literacies upon which it sits. To tackle this, it is vital to facilitate a series of professional development opportunities, to further support staff autonomy and community-based discovery and exchange and to explore how the LDF can apply to different subject disciplines. Naturally, much of this room to flex and grow was integrated into the original design.

The LDF's longevity will depend upon institutional appetite to stay the course, and persist with innovation, in the face of challenges from a sector workforce who find change unsettling. Yet given the constant flux of UK Higher Education, change is perhaps the only certainty, and the sooner we become comfortable with the uncomfortable, the better.

Case Study 4.4: Embedding Proctoring Tools within the Virtual Learning Environment

DAVID HUNT, TRACEY WEBB AND STEPHEN PYNE

The use of online proctoring surged during the COVID-19 pandemic (Grajek, 2020) as Higher Education institutions moved their teaching and learning entirely online, and Professional, Statutory, and Regulatory Bodies (PSRB) stipulated the invigilation of summative exams to meet their awarding requirements. At Bournemouth University, the departments of Design and Engineering (D&E) and Law were given dispensation by their professional bodies to provide online invigilated exams. After a review of online proctoring technologies, a license was obtained for Honorlock due to its functionality, cost and compatibility in terms of its integration with our Brightspace VLE. The tool was adopted at speed to facilitate, for these departments, online proctored exams as the summative assessments for students across all levels in the 19/20 and 20/21 academic years.

Description

Honorlock is an online proctoring service which combines Artificial Intelligence (AI) software with real-time, technical support from human invigilators. Exam questions are built within Brightspace's quiz tool, so students access their exams via Brightspace using the Chrome browser and the downloaded Honorlock extension. The exam is accessed at a set date and time, usually off campus, using a personal device of a designated specification. Students must have an active webcam to undertake the exams. Proctoring settings are tailored per exam, including options to enforce ID checks and room scans. A browser guard can also be used to restrict activity to only allow access to exam content and permitted URLs.

Students with additional requirements are catered for via further settings, for example those requiring breaks or other considerations. The Honorlock AI software monitors students for the duration of the exam session and alerts a human proctor to intervene if any potential problems are detected in relation to the stipulated settings. For example, this may happen if additional voices are heard in the room, or a face moves out of the webcam frame. Screen activity can be recorded and is available post-exam for up to one year and includes flags highlighting suggested areas for tutor review. It is worth noting that the exam activity takes place completely within Brightspace along with marking and grade release. Honorlock therefore functions purely as a proctoring overlay for the exam.

Application

Following a short review process between Faculties, the IT department and the Learning Technology teams, Honorlock was selected, and once licenses were obtained, we integrated Honorlock into the Brightspace test environment for the evaluation of its functionality and scope. This was found to be satisfactory, and Honorlock was subsequently integrated into the production site where it could be easily enabled on specific units as required. A dummy module with test students was created, and used by the Learning

Technologists, for further testing and to explore configuration settings. This space also served as an information repository including good practice guidance on setting up exams and student support resources to be shared on teaching units.

It was recognized that online exams, compared to paper-based exams, require more systematic and effective design (Cramp *et al.*, 2019, p. 1). This proved to be the case as the traditional face-to-face exam papers had to be converted for use with the online Brightspace quiz tool. The questions were predominantly a combination of multiple-choice and written response questions, and were adapted for the quiz tool, with reference to appropriate guidance and instruction from the module's assignment brief.

Each exam's settings were tailored to the individual requirements of that exam, for example some were 'open book' and others permitted an on-screen calculator provided by the Honorlock system. As student instructions, and consequently the appropriate Honorlock settings, differed depending on the assignment, liaison and discussion with teaching and Program support staff culminated in prepopulated spreadsheets listing the recommended, and optional, settings that had been agreed in advance. This spreadsheet was used by the Learning Technologists setting up the exams, thereby ensuring accuracy and reducing the risk of errors when the exams were recreated in Brightspace. Additional learning support time allowances were entered in the Brightspace quiz tool with special accommodations, such as extra breaks, listed per student, and noted within the Honorlock settings.

Restrictions for web access and the whitelisting of specific online publications proved problematic as some publishers required students to sign into the entire website to access specific online books or publications, thereby allowing students to access other unrestricted areas. This was mitigated to some degree by informing students that screen recordings of their browser activity were being captured and could be reviewed by the teaching staff as required.

Being accustomed to working with in-person invigilated written exams, it became clear that the teaching and marking staff were unfamiliar with the Brightspace quiz tool and had minimal understanding of how Honorlock functioned. Consequently, due to the short period of time available for converting exams, most of the exams were created by the Learning Technologists alongside delivering training sessions and writing detailed in-house guidance for Honorlock. Teaching and Faculty admin staff also required training relating to using the Brightspace quiz set-up and marking processes. It was interesting to note that, even after training, the confusion between Honorlock and Brightspace as two distinct but linked systems persisted, with staff continuously referring to the exams as 'Honorlock' rather than as the actual assignment or exam.

Similarly, the students were not used to this style of exam, so clear communications were shared via the Brightspace module explaining the new processes. This included instructional videos, written guidance and Zoom webinars with demonstrations. Additionally, mock exams were created which closely matched the actual exam in set-up and appearance. Students were strongly advised to participate in these mock exams to familiarize themselves with the Honorlock process. This was also used as an opportunity to check the functionality of the students' computers, so that any issues could be addressed before the main exam. Take-up of the mock exams was monitored, and students encouraged to engage further as required.

Some students expressed privacy concerns at what they perceived of as the installation of spyware on their computers; however, they were directed to the Honorlock privacy statement and reassured that no software was being installed, and that they simply needed a Chrome browser extension which they could later disable or remove once the exams had concluded.

Some technical issues were experienced and, while the Honorlock support teams were able to address most issues, there were a few problems that had to be managed by the university. These mainly consisted of pre-Windows 10 laptops and Chromebook laptops that were not capable of running the Chrome extension. Some students didn't have a working webcam, and others lacked a private space for sitting the exam. Poor Wi-Fi/internet stability was another common issue, and in a couple of instances, we had situations including students accessing the exam at work using business-provided laptops with download restrictions that prevented the use of Honorlock.

Arrangements were made to mitigate these issues as much as possible. For example, the university loaned out equipment such as webcams and laptops where practicable. Due to the large student cohorts in the D&E department, students with significant access issues on the day of the exam were provided with the opportunity of sitting their exam via Zoom, invigilated and monitored by members of the teaching team. This was a last resort to enable those with unresolvable technical difficulties to continue with the exam on the day, and to alleviate the stress for participants. This was only viable due to the small number of students affected.

As this was a new system, while students had been instructed to contact Honorlock as a first port of call for any issues with the authentication process, all the exams were synchronously monitored by a Learning Technologist to support both staff and students through the process and to intercept any issues. Additionally, for D&E staff and students, a collaborative space was set up on Microsoft Teams so that students could easily raise any concerns or technical issues, and Learning Technologists and staff could respond expediently at point of need, with communications shared with the whole cohort. This online support proved to be valuable for signposting students to Honorlock support, and in providing reassurance, particularly at the start and end of the exam process.

Impact

The measurement of impact was derived from various sources including Honorlock's in-built metrics and reporting tools, anecdotal feedback from academic staff, reviewing the interactions and volume of student enquiries into the Microsoft Teams support channel, and ultimately student attainment levels evidenced by exam results. While quantitative metrics formed an important aspect of measuring success, the qualitative and humanistic impacts were equally considered. Faculty staff sought feedback from their students following the exams, and overall responses were positive. Working closely with staff and students end-to-end through the entire process, the Learning Technology team were aware of, and constantly mitigating against, any negative impacts from implementing the technology.

The primary benefit of using exam proctoring software was that we were able to successfully deliver invigilated summative exams online during a national lockdown and comply with COVID-19 restrictions in force at that time. This included international students and students living abroad, who were unable to travel due to lockdown restrictions. This approach introduced a flexibility which enabled them to complete their courses despite restrictions. There were minimal exam resits, with most students achieving pass grades on their first attempt.

The first exam generated a multitude of questions from students, including technical support requests, and instances of students being unable to access exams. This resulted in students becoming stressed and anxious at the point of undertaking their exam. It was evident that the additional stress associated with technicalities of the start-up process, concerns over losing exam time and the additional cognitive load above the expected baseline requirements (Milone *et al.*, 2017) required timely support. Honorlock served as the first line of support for students experiencing software problems, and they were able to resolve most of the issues quickly. Learning Technologists liaised closely with Honorlock, who were very receptive, feeding back issues and seeking solutions around functionality, which led to Honorlock improving their live chat response times in line with agreed service-level agreements (SLAs).

Clear and concise communications were posted via announcements on the VLE including specific and tailored instructions for students with additional learning needs where extra exam time was allocated in line with institutional policy. Exam instructions, question layouts and question texts were all updated, ensuring a robust and streamlined process. This change of approach was received positively by students resulting in noticeably improved attitudes in how they approached subsequent exams. Changes to the communication strategies were particularly pertinent at the time to mitigate against students sharing negative perspectives toward the online exam experience with their peers.

To alleviate stress on students, Microsoft Teams channels were set up for the duration of each exam, to provide a space for them to ask support questions and receive immediate responses from academic staff and Learning Technologists. Most students were partaking in multiple exams, and by providing alternative support solutions, including the fallback option of undertaking a non-Honorlock exam proctored over Zoom, students quickly adapted and were reassured that they would be supported though the exam process (Shraim, 2019).

A notable change was how quickly students who were taking multiple exams became more confident with using Honorlock. This was measured by the consistently decreasing number of issues flagged by students and the reduction in the volume of support queries coming through the Microsoft Teams support channel. The creation of clear and concise guidance and the provision of robust support mechanisms which factor in human interactions were all key in supporting those taking remote proctored exams (Ish-Horowicz, 2021).

To effectively support academic staff and students through the new processes, the impact on time and resources for the Learning Technologists was considerable. There was a heavy reliance on the team to deliver the Honorlock solution at short notice, which required an initial upskilling to their skillset and an ongoing agile approach to deal with multiple last-minute changes. Academic staff required varying levels of support through every step of the process, from redesigning exam questions adapted to an online environment, to setting up exams in full on the VLE.

It was essential for the Learning Technologists to liaise with institutional stakeholders, notably Faculty management, teaching teams, IT and the exams team. Bringing in the exams team was critical in ensuring solutions and recommendations were centered on existing policy. This resulted in the adaptation of exam policies and procedures, establishing the roles and responsibilities for future online proctored exams, and formalizing the new processes.

Case Study Conclusion

Following the pandemic, and the return to predominantly face-to-face teaching, usage of online proctoring has significantly reduced, but Honorlock remains a tool in our arsenal which we can employ at short notice. For example, an on-campus exam was recently delayed for a group of apprenticeship Nursing students, and as these students tend to live away from campus, they were given the alternative of taking a proctored online exam from home.

The Honorlock licensing and pricing model allows us to adapt, and be agile, to changing requirements, and to provide this sort of flexibility for students at short notice. Honorlock is still being used for summative assessments in the Law department where it is common for students to work in a law practice, and so attend courses remotely. Furthermore, the availability of online proctoring means summative exams can be conveniently undertaken remotely, while still meeting the requirements for PSRB.

These benefits need to be weighed against some of the challenges that implementing an online proctoring service also brought. The experience has proven to be very resource-intensive for the Learning Technologists, including upskilling, online exam design, the development of delivery of guidance and training and the implementation of recommended good practice for situations in which exam briefs and parameters differ each time. Additional support for the marking processes was also required, alongside set-up and wash-up meetings, ongoing feedback and liaison with the supplier and collaboration with the exams team on roles and responsibilities.

Both staff and students required a lot of support and this human element, with the associated need for reassurance that it provides, remains a key part of successful implementation (Ish-Horowicz, 2021). The high-stakes nature of summative exams, and the additional cognitive load of navigating the technology (Cramp et al., 2019), needs to be mitigated to ensure a positive experience for the students. The debate around the ethical use of online proctoring, and the invasiveness for students into their privacy and personal space, continues. Overall, the student feedback collated was positive.

It has been argued that cheating is a pedagogical issue, not a technological one (Flaherty, 2021). But with the advent of Generative AI tools, capabilities readily available to students, and their potential for use with exams, the use of technology is still being looked at to ensure robust online environments for summative assessments, and to mitigate against academic misconduct.

Case Study 4.5: Using an Experiential Digital Learning Platform to Enhance Student Employability

ANDRINA HALDER

Students learn better when they are engaged through practice. As such I believe in experiential learning, and exposing the students to meaningful hands-on experience that can then be translated and understood using academic knowledge. In this sense, experiential learning is about the strategic use of activities in which the learner needs to be able to apply the knowledge (Salmon, 1989). This approach helps the students as they engage more willingly and enthusiastically. I believe in inspiring students when I teach, and my passion is to bring the workplace into the classroom.

As such, to integrate experiential learning into the course curriculum, as the Course Leader of the BSc Digital Business Management course, I took the initiative to involve the students in Riipen (https://www.riipen.com) which is an experiential digital learning platform. The students were studying a consultancy-based module. Riipen was one of the initiatives taken by the careers team in the school, and this module was the pilot to test it. Using this platform, the students have an opportunity to work with business owners based in the USA, and so gain hands-on experience to practice their acquired theoretical knowledge, demonstrate employability skills and network with employers. The students expressed satisfaction with the module, and the fact that they could work with business owners, and solve real-world business issues, was important to them.

Description

Riipen is a work-based digital learning platform that helps educators, organizations and learners to collaborate on real industry projects to bridge the gap between Higher Education and employment. It integrates educators, business organizations and students under one platform. The educators upload the academic subject topics and learning outcomes to the platform and enter the request for placements. The software then matches the subject-specific learning outcomes with the project requirements of the businesses and suggests suitable business projects for possible placements. The educators can choose from among the best-suited business projects and communicate directly with the business project owners.

Once the initial meeting confirms that both parties (educators and the business project owners) are satisfied, the students are then invited to the projects. The students have the opportunity to choose suitable business projects according to their interests and learning objectives. The students are introduced to the project owners via online meetings, and the project owners present the details of their project. Future meetings are managed by the students and the business project owners under the supervision of the educators. The students then work on the solutions under the supervision of the educators.

The project owners suggest the format for delivering the project solutions, and they are usually in the format of presentations followed by a business report, supported by academic references to theories or concepts. Alongside the educators, the business project owners also can provide both feedback and marks, relating to the effectiveness of the project solution delivered by the students. Currently, Riipen provides Workforce Development, Work-Based Learning Programs and Project-Based Internships. The Riipen platform also can provide two-to-eight-week internships.

Application

My teaching interest is Employability and Experiential learning as a means for student engagement. My pedagogy is informed by practice, and my main aim is to bring the workplace into the classroom through my teaching pedagogy. As such, facilitating employability through experiential learning is one of the objectives in each module that I design and teach.

While developing and leading the Professional Practice (business consultancy) module delivered as part of our Digital Business Management degree course, I used the Riipen platform to promote experiential learning (Gibbs, 1988; Kolb, 1984). Riipen incorporates live projects, and the students have the opportunity to work with the business owners.

Initially, I had a meeting through my university with the Riipen team to understand my role as an educator before I registered on the platform. I then uploaded the consultancy-based module specification, and learning outcomes, to facilitate the Riipen team to match business projects with my learning requirements. Later, I received notification of matched business projects through the Riipen platform.

The business projects were based in the USA. I had the opportunity to choose a suitable project based on the learning outcomes, and I invited students for remote placements. The projects selected involved some 'for profit', and some 'not for profit', organizations. This helped the students to understand the business dynamics of both types of organization. As it was an international collaboration, the students were not paid for these placements. The students within their teams had the opportunity to choose their projects from the ones that I had selected.

Once the projects were finalized, the students met the project owners, and carried out the agreed work. Thereafter, under the supervision of the business project owner and myself, the students had the facility to set up meetings. Two assessments were created based on the project timeline and academic learning outcomes. The final assessment task was to provide the full report of the project solution. The students had the experience of applying the theories that they had learned in the classroom to practice.

The students had to complete a consultancy-based assessment and receive feedback and marks from the business owner and from myself as the module lecturer. The feedback has helped the students to understand both perspectives, i.e., what is expected of them in the business world, and academic settings, and how to integrate this learning into practice. The Riipen platform has helped find experiential learning projects to integrate into this module curriculum and, therefore, has enabled students to gain real-world experience, and ultimately to improve their employability outcomes.

Impact

The use of the Riipen platform has been very successful. This initiative promoted employability and provided all the students with the opportunity to demonstrate their employability skills, as well as to practice their acquired theoretical knowledge. This initiative has helped bring the workplace into the classroom. The students showed greater satisfaction with the module as they learned through 'real-life' experiences. They found this experience invaluable as this has helped them to build skills that employers desire. In terms of assessment and feedback, the inclusion of feedback from business owners has provided the students with a holistic understanding of their work, as it presented not only the perspective of the academic standard, but also the viewpoint of what is required in real-world business practice.

The student module survey showed 100% satisfaction with this module and the course achieved 90% student satisfaction in the 2022 NSS. Some insights from the student module survey are provided below:

> *I really love the fact that we are able to practice what we have learned ... with real companies. This will help me in the future in terms of my CV and my experience.*
>
> (Student, 2022)

> *To be in collaboration with real companies, real stakes [and] challenging tasks.*
>
> (Student, 2022)

Discussion

In my experience, the use of the Riipen platform has multiple benefits. For example, taking an educator's perspective, the use of Riipen has enhanced the learning and teaching aspects. Here are some examples:

- Riipen has helped drive student engagement up by helping the students to develop employable skills, and to improve graduate employment outcomes, through working on real work-based projects;
- The platform has saved time in finding relevant employers by giving access to thousands of organizations, and experiential learning projects, in just a few clicks;
- The use of Riipen has strengthened the reputation of the institution by supporting our strategic plans for innovation, and our commitment to employability, by integrating theory and practice within work-based projects;
- The platform has helped to enhance course content and curriculum, and real-world experiences, by applying an experiential learning approach to drastically improve educational outcomes.

Moving to the student's perspective, the use of Riipen has facilitated the students in some of the following ways:

- To apply what they have learned in the classroom by completing projects for real companies and organizations;
- To develop employable skills, and a professional network, by gaining career clarity, real-world experience and an opportunity to connect with industry experts and so to position themselves for a thriving career;
- To add real value to employers by helping the business project leaders to achieve their goals, while expanding their field of study;
- To make a positive impact by contributing unique ideas to organizations to help them to innovate and succeed.

Lastly, the use of Riipen has helped the business project owners in the following ways:

- To accomplish more for their organization, and grow their business, through the completion of projects with students who get college credit for completing tasks;
- To shape the future of business, and future business leaders, by having an opportunity to mentor students, and help educators to develop rising

leaders with the potential to make a future impact in their communities and worldwide;

- To discover, and recruit, rising talent, by identifying and engaging with diverse candidates before they enter the job market;
- To cultivate innovation in the workspace by bringing fresh ideas, and new perspectives, to their organization, and by working with student talent from various locations and backgrounds.

Like any other aspect of technology, the use of Riipen is not free from challenges. One of the challenges was that, due to the busy schedule of the project owners, it was challenging to set up multiple meetings whenever the students had queries. Initially, we agreed to one meeting per month. To mitigate this, we introduced an asynchronous approach in which the students emailed their queries to the relevant project head, and then the project head would reply via email later.

Case Study Conclusion

At the moment, Riipen is the world's largest experiential learning marketplace. The experiential learning platform has supported my pedagogy of practice-based teaching to promote student engagement. As an educator, the platform also helped me to easily connect with businesses globally, and to find work-based projects for my students. Moreover, this has helped my students to shape their understanding and experience of the world of work. Additionally, while using this platform, the students could prepare for the upcoming challenges in the real workplace. This benefit is invaluable, and provides greater experience for the students, educators and business owners alike. Currently, Riipen is facilitating 31,000 business and not-for-profit projects. Going forward, this work-based platform will thrive in bringing educators, students and business owners under the same network, and so help all three stakeholder groups to develop innovative education solutions.

References

Abd Wahab, A., 2016. *Designing an Information Infrastructure to Support Research Degree Programmes: Identifying Information and Technology Needs*. PhD Thesis. Newcastle: Newcastle University.

Allsop, J., Young, S.J., Nelson, E.J., Piatt, J. and Knapp, D., 2020. Examining the benefits associated with implementing an active learning classroom among undergraduate students. *Teaching and Learning in Higher Education*, 32(3), 418–426.

Assinder, W., 1991. *Peer Teaching, Peer Learning: One Model*. Oxford: Oxford University Press.

Bournemouth University, 2023. *Code of Practice for Research Degrees*. Poole: Bournemouth University.

Brown, A., Lawrence, J., Basson M. and Redmond, P., 2022. A conceptual framework to enhance student online learning and engagement in Higher Education. *Higher Education Research and Development*, 41(2), 284–299.

Bulat, A., 2018. *The UCL Good Supervision Guide*. London: University College London.

Capp, M.J., 2017. The effectiveness of universal design for learning: A meta-analysis of literature between 2013 and 2016. *Inclusive Education*, 21(8), 791–807.

Casey, C., Harvey, O., Taylor, J., Knight F. and Trenoweth, S., 2022. Exploring the wellbeing and resilience of postgraduate researchers. *Further and Higher Education*, 46(6), 850–867.

Central Queensland University, 2024. *CQUniversity Strategic Plan. We Change Lives*. Rockhampton, Australia: Central Queensland University.

Cramp, J., Medlin, J.F., Lake, P. and Sharp, C., 2019. Lessons learned from implementing remotely invigilated online exams. *University Teaching & Learning Practice*, 16(1), 9–28.

Flaherty, C., 2021. Big proctor: Is the fight against cheating during remote instruction worth enlisting third-party student surveillance platforms? *Inside Higher Ed*, May 10.

Friedrich-Nel, H. and Mac Kinnon, J., 2019. The quality culture in doctoral education: Establishing the critical role of the doctoral supervisor. *Innovations In Education and Teaching International*, 56(2), 140–149.

Gibbs, G., 1988. *Learning by Doing: A Guide to Teaching and Learning Methods*. Oxford: Oxford Further Education Unit.

Gower, O., 2021. *Research Supervision Survey – 2021 Report*. Lichfield: UK Council for Graduate Education (UKCGE).

Grajek, S., 2020. EDUCAUSE COVID-19 quickpoll results: Grading and proctoring. *EDUCAUSE Review*. April 10.

Gunawardena, C., Frechette, C. and Layne, L., 2018. *Culturally Inclusive Instructional Design: A Framework and Guide for Building Online Wisdom Communities*. New York: Routledge.

Gunnarsson, R., Jonasson, G. and Billhult, A., 2013. The experience of disagreement between students and supervisors in PhD education: A qualitative study. *BMC Medical Education*, 13(134), 1–8.

Heard-Lauréote, K. and Buckley, C., 2021. 'To be relied upon and trusted': The centrality of personal relationships in a successful cross-team institutional change project. *University Teaching & Learning Practice*. 18(7), 7–24.

Heard-Lauréote, K. and Buckley, C., 2022. Exploding hierarchies for educational change: Leveraging 'third spaces' within Solent University's Transformation Academy. *In:* Jamil, G. and Morley, D. (eds.), *Agile Learning Environments Amid Disruption.* Cham, Switzerland: Palgrave Macmillan, 35–49.

Hmelo-Silver, C.E., 2004. Problem-based learning: What and how do students learn? *Educational Psychology Review,* 16(3), 235–266.

Ish-Horowicz, S., 2021. *A Learning Technologist Sits a Proctored Exam.* Bicester: Association for Learning Technology.

Jackson, L.H., 2023. Developing a learning and teaching leadership profile in a specialist arts institution. *In:* Hosein, A., Rao, N. and Kinchin, I.M. (eds.), *Narratives of Becoming Leaders in Disciplinary and Institutional Contexts.* London: Bloomsbury Academic, 101–118.

Kolb, D.A., 1984. *Experiential Learning: Experience as the Source of Learning and Development* (Vol. 1). Englewood Cliffs, NJ: Prentice-Hall.

Manathunga, C., 2005. Early warning signs in postgraduate research education: A different approach to ensuring timely completions. *Teaching in Higher Education,* 10(2), 219–233.

Masuku, V.Z. 2021. Becoming a research supervisor: Reflections on a postgraduate supervision course. *Teacher Education and Curriculum Studies,* 6(4), 143–150.

McGloin, R.S., 2021. A new mobilities approach to re-examining the doctoral journey: Mobility and fixity in the borderlands space. *Teaching in Higher Education,* 26(3), 370–386.

Metcalfe, J., Wilson, S. and Levecque, K., 2018. *Exploring Wellbeing and Mental Health and Associated Support Services for Postgraduate Researchers.* London: Vitae.

Milone, A.S., Cortese, A.M., Balestrieri, R.L. and Pittenger, A.L., 2017. The impact of proctored online exams on the educational experience. *Currents in Pharmacy Teaching and Learning,* 9(1), 108–114.

Müller, A., 2022. *Supporting Students in an Online Environment.* Melbourne, Australia: Tertiary Education Quality Standards Agency.

Polkinghorne, M., Taylor, J., Knight, F. and Stewart, N., 2023. Doctoral supervision: A best practice review. *Encyclopedia,* 3(1), 46–59.

Race, P., 2007. *The Lecturer's Toolkit: A Practical Guide to Assessment, Learning and Teaching,* 3rd edition. Abingdon: Routledge.

Salmon, P., 1989. Personal stances at learning. *In:* Werner Weil, S. and McGill, M. (eds.), *Making Sense of Experiential Learning.* Milton Keynes: Open University Press, 230–244.

Shraim, K., 2019. Online examination practices in Higher Education institutions: Learners' perspectives. *Turkish Online Journal of Distance Education,* 20(4), 185–196.

Stone, C., 2017. *Opportunity Through Online Learning: Improving Student Access, Participation and Success in Higher Education.* Perth, Australia: Curtin University.

Stone, C., 2019. Online learning in Australian Higher Education: Opportunities, challenges and transformations. *Student Success*, 10(2), 1–11.

Taylor, S., 2019. *Good Supervisory Practice Framework*. Lichfield: UK Council for Graduate Education (UKCGE).

Turnbull, D., Chugh, R. and Luck, J., 2020 Learning management systems, an overview. *In: Encyclopedia of Education and Information Technologies*, Cham, Switzerland: Springer, 1052–1058.

Innovative Applications of Technology to Improve Teaching Standards

5

The following five case studies describe innovative applications of technology to improve teaching standards. Each case study presents the personal perspectives of those involved.

Case Study 5.1: Using Online Platforms for Assessment and Feedback

LINDA LEFIÈVRE AND MARK HANCOCK

The education sector has undergone swift adjustment and transformation in the last four years, attributed primarily to two significant factors. First, the COVID-19 pandemic prompted rapid adaptation and digitization in teaching and assessment methods (Adedoyin and Soykan, 2023). Second, Generative Artificial Intelligence (GenAI) advancements have raised concerns regarding academic integrity, prompting a shift toward redesigning assessments (Hodges and Ocak, 2023). This focus on enhancing the quality and authenticity of assessment has accelerated change (Fuller et al., 2022; Mate and Weidenhofer, 2021). The rapidly evolving landscape of Higher Education has presented challenges and opportunities in adapting to modern technologies and addressing various needs to ensure students acquire essential graduate skills.

DOI: 10.4324/9781032635248-6

The response to the pandemic in 2020 prompted an unprecedented shift to online teaching in Higher Education across the globe. During the immediate response, most universities adopted an Emergency Remote Teaching approach which was unplanned, and so forced a rapid transition into the digitalization of teaching content and online delivery, with a limited understanding of the pedagogy that underpinned the technology being used (Castañeda and Selwyn, 2018; Hodges *et al.*, 2020; Lockee, 2021). This transition was followed by intermediate actions focusing on delivering remote online assessments prioritizing student progression and graduation (Tuah and Naing, 2021). Many institutions, including the University of Birmingham, repurposed their Virtual Learning Environment (VLE) for online assessment, pushing its capabilities, design constraints and functionalities beyond their original teaching-centric design (Kozaris, 2010; Hussain *et al.*, 2020; Jaam *et al.*, 2021). Due to time constraints, we moved our traditional campus-based exams to the VLE platform, despite its limitations, and therefore this was not necessarily the most suitable or efficient strategy (Mate and Weidenhofer, 2021).

In the long term, various adaptations and campus-based programs returned to traditional in-person teaching. Nonetheless, the adoption of online assessments continued due to their flexibility as they offered various advantages for both academics and students (Pettit *et al.*, 2021; Mate and Weidenhofer, 2021). Institutions transitioned to dedicated online assessment platforms with tailored functionalities and versatility, which have now become integral in supporting assessments.

In 2023, the rapid development and widespread use of GenAI, including large language models like ChatGPT, have introduced new possibilities and challenges within the education sector. However, GenAI's most noteworthy influence in education is evident in assessment, especially affecting traditional assessments and profoundly impacting academic integrity (Hodges and Ocak, 2023). This reinforces the urgency and importance of developing more authentic assessments. In this context it relates to the development of real and transferable skills which can be gained by aligning learning objectives and real-world expectations (Appiah and van Tonder, 2018; Hatzipanagos *et al.*, 2020; Huber *et al.*, 2024; Olasina, 2023).

The positive aspects of both crises described above provided the opportunity to leverage digitalization and GenAI, to enhance student support and to engage in a comprehensive review of assessment and feedback practice. In addition to a minimum standard feedback provision, integrating enhanced technology and GenAI within assessment platforms provides students with quicker, real-time feedback, allowing for efficiency improvements (Leibold and Schwarz, 2015; Al-Bashir et al., 2016; Lee, 2023).

This approach can also streamline administrative tasks by cutting grading time for educators (Leibold and Schwarz, 2015; Appiah and van Tonder, 2018; Cavalcanti et al., 2021; Pettit et al., 2021). Balancing the benefits of technology, with the human aspects of education, remained a key focus for educational institutions during this transformative period, and it paved the way for innovation, collaboration and personalized learning experiences (Lee, 2023).

In this case study, we will discuss our experiences with online assessments, and explore how they offer opportunities to enhance student attainment. We will propose that digital assessments present another avenue to address students' need for improved feedback, as voiced by the National Student Survey (NSS) (Buckley, 2021).

Description

Despite recognizing that the VLE was not primarily designed for assessments, our heavy reliance upon it limited our exposure to, and experience of, other possible assessment online solutions and their potential benefits. As we broadened our exploration, it became evident that expecting a single solution to fulfill all our institutional needs, across various types of assessments and questions, was unrealistic.

Initially, the small-scale adoption of different tools focused on a selection of degree program needs for appropriate exam question types, such as multiple-choice and short answer questions, and additional specific features, including question bank software. The additional need for lockdown browsers involved exploring the sector's position on remote proctoring, and whether our internal academic and legal positions aligned to ensure an appropriate invigilation provision (Fuller et al., 2022; Huber et al., 2024). Incorporation of GenAI into assessment was also taken into consideration, not only from a design perspective but also for enhanced machine-based marking support and, potentially, even for feedback provision (Lee, 2023).

Identifying a solution required us to accommodate various assessment modes across disciplines and diverse marking approaches. Additional functionalities were also identified based on the study year and assessment weighting. These features encompassed double marking, blind marking, moderation and tools for annotation, including the ability to highlight or draw on digital text and images. We also identified varied marking criteria within a single module and an extensive use of rubrics.

Improving feedback provision was a key driver for this project as this was intricately linked with the strategic requirements associated with the NSS assessment and feedback scores and subsequent national rankings (Buckley, 2021). The technology had to facilitate feedback in a way that considered equity and accessibility, linking to the importance of academics giving, and students receiving, and acting on any feedback provided (Leibold and Schwarz, 2015). Offering a variety of feedback methods such as audio, video and even utilizing GenAI for creating feedback and assigning grades was therefore essential (Leibold and Schwarz, 2015; Al-Bashir et al., 2016).

Application

Before the pandemic, the transition toward digital transformation consistently faced obstacles, resulting in very few large-scale approaches being implemented. This was frequently due to a limited understanding of digital pedagogy, digital transformation and inadequate consideration of the transformative process. Practices therefore varied within our institution, and across the sector, as digital assessment had not yet been fully adopted, e.g., in achieving scaled consistency in online marking was considered innovative. As a result, institutional practices were not aligned, making it challenging to learn from shared experiences. This became evident when interacting with institutions conducting small pilots on digital assessment platforms. At the surface level, their experience seemed positive, but delving deeper, a different story was revealed.

Internal challenges were identified, as there was a need to consider the assessment practices of different academic disciplines and their unique approaches. Initially, we attempted to categorize requirements in the hope of identifying a 'one-size-fits-all' solution that would address all assessment needs. However, it soon became apparent that a range of digital assessment tools would be more appropriate. This realization allowed us to understand better how to meet the specific needs of different discipline groups at a more granular level, rather than broadly categorizing them as STEM or non-STEM.

Throughout our experience, the need for more frequent feedback provision was highlighted. We identified the need for a scaffolded and continuous feedback approach supported within a digital assessment platform. This approach allowed us to offer support to students from a formative perspective, highlighting the benefits of the platform. GenAI brought many positive elements for us to consider, such as how automated marking might help reduce academic workload. Integrated GenAI produced templated assessments and marking tools, including prepopulated rubrics that could potentially enhance the development of assessment and marking approaches, and feedback provision (Lee, 2023).

Over recent years, academic practice has transitioned from paper-based assessments to digital approaches to assessment. This shift led to a rise in the use of digital assessment tools and engagement with new digital platforms, diverging from the VLE with the desire for end users to have a similar, or equivalent, experience regardless of the platform. Within Higher Education, online assessments have now become the standard practice.

Impact

Many of the lessons learned are connected to internal factors such as strategic priorities relating to data and integration, internal procedures and policies related to procurement processes and institutional needs concerning software functionality. These themes include staff engagement, the existing support structure for implementation and the budget allocation necessary to fulfill these objectives. We encountered nuanced requirements that needed capturing in our scope. Disciplines tended to work in silos, with added challenges and complexity when regulated by external bodies.

Gathering functionality requirements therefore proved to be challenging across disciplines. We considered local approaches, and how extensively institutional assessment frameworks had been interpreted at a micro level, e.g., in accommodating diverse marking and moderation practices. This included considerations of what markers could view when double marking was needed, the type of feedback provided and how and what the student would be able to see once the marking had been complete.

The diversity of assessments, and their differences, were all considered during the requirements gathering phase at the institutional level, a task that had never been accomplished before. This comprehensive analysis led us to conclude that providing a single digital assessment solution would not suffice to meet our needs, particularly as we failed to identify one single platform that met most of our requirements, even after extensive research and engagement with digital assessment solution procurement frameworks.

Another critical consideration was ensuring the seamless integration of the assessment platform with our existing systems, including our VLE, gradebook and student record systems. Despite a robust procurement process, we discovered that receiving positive confirmation of a learning tool's integration capability did not ensure that the desired level of functionality would be achieved once implemented.

The procurement process in Higher Education is intricate, balancing legislative requirements with efforts to innovate. Scoping security considerations, data governance and approval from a vast number of stakeholders took much longer than anticipated. Departments working in silos meant a collective approach took time and the upskilling of staff. We also needed to balance our understanding of the technicalities of data processing with how institutional risk and reputation were being prioritized in the decision-making process.

Digital literacy is crucial for both students and academics to successfully implement an institutional digital assessment solution, as highlighted by Hodges *et al.* (2020). At the outset of our project, it became apparent that there was a need for additional work in this area. Considering the digital skill set, this realization unveiled supplementary requirements indirectly tied to our experiences. There was also a less recognized need to address the sector-wide perception of digital literacy, especially when interacting with a 'different' or 'new' digital platform, whether for assessments or more general use (Montenegro-Rueda *et al.*, 2021). To address these issues, we introduced basic-level training and ongoing support.

Post-pandemic, online assessments continue to benefit the education sector (Hatzipanagos *et al.*, 2020; Pettit *et al.*, 2021). Although setting up, and conducting, online exams is more intricate than traditional paper-based methods, the diversity in assessment types and innovative feedback mechanisms that can be used caters to diverse learning styles and preferences. This approach therefore offers a more holistic view of a student's capabilities.

While online platforms change the 'how' of the teaching and learning journey, they do not change the 'why' (Mehanna, 2004; Castaneda and Selwyn, 2018). Pedagogically, assessment and feedback are foundational as they form a dynamic dialog between the educator and the student, fostering learning and helping students identify gaps to hone their skills further, and pinpoint areas they need to refine (Meyen *et al.*, 2002).

Drawing from our experience with various online assessment platforms, we would argue that their most profound impact is equipping academics with the tools, and the capacity, to bolster the quality and timeliness of feedback return (Montenegro-Rueda *et al.*, 2021). This would improve student satisfaction and mitigate the workload for academics (Mate and Weidenhofer, 2021; Lee, 2023). Integrating Technology-Enhanced Feedback, and GenAI-supported feedback, into assessment platforms is an advancement in the education sector that aim to further support the optimization of this feedback process (Lee, 2023).

Technology-Enhanced Feedback involves tools and platforms that streamline, and automate, certain aspects of the feedback process, thereby providing automation, consistency and instant feedback to the students. However, operationally it is limited as it functions within predefined parameters, and does not offer in-depth feedback (Cavalcanti *et al.*, 2021). GenAI uses advanced AI to analyze, predict and generate feedback tailored to individual student needs, making it more inclusive (Lee, 2023). Advanced GenAI feedback systems are only as good as their training data, and as a result they may sometimes misinterpret nuanced and empathetic human expressions, or cultural and biased contexts.

Moreover, the analytical capabilities inherent in many online platforms offer another layer of support. These analytics can spotlight trends in student performance, illuminate areas where many students grapple with challenges and even suggest potential instructional strategies (Lim *et al.*, 2021; Banihashem *et al.*, 2022). Armed with such insights, educators are better positioned to fine-tune instruction, modify curriculum design and ensure that learning experiences are rigorous and supportive.

Case Study Conclusion

Our experience has made it clear that an institutional move toward embracing digital assessments brings both prospects and hurdles. This is evident from the obvious burden that the pandemic placed on the rapid digitization of Higher Education, and the swift changes brought by the sudden availability of GenAI. While both have been transformational for the educational sector, they have also called into question our belief that a digital assessment strategy, backed by strong engagement and transparent accountability, would smoothly facilitate the implementation of digital assessment at an institutional level. We may have misjudged the extent to which this shift could be realized.

Exploring software solutions at scale can be an approach that may be used to increase the adoption of digital assessment. The sector needs to appreciate the operational challenges, including procurement legislation and the bureaucratic internal governance processes, so that can undertake rigorous proof of concept studies, rather than procure one solution that will not meet everyone's requirements. This would allow us to explore more fully what is possible for implementation at scale, and so identify new future-proofed pedagogies that can be combined with the powerful impact brought about through GenAI.

The shift to online assessment necessitates academics to adapt and re-evaluate traditional practices. Too frequently, academics persist with outdated assessment models on modern platforms, and traditional delayed feedback that can hinder students' real-time learning. Online platforms are merely tools. The onus is on the instructors to embed the appropriate pedagogy. In taking this approach, we highlight the importance of the student experience within assessment, particularly feedback engagement and how their needs are integrated into this.

Academic engagement needs to underpin all the above, driven by institutional strategic priorities, acknowledging external factors such as national and global levers, with accountability around digital assessment transformation. Real-time academic motivation, through greater engagement, hints that this change is possible. We are still 'work in progress' and continue to learn. We are committed as an institution to advance and scale up, but it comes with many challenges. It is not just about moving platforms; it requires considerable effort.

Case Study 5.2: Using Technology to Evaluate Student Learning Gain

MARTYN POLKINGHORNE, GELAREH ROUSHAN AND JULIA TAYLOR

This case study relates to Higher Education delivered in the UK where the increasing cost of tuition fees is raising questions about the overall value for money of a university degree-based education (Polkinghorne *et al.*, 2017a). The consequence of this change in attitudes is that students have started to view themselves as consumers (Roohr *et al.*, 2017). As a result, the process of marketizing Higher Education is now happening (Chapleo and O'Sullivan, 2017).

To address these issues, and respond to student expectations, we recognized that university leaders need to understand how students perceive the education that they receive. This perception goes beyond grades awarded and progress attained. It relates to the usefulness of the educational experience delivered in terms of developing transferable and subject-specific skills, raising awareness regarding the global challenges that we need to face together, and understanding how student learning relates to an individual's future employability trajectory.

These are all issues we were aware of, and so we decided to investigate how we could better understand student perceptions theoretically, and the implications of this upon our own practice. Many colleagues across the sector were starting to consider the merits of student learning gain (Howson and Buckley, 2020), and trying to agree on how to define and evaluate it (Evans *et al.*, 2018). The UK Office for Students now refers to learning gain under the label of *educational gain*.

The most common understanding of student learning gain is that it refers to the improvement that a student makes in their knowledge, skills and understanding over a specific period (McGrath *et al.*, 2015). As such, it is a measure of how much a student has advanced academically from one point in time to another. Typically, changes in student learning gain might be assessed over the duration of an activity, a taught module or across an entire degree program. This concept of learning gain is important because it enables educators, institutions and policymakers to assess the effectiveness of educational programs, teaching methods and the taught curriculum. In other words, if we better understand the learning of our students, then we can improve our teaching delivery to ensure that more students have access to an enhanced learning experience (Tight, 2021).

Learning gain is typically evaluated in various ways, including pre- and post-module evaluation, standardized tests, formative and summative assessments and sometimes even observations (Jones-Devitt *et al.*, 2019). To complicate this further, students will start a taught module with a variety of different levels of knowledge based upon their own personal educational experience, and so any evaluation of learning gain has to take this into account to ensure that the development of the student is being considered *per se*, and not the student's achievement and attainment (McGrath *et al.*, 2015).

By assessing learning gain, we knew that we could start to make data-driven decisions to enhance teaching strategies, tailor interventions for individual students and create opportunities for more personalized learning (Polkinghorne *et al.*, 2017a). Instead of simply considering learning gain as being the distance traveled by a student between two points in their learning journey (McGrath *et al.*, 2015), we created a new model (Polkinghorne *et al.*, 2017b) in which we took an alternative perspective, as we wanted to capture both a student's theory-based distance traveled (i.e., explicit knowledge based upon theories and models) and also their practical experience-based journey traveled (i.e., tacit understanding relating to personal experience and know-how), as in reality every student needs to have a blend of both to ensure that they can both understand and apply their knowledge.

This case study now considers how we applied this model and used technology to evaluate the learning gain of our students, how the results revealed to us insights into our teaching that we did not already know and how we were able to integrate these findings into our continuous improvement process to enhance our future teaching delivery.

Description

For the research reported in this case study, we have used the Jisc Online Surveys tool (https://www.onlinesurveys.ac.uk/about/), which Jisc (Joint

Information Systems Committee) makes available for universities to utilize for research purposes, such as gathering feedback from students, staff and other stakeholders.

Jisc is an organization that provides digital services to the UK education sector. In particular, it has helped advance the digital infrastructure used by Higher Education, including high-speed internet connectivity, network services and cybersecurity measures. Furthermore, Jisc provides consultation, training and guidance to universities to help them make informed decisions about technology integration and digital strategies.

Jisc supports research, including providing tools and services to aid data management and digital preservation. Regarding data services, Jisc offers analytics and visualization tools to help universities gather insights from various data sources, enabling evidence-based decision-making.

The Jisc Online Surveys tool can create surveys with various question types. They can then be distributed using email invitations and web links, or the surveys can be embedded within an organization's VLE. The service provides a user-friendly platform that enables the quick and easy customization of surveys, with features for the distribution to targeted audiences and automated data analysis.

One key aspect of the Jisc Online Surveys tool is that the design themes used in a survey can be customized to comply with organizational branding and identity. From the participants' perspective, the surveys are easily accessible using a wide range of devices, and automated reminders can be included. Together, these two factors can significantly improve engagement levels in the target audience group.

Jisc has undertaken work on advanced cybersecurity measures across the Higher Education sector to ensure the ongoing protection of participants' data. For these reasons, Higher Education often prefers the Jisc Online Surveys tool to commercially available alternatives.

Application

We decided to run a series of pilot activities to test our learning gain model, using the Jisc Online Surveys tool as our data collection and analysis platform. In particular, we wanted to know how students perceived their own learning in the following range of scenarios:

1. When undertaking group-work-based taught modules (Polkinghorne et al., 2023);
2. When undertaking individual assessment-based taught modules (Polkinghorne et al., 2021a);

3. When undertaking autonomous project-based modules (Polkinghorne et al., 2021b, 2022);
4. When studying in the first year of their undergraduate degree studies (Polkinghorne et al., 2021c; O'Sullivan et al., 2022);
5. When studying in the final year of their undergraduate degree studies (Leidner et al., 2022).

In all cases, the pilot tests were undertaken with the full support of the academic teaching team for the modules included, and to align with our ethical approval from Bournemouth University (BU), we were not allowed to analyze the data until the students had completed the particular year of study being considered. All data collected was anonymous.

Students volunteered and were asked to reflect on how they considered their own learning to have advanced. We designed the questions around the intended learning outcomes for the module being studied, as we found that this provided the most tangible information for us to use to evaluate the effectiveness of the teaching provided. The question design reflected Bloom's revised taxonomy of higher-order thinking skills (Anderson and Krathwohl, 2001).

Examples of questions relating to distance traveled from different surveys are: "How much has your understanding of leadership increased?"; "How much has your understanding of marketing principles increased?"; "How much has your understanding of research design increased?"; "How much has your understanding of business interconnectivity increased?".

Examples of questions related to the journey traveled from different surveys are: "How much has your ability to analyze ethical challenges improved?"; "How much has your ability to apply marketing techniques improved?"; "How much has your ability to apply research methods to projects improved?"; "How much has your ability to assess performance and talent improved?".

Impact

In terms of learning and teaching, using the Jisc Online Surveys tool as our data collection and analysis platform was quick and easy to understand and apply. The distribution options enabled us to set the optimal time and method for reaching out to students for each teaching module, which maximized our potential returns. We could then monitor student engagement in real time to ensure the sufficiency of data collection, which was important, as we needed the results obtained to be meaningful.

Because of the anonymous nature of the surveys, the automated reminders sent by the system were very helpful to us as this was not something that we could undertake without knowing who had already responded and who had not. In an era when many students suffer from survey fatigue, we thought this type of targeted action was particularly important.

Considering the results obtained, alongside expected and predictable results, there was a scattering of interesting insights into how students perceived their own learning. For example, students engaged in group-work recognized the acquisition of vital transferable skills such as communication and planning. However, they also disclosed that they believed that, consequently, their subject-specific learning had been compromised. This insight underscored the potential pitfalls of excessive reliance upon group-work within a university context and emphasizes the necessity for a well-balanced array of learning opportunities.

Certain students reported notable gains in perceived learning across the spectrum, while others indicated significantly fewer advancements. This observation prompted us to bring to the attention of the teaching team the importance of engaging students through a diverse range of activities, acknowledging the numerous ways in which students absorb knowledge.

In a few instances, students who reported substantial perceived learning in terms of distance traveled showed markedly less progress in terms of journey traveled. Conversely, the opposite was also evident. When considered together, this suggests that some students are more receptive to learning theory, while others prefer to learn more practical knowledge. This revealed the imperative for the academic team to carefully consider their approach to presenting instructional material, such as integrating case studies within their teaching to illustrate practical applications of theory.

After each initial survey for a teaching module, we engaged in discussions with the teaching team about the outcomes, resulting in agreed-upon actions that were then executed. The subsequent surveys of students conducted with the next student cohort demonstrated shifts in their responses. Higher levels of perceived learning were reported, notably in the areas where changes had been implemented.

Data had been collected from in-person teaching activities before the global pandemic in 2020. Due to the subsequent closure of university campuses, and the transition to online instruction for a few academic years, we continued data collection to gauge potential shifts in learning behavior (Leidner et al., 2022; O'Sullivan et al., 2022).

Interestingly, first-year undergraduate students indicated a decline in their perception of their own personal learning once the shift to online instruction occurred during the pandemic. Conversely, final-year undergraduate students, particularly females, reported an improvement. This discrepancy is thought to arise because, at the commencement of their degree programs, students transitioning from secondary education are accustomed to a higher level of structure (Carpenter and Western, 1984), which was attenuated by online learning. In contrast, final-year students have matured into self-directed learners (Singaram *et al.*, 2022) and therefore the increased availability of online materials and recordings facilitated their self-study endeavors.

These findings have significantly impacted on our thinking and planning for future educational activities. By integrating the findings into our annual continuous improvement process, we have been able to introduce controlled and targeted change, which means that, over time, we can incrementally improve the effectiveness of our teaching and the resulting learning of our students.

Case Study Conclusion

This case study delves into the evolving landscape of Higher Education within the UK, where the shifting dynamics of tuition fees and student perspectives have forced universities to explore the concept of students as consumers. This transformation has triggered the marketization of Higher Education, prompting the need for institutions to re-evaluate the educational value that they provide. Recognizing the imperative to address these shifts and respond to student concerns, we tried to understand how students perceive their education beyond traditional metrics such as grades and progression.

Leveraging the Jisc Online Surveys tool, a versatile platform for data collection and analysis, we orchestrated a series of pilot activities with a range of educational scenarios ranging from group-work to autonomous projects. In each scenario, we aimed to understand the students' perceived trajectories for their own learning. Notably, our model encompassed both the theoretical (distance traveled), and the practical (journey traveled), dimensions of learning, accounting for explicit knowledge and tacit understanding.

The impact of our endeavor extended to the learning and teaching landscape. Utilizing the Jisc Online Surveys tool streamlined data collection and analysis, optimizing engagement and enabling informed decision-making. Our findings revealed a spectrum of insights that led to focused interventions and improvements, contributing to a progressive evolution in our teaching methods.

Ultimately, this case study underscores the importance of dynamic engagement with the student community to better understand what students think about their own learning. By integrating these insights into our continuous improvement framework, we have empowered ourselves to incrementally enhance teaching methodologies, and so optimize student learning experiences. As the educational landscape continues to evolve, the significance of data-driven, evidenced-based understanding of our students will become increasingly apparent, enabling us to navigate the ever-changing currents of Higher Education with insight and innovation.

Case Study 5.3: Using Point-of-View Cameras to Support Teaching, Assessment and Feedback

GRAHAM FRENCH AND RHYS COETMOR JONES

Teacher education programs frequently adopt andragogical approaches that value modeling and direct experience as teaching tools (Loughran and Hamilton, 2016) and so embrace constructivist epistemology (Richardson, 1997). While this is often tempered with classroom or lecture-based instruction, it is perhaps most prevalent in pre-service programs for physical education (PE) (Byra, 2006; Capel and Blair, 2007; Kirk, 2010) and adventure education (AE) (Backman, 2015; Brown, 2006; North, 2020). However, when the global COVID-19 pandemic enforced restrictions on teaching practices at Higher Education institutions in early 2020, these modeling and direct experience sessions were significantly curtailed, and in some cases completely prohibited.

Our university was not alone in facing challenges with overseas students being unable to attend sessions. We had mixed groups of students to teach that comprised of those present and able to attend, and those unable to attend other than online sessions. Working on the PE and AE postgraduate initial teacher education (ITE) programs at Bangor University, we sought alternative ways to provide students with the required experiences.

We viewed this situation as an opportunity to develop our practice with andragogic approaches that would enhance, rather than just replace, what had gone before. This case study details this development, including a description of the technology we used, how this was applied and developed during post-COVID restrictions and a brief evaluation of the impact of this new practice.

Description

The approach we adopted was to use Point-of-View (POV) cameras to record student-perspective videos of practical PE and AE sessions. These videos were presented unedited in a multi-screen format, through the university's secure VLE. The lack of editing was important to present an authentic student-eye view of sessions, without the direction or potential bias that editing can bring (Ruby, 1995). Permission for recording sessions, and subsequent sharing of the videos, was obtained from participants, and approval for this practice was gained through our faculty director of teaching and learning. Any students who did not wish to be recorded were placed into groups without cameras, but they still participated in the same learning sessions as other students.

A POV camera is a small video camera, typically not much bigger than a smartphone. It is usually worn on a headband, wrist strap or chest harness. There are many models and styles, but one of the originals is the GoPro Hero series. In practice, GoPro is becoming the generic name for all POV cameras (French, 2016a, b). A POV camera is a point-and-shoot device, the operation of which involves simply an off/on switch leaving the camera's electronics to do the rest to optimize the footage recorded (image stabilization, autofocus, sound isolation, etc.). The challenge of ensuring the camera is pointing at what the user is seeing is addressed by using a wide-angle fisheye lens, to give approximately 170 degrees of field of view, and wireless connectivity to allow the camera to transmit its signal to a suitable app on a smartphone for checking.

A POV camera is less obtrusive than a handheld camera, as it is small and worn on the body, and such cameras are popular and familiar to sports participants (French, 2016b). They are waterproof, resistant to impacts and wearable. Most have a battery life of several hours' continual recording and can easily collect this amount of video footage on a high-density compact memory card. These characteristics make them ideal for filming where conventional cameras may be unsuitable or unwieldy. French (2016a) noted that an unobtrusive approach to using video is important, as the process of being observed by a camera can alter behavior (Cromdal, 2000; Foucault, 1991; Sparrman, 2005). The use of POV video allows complete participation by the wearer (camera-operator), which is important to further reduce the effect the camera has on the subject's behavior.

Application

We ensured there was at least one camera between two students so one could wear the camera and give the point of view, and one could be 'in shot'. In many cases involving group-work, we found that fewer cameras captured the session well, and made presenting the footage more straightforward.

Students were given a choice of wearing a camera, and whether to use a head strap or chest mount. It became regular practice at the start of practical sessions in AE and PE for students to collect a camera with other equipment, put it on and start recording. During some AE sessions, students found it easier to mount cameras on their kayak, handlebars or rucksack strap. There was no concern over damage through contact as we were initially restricted to non-contact activities.

After every session, one of us downloaded the footage from the memory cards and then uploaded the files to the VLE. Student feedback identified a need for more than one group's footage to be visible at once. This meant students who had attended, and were watching the footage back to evaluate learning, could gain experience of other groups' sessions, and those who were unable to attend could also contribute. Through a process of trial and dialog with the students, we settled on splitting the screen into four equal sections, having a different group in each quadrant. This took a little more time to facilitate, as although we were not altering the content or sequence, some editing software was needed in incorporating four camera images on one screen. However, this did not add a great deal of complexity as many video editing apps have picture-in-picture functions to allow this.

At first, we utilized the videos to allow students who were unable to attend to catch up on the content they had missed, similar to the lecture capture process used in many educational institutions (Prince, 2016). This also enabled students who did not attend to take part in critically reflective activities based on the practical sessions. Student feedback from those unable to attend demonstrated the value that the recordings had in allowing absent students to feel part of a community of learners, and gain insight into how the activities were taught, mimicking the modeling aspect of our pre-COVID teaching. There was some aspect of a shared experience through the footage because it was unedited, and so captured all the conversations and moments, much of which had gone unnoticed in the actual sessions.

As the bank of session footage grew, we also began to use the video in a more reflective way, with one of us scanning the footage and selecting critical incidents within the session that we could then highlight (watch back) in our classroom/online sessions. This allowed direct examples of teaching techniques, and rather than spending time trying to remember what happened, students were able to engage in a critical discussion of the incidents. This was particularly useful when considering assessment for learning tasks that had been set relating to how participants responded, and how the student teachers evaluated the evidence thus gained.

Impact

We utilized several features of the VLE to gauge impact, and worked with student representatives, as well as whole class feedback sessions, to develop the use of POV videos through the 2019–2020 cohort and with subsequent groups. The VLE recorded the number of views each video gained, which could be seen at an individual level, as well as by cohort. Unsurprisingly students who were unable to attend viewed the videos most frequently, and there were a high number of views across the cohort in the week following the session.

Practical sessions occurred one day per week, and were closely linked to classroom/online sessions, so it is likely that, as the next practical occurred, students moved to that video. However, there were still a high number of views spread across the year (compared to the size of the cohort), especially when assignments that related to specific pedagogies, and how children learn, were due for submission. Students may have been using the direct experience videos to relive and reflect on their practical sessions, or they may have been looking for the application of subsequent pedagogical approaches and ideas in earlier pedagogy modeling sessions.

In the first few weeks of using the POV cameras we asked students what they thought of the latest video, and how they were using it in the classroom and online sessions (and in their independent learning), and we acted on feedback if there was a consensus. From this initial feedback, we concluded that the four-way split of the screen was the most helpful, and that while audio was important during direct instruction, it was what the students could see that they found most useful. Students shared that, when they were absent, they used the videos to gain some feeling of what had been covered in the sessions they missed, and how their peers viewed the session content. This allowed them to play a greater part, and contribute more meaningfully, to subsequent classroom and online reflective sessions.

They also liked the ability to watch excerpts and look for critical incidents. After we started using these critical incident excerpts in classroom sessions, students could identify these more readily by watching footage. The ability to identify critical incidents in classroom observation is seen as an important step in a student teachers' development (Dinsmore and Wenger, 2006; Oosterheert and Vermunt, 2001). With this first group and subsequent cohorts, this learning happened sooner, compared to our previous experience with similar cohorts, by several weeks. Admittedly we currently have little quantitative empirical data on this, which is an area for further investigation.

Realizing that this use of video was moving beyond our original expectations of replicating practical sessions and providing an additional andragogical tool for use with student teachers, after the first cohort had graduated, we reflected on how we could further enhance our practice as teacher educators. We were engaging in a professional development exercise involving lesson study (Lewis *et al.*, 2009), and this approach aligned with the collaborative planning and reflection we had used in our preparation phase. Subsequent iterations of the use of POV cameras incorporated our own reflections and student feedback (including viewing metrics from the VLE). Together with feedback from other colleagues as part of the lesson study work, this led us to use some fixed-point video, which used the same cameras with the wide-angle fisheye lenses, for contact sport sessions once COVID restrictions had relaxed in the following years. We also used them for longer fixed-location AE sessions such as rock-climbing at a climbing wall. While this was not as effective for capturing student experience as it was not as immersive, it still allowed critical incidents to be exemplified in later teaching.

The final development of the practice was to try to replicate the direct experience of observing real teachers with real children, rather than students role-playing, which is noted as being an essential part of a student teacher's development. As COVID-19 restrictions relaxed, teaching could resume. Even though children could go back to school, it was still not possible to send groups of student teachers into schools to observe teaching. We approached some of our partner schools, and identified hubs of effective pedagogic practice, and asked them to record sessions using POV cameras from the teacher's perspective.

We gained permission from the school authorities, parents and children to capture video, and stored this on the university's cloud drive system which is approved by the ethics committee as suitable for such data. Access was provided via the VLE, and the data was kept in line with the GDPR (General Data Protection Regulation) policies of the university. This data provided further opportunities for student teachers to develop their observational skills, such as looking for critical incidents, and gain some experience of the physical actions and speech of a teacher in a PE or AE session.

Case Study Conclusion

The use of POV video is becoming more widely accepted in sporting environments (French, 2016b) and thus the effect of being filmed on participants is growing less significant. Familiarity with social media platforms, and video sharing sites, such as YouTube and Tik-Tok, has also reduced the novelty value of being filmed such that some of the effects that Sparmann (2005) noted are now uncommon. Although developed as a response to the challenges raised by the COVID-19 pandemic and its associated restrictions, the use of POV video has been demonstrated as being an effective tool for developing student teachers' observation abilities, and in the identification of critical incidents, thereby providing a record of their personal, and group, experience during practical sessions. These can be referred to, and relived, for reflective and evaluative purposes, and provide exemplar materials and incidents that can be used when teaching, and for providing feedback to student teachers of PE and AE.

Further work is needed to collect a wider variety of empirical data, and to investigate cognitive outcomes with student teachers, to support some of the early findings from the lesson study work, which itself is an ongoing process. This will provide further opportunities to reflect on and develop this andragogic approach as we seek to ascertain whether, and how, this practice can be adopted across subject session delivery beyond PE and AE.

Case Study 5.4: Supporting New Teaching Staff to Navigate the Virtual Learning Environment

MARY JOY GUEVARRA, SCOTT HEDGER AND ALLARD LUMMEN

In today's rapidly evolving educational landscape, integrating technology within training and education has become not just a preference, but a necessity. This case study details a project initiated by our Technology Enhanced Learning (TEL) development team at BU. Our objective was to reshape the induction for new teaching staff members by helping them gain a comprehensive understanding of our Brightspace VLE.

Higher Education institutions like BU are working diligently to make the most of online learning tools. Nevertheless, we often encounter challenges in training our teaching staff effectively. This includes limitations with traditional text-based resources when engaging faculty members and helping them fully grasp the intricacies of the VLE.

Recognizing the need for a significant transformation, the TEL development team embarked on a creative journey that culminated in creating 'Brightspace Foundations' which is a set of instructional video guides. These videos aimed not only to educate, but also to create an engaging learning experience. We combined essential information with a friendly and relatable approach. The underlying idea was straightforward yet impactful, i.e., we were trying to craft an experience that resonated with our teaching staff and to foster enthusiasm and confidence in using the VLE.

Our commitment to convenience and personalization was at the core of the Brightspace Foundations project. We intentionally designed the videos as brief, self-paced lessons. This design choice empowered teaching staff to learn whenever, and wherever, they had the time. To enhance the learning process, we incorporated self-assessment questions. These questions helped staff to monitor the progress of each learner and enabled each of them to refine their understanding as they progressed.

The influence of the new approach extended beyond the implementation phase. By analyzing data from the VLE, and gathering insights through surveys, we comprehensively understood its effectiveness. These valuable insights served as guiding lights, informing our plans for future improvements. This iterative method ensured the continuous enhancement of the training process for our teaching staff.

This case study is not confined to surface-level observations; it is proof of the effectiveness of a comprehensive approach to training. Brightspace Foundations not only captured the attention of new teaching staff but also fostered a dynamic and interactive learning environment within our online platform. By incorporating visual and interactive tools, Brightspace Foundations piqued the interest of new teaching staff and so created an environment where learning was engaging and inclusive.

This project provides valuable insights into the process of redefining faculty training in an education landscape driven by technology. It celebrates innovation, while acknowledging the challenges that accompany change. In the ever-evolving realm of Higher Education, this is an example that redefines how we can deliver exciting, effective and continually evolving academic training.

Description

Instructional video guides are resources designed to facilitate the acquisition of new skills, knowledge enrichment and the mastery of specific tasks (Winslett, 2014). Leveraging the combination of audio-visual elements, they can be used to engage learners through a captivating and interactive format. The primary objective is to demystify intricate concepts, enhance accessibility and enhance enjoyment along the learning journey.

The core components of instructional video guides typically comprise meticulously crafted pre-recorded videos. These videos effectively demonstrate intricate processes and techniques, spanning a wide range of subjects such as software tutorials, DIY projects, fitness routines, cooking recipes, language learning and more. The presentations are fortified with clear explanations, insightful annotations and on-screen graphics, which together elevate the learning experience.

The primary purpose of instructional video guides is to simplify complex concepts and so make learning more accessible and enjoyable. By including audio-visual elements, they offer a multi-sensory learning experience that can be highly effective in retaining information. Watching demonstrations, and following along with the instructions, allows users to grasp concepts more easily, understand the correct sequence of actions and observe specific details or nuances.

Instructional video guides can be made accessible through various platforms such as websites, video-sharing platforms, dedicated training portals and online learning environments. This flexibility empowers users to tailor their learning journey according to their own rhythm. The ability to pause, rewind, replay or revisit specific segments empowers individuals to accommodate their own specific needs and unique learning styles.

Inclusivity is at the forefront of the design process, and the instructional video guides frequently incorporate features that enhance accessibility. Closed captions and subtitles cater for learners with hearing impairments, while translation options into diverse languages broaden their reach. The guides are compatible with various devices, encompassing computers, tablets and smartphones, ensuring learning can be delivered seamlessly with minimal barriers to accessibility (Anderson and Ellis, 2001; Harrison, 2015).

Instructional video guides are a versatile medium for education, facilitating the acquisition of skills and knowledge in an engaging and efficient manner. Whether pursued for personal enrichment, professional growth or sheer curiosity, these guides emerge as indispensable resources that propel individuals toward their educational aspirations. This case study celebrates the pivotal role of instructional video guides in reshaping current educational approaches so that they foster effective knowledge acquisition.

Application

We provided all members of our staff with access to Brightspace Foundations through a specific module within the VLE. New members of staff were also presented with a welcome email from their faculty, which included a direct link to Brightspace Foundations to encourage participation. This module was designed to help our staff members understand the basics of the VLE, and we wanted it to be available not only to new employees, but also to existing staff who needed a refresher.

All videos were produced in a particular format. Instead of a voice-over, the beginning of each video displayed the speaker in front of a green screen to add a more individualized touch. The videos started with an overview of the topic, followed by a table of contents including video timestamps, enabling users to navigate to specific sections of the video if they preferred not to watch it in its entirety.

To ensure everyone was engaged and understood the material, we incorporated short knowledge quizzes after each video in Brightspace Foundations. This allowed the viewers to see how well they understood the content, and allowed them to review it, before continuing with the next topic. By including these quizzes throughout the module, we aimed to help our staff retain the information they had learnt by reinforcing the key concepts.

In addition to knowledge quizzes, each member of staff was provided with a sandbox area where they were free to practice the relevant material in a safe environment. This allowed for the exploration of content without having to worry about impact upon others.

At the end of the module, we asked viewers to complete a survey to gather feedback on its effectiveness, and gauge how this form of guidance was received. This survey allowed us to gain insight into which aspects worked well so that we could identify areas that could be improved for future cohorts.

Overall, our goal with Brightspace Foundations was to provide our staff with accessible and comprehensive training on the basics of the VLE. While we wanted our videos to contain all the necessary information, we also aimed for the videos to be under five minutes to make the content more inviting and approachable. We aimed to stimulate continuous learning and improvement by including knowledge quizzes and a survey.

Impact

We found multiple advantages of providing VLE training via guidance videos instead of face-to-face training. The primary advantage of giving users episodic, bite-sized instructional videos was in their ability to exercise discretion when selecting the videos, thereby enabling a personalized viewing experience in terms of timing and pace. It also meant they could quickly return to them if they had to complete a task within the VLE and needed a refresher on how to do it.

Providing users with a personal sandbox area within the VLE, and adding short quizzes after each video, allowed users to practice and evaluate their knowledge. The short quizzes garnered excellent levels of engagement, with some users attempting the quiz multiple times to achieve a pass mark, even though the quizzes were not mandatory. Moving away from face-to-face training allowed our Learning Technology colleagues to utilize that time to concentrate on other projects. It meant that the new teaching staff received a consistent approach to the training that they received.

Another huge advantage, more for us than for the users watching the videos, was the ability to gather analytics on video views and completion. A year after implementing Brightspace Foundations we gathered our first set of analytics for each video to review user engagement. It was immediately obvious from the analytics data that user completion was at its highest percentage for videos under five minutes, and this gradually became worse as video length approached ten minutes. This reflects the findings by Guo *et al.* (2014) who found users' median engagement time is at most six minutes, regardless of total video length. The statistics also gave us a better understanding of the topics new teaching staff were most interested in learning about. The highest completion rate was for Module Introduction (91%) and Introduction to the VLE (90%).

We also provided users with a short four-question survey with the chance to provide written comments to gain further feedback and help us plan for future video guidance projects. The feedback from the respondents revealed several key insights:

- 90% of respondents said that the video durations were suitable;
- 78% of respondents found the introductory segments at the beginning of each video to be highly beneficial in helping them determine the relevance of the content to their roles or tasks that required guidance;
- 45% of respondents regarded the short quizzes as 'very helpful', while an additional 55% considered them 'somewhat helpful';
- 66% of respondents were in strong agreement about the value of the Brightspace Foundations module, while 34% still acknowledged its usefulness.

Case Study Conclusion

After reviewing the video analytics and user feedback, ensuring where possible that our video guides were less than five minutes has had a positive impact on user engagement, and helped shape the way we think about creating future guidance videos. It also helped us realize what processes are more important to highlight than others to keep within that five-minute time limit. On reflection, we would like to review the content within some episodes in the series to see if there is anything that can be done to reduce the duration of them as some still approach ten minutes in length.

The success of this project has led to plans for a second series of videos concentrating on more advanced tools and features in our VLE. We hope this will help raise awareness of tools and features that existing users may not have been aware of, or which they had not used before because of a lack of existing video guidance material being available.

There are also plans to create a set of video guidance for professional and support staff, concentrating on specific tasks they are required to complete on the VLE that are not typically performed by teaching staff.

This project has been a great way to showcase the innovative video creation and editing capabilities of our Learning Technology team members to our academic community. We have already had many staff contact us to assist with creating short videos for their own teaching content, including the use of green screen technology.

Case Study 5.5: Implementing a Framework for Digital Pedagogies to Enhance Student Learning

TIM GALLING, GELAREH ROUSHAN AND TRACEY WEBB

The accelerated change to a reliance upon digital tools for learning and teaching impacted upon the pedagogical approaches used at BU and provided us with opportunities to think differently regarding how we engage our students. A Digital Pedagogies Framework (DPF) was developed to further enhance both the consistency of the student learning experience and the quality of teaching delivery and assessment requirements. The framework aimed to promote staff digital literacy at BU regarding our Brightspace VLE and associated digital tools, and so increase the opportunity for students to enhance their digital awareness through active engagement with digital learning tools within their teaching modules.

Our DPF was created with reference to existing frameworks and models used within Higher Education, but it was then tailored specifically to our institutional needs. The framework was successfully rolled out to faculties in the summer of 2020, and academics were supported to embedding the framework in their teaching. This was a complete step change for BU as we had previously used the VLE as simply a repository of learning materials with little or no innovation embedded (Anderson, 2020). This was therefore a significant initiative given the subsequent challenges of the COVID-19 pandemic, however the framework was in planning prior to this, and landed opportunely following the enforced pivot to online teaching and learning.

We devised the framework to offer a structure for excellence by enhancing the design and development of our education standards and education practices. It was recognized that staff required more than a basic competency in the use of the digital tools available to them, and so we wanted them to embrace new technologies, and new pedagogical approaches, that together would enable them to develop their teaching, and create an excellent and consistent student learning experience.

We designed the framework into six key thematic areas: (1) Module Roadmap and Learning Design; (2) Inclusivity and Accessibility; (3) Curriculum Content Design; (4) Assessment and Feedback; (5) Communication and Engagement; and (6) Monitoring and Review. Each theme introduced a set of guiding principles and included a list of criteria to help scaffold module design on the VLE, including suggested digital tools to facilitate pedagogical approaches, and the provision of direct links to supporting guidance for those tools.

To help embed implementation of the framework, each theme included a checklist that staff could work through as they built their modules. The framework sat on the VLE, making it easily accessible for staff to review, and as a showcase itself of some of the VLE's functionality. An additional section was included to incorporate exemplary pedagogical approaches from academic colleagues at BU, and to showcase videos of staff in conversation discussing innovative teaching approaches with the VLE and associated digital tools.

Since launch, the framework has become the backbone for good practice guidance in relation to our VLE, and its key messages are reinforced each year within the master template used for supporting faculties to build their teaching modules at the start of semester. This approach also helps to ensure consistency across modules which helps students to access and understand the materials and learning opportunities being provided.

Application

We introduced the framework to faculties in stages, tailoring it to subject disciplines in turn, and presenting the key themes alongside illustrated examples of good practice within their specific areas. Using this approach, educators could understand the practical application of the framework to their module design, and they could share approaches with their peers.

It was delivered within a fully supportive space in which staff at all levels of digital abilities were encouraged to embrace it, and understand it, and use it to support their practice.

A key challenge in uptake in the adoption of the framework was a lack of co-ordination and consistency in an agreed approach for embedding the framework within the curriculum. Therefore, where departments, or degree programs, made a conscious effort to adopt all areas of the framework in their teaching practices, student feedback would reflect a more positive learning experience. As highlighted by Porter *et al.* (2014) a structured and systematic approach increases the success of adoption and implementation of such frameworks.

The framework had been aligned with the institutional peer observation process to form a part of the departmental annual monitoring actions plans. Using the JISC Online Surveys tool for data collection, questions were asked relating to the themes of the DPF, and the guidance was updated based upon the feedback received. This enabled peer observation to include a review of teaching material on the VLE including both synchronous and asynchronous teaching. Our experience showed that adoption of the DPF was influenced by context-led disciplines and their readiness to enhance their own education practices (Crawford *et al.*, 2020).

While aspects of the framework were expected to be applied in different ways in various discipline areas subject to the normal pedagogical approach taken, there were specific elements that were necessary to provide a consistent experience for students across their modules of study. To ensure these requirements were met, we developed automated reporting to check the progress and completion of specific areas stipulated in the framework. Examples include checking teaching staff had access to modules, and that module information documents, e.g., intended learning outcomes, assessment briefs and a 'welcome' announcement, had all been posted. The overall report, which was refreshed daily, indicated a level of 'readiness for teaching' for each VLE unit and was made available to Program Leaders, Department Heads and Faculty Executives, thereby enabling them to monitor the preparation of VLE modules prior to the start of a teaching term, and then take action where required to ensure key tasks were completed.

The framework will continue to be reviewed and updated annually as digital tools and practices evolve, and as new feedback is collated from staff and students. For example, the framework now also considers Universal Design for Learning (UDL) guidance and key accessibility considerations. These updates are reflected in the master template design each year that forms the basis of all curricular modules, reinforcing good module design, and promoting consistency.

Impact

Our initial idea of establishing a minimum baseline level for all module content on the VLE was surpassed early on when departments sought to elevate modules across their program areas with higher requirements. We have seen a continued appetite for embracing digital pedagogical approaches. Confidence in the framework has also been evidenced by suggested inclusions from other areas of the university, for example adding a reference to the United Nations Sustainable Development Goals (UNSDGs). Increasingly, the framework is being seen as being a space to engage staff with key initiatives related to the curriculum.

The framework leveraged the usage of VLE tools. Following the introduction of the framework, increased sustained activity was recorded in areas including use of the online quizzes, discussion boards, creation of video content (including recording of teaching sessions) and other recommended tools. As with any online learning tool, usage statistics from this period do indicate an increase in engagement partly as the result of online learning during the period of the COVID-19 global pandemic when campuses were closed during national lockdowns.

We have seen that the uptake in the adoption of specific digital learning tools can be more prominent for specific disciplines where teaching approaches are more closely aligned to the capabilities of specific online tools. An example of this is the online quiz being used for formative math-based assessment on design and engineering courses. We have also seen an increased uptake in the adoption of online learning tools through best practice being shared at a peer-to-peer level. These trends may be subject to the specific successes of an academic colleague that may inspire others or may be driven by departmental initiatives. The impact on student learning has also been evident in student feedback where academics are adopting the framework:

> Brightspace has been a very useful software throughout the course as there are a lot of course materials available, and it is easy to use and navigate.
>
> Level 6 student 2023

Case Study Conclusion

Being committed to the enhancement of education quality, and to encourage educators to further embed a more consistent pedagogical strategy, we engaged with key stakeholders, including academic faculties and our

Student Union, to design, develop and implement a DPF underpinned by sector benchmarks. We used a thematic approach for more student-centered pedagogical practices, and we developed an education enhancement plan for academic staff development. Using the context of our framework, we supported faculties and incorporated a series of thematic staff development sessions, including session alignment with faculty and departmental education quality and enhancement priorities.

The Student Union subsequently embedded the DPF in their evaluation of our institutional student feedback survey which demonstrated the positive impact of pedagogical practices proposed in the framework on the student learning experience.

The DPF has become central to scaffolding our offering as a center for innovation and excellence in learning. The DPF themes give structure to our online support and guidance materials, as well as framing our staff development workshops and resources. The framework itself is embedded in new starter communications so that all new academic staff are introduced to it when they join BU.

As we continue to build data around tool usage and VLE activity, we will look to evaluate the impact of the DPF on the student learning experience at BU, by mapping application metrics of the framework against student engagement, attainment and satisfaction metrics. This work will further evidence the benefits of the framework but also serves to identify best practice with online and blended approaches that have produced high engagement, attainment and satisfaction which can be fed back into the continuous development of the framework.

References

Adedoyin, O.B. and Soykan, E., 2023. COVID-19 pandemic and online learning: The challenges and opportunities. *Interactive Learning Environments,* 31(2), 863–875.

Al-Bashir, M., Rezaul, K. and Rahman, I., 2016. The value and effectiveness of feedback in improving students' learning and professionalizing teaching in higher education. *Education and Practice,* 7(16), 38–41.

Anderson, A.J. and Ellis, A., 2001. Using desktop video to enhance music instruction. *Australasian Journal of Educational Technology,* 17(3), 279–294.

Anderson, L. and Krathwohl, D., 2001. *A Taxonomy for Learning, Teaching, and Assessing: A Revision of Bloom's Taxonomy of Educational Objectives.* New York: Longmans.

Anderson, V., 2020. A digital pedagogy pivot: re-thinking higher education practice from an HRD perspective. *Human Resource Development International,* 23(4), 452–467.

Appiah, M. and Van Tonder, F., 2018. E-assessment in higher education: A review. *Business Management & Economic Research*, 9(6), 1454–1460.

Backman, E., 2015. Teaching trainee teachers about outdoor education. *In:* Humberstone, B., Prince, H. and Henderson, K.A. (eds.), *Routledge International Handbook of Outdoor Studies*. London: Routledge, 121–130.

Banihashem, S.K., Noroozi, O., van Ginkel, S., Macfadyen, L.P. and Biemans, H.J.A., 2022. A systematic review of the role of learning analytics in enhancing feedback practices in higher education. *Educational Research Review*, 37, 100489.

Brown, M., 2006. Adventure education and physical education. *In:* Kirk, D., Macdonald, D. and O'Sullivan, M. (eds.), *Handbook of Physical Education*. New York: SAGE, 685–702.

Buckley, A., 2021. Crisis? What crisis? Interpreting student feedback on assessment. *Assessment & Evaluation in Higher Education,* 46(7), 1008–1019.

Byra, M., 2006. Teaching styles and inclusive pedagogies. In Kirk, D., Macdonald, D. and O'Sullivan, M. (eds.), *Handbook of Physical Education*. New York: SAGE, 449–466.

Capel, S. and Blair, R., 2007. Making physical education relevant: Increasing the impact of initial teacher training. *London Review of Education,* 5(1), 15–34.

Carpenter, P. and Western, J., 1984. Transition to higher education. *Australian Journal of Education*, 28(3), 249–273.

Castañeda, L. and Selwyn, N., 2018. More than tools? Making sense of the ongoing digitizations of higher education. *Educational Technology in Higher Education*, 15(22), 1–10.

Cavalcanti, A.P., Barbosa, A., Carvalho, R., Freitas, F., Tsai, Y.-S., Gašević, D. and Mello R.F., 2021. Automatic feedback in online learning environments: A systematic literature review. *Computers and Education: Artificial Intelligence*, 2, 100027.

Chapleo, C. and O'Sullivan, H. 2017. Contemporary thought in higher education marketing. *Journal of Marketing for Higher Education,* 27(2), 159–161.

Crawford, J., Butler-Henderson, K., Rudolph, J., Malkawi, B., Glowatz, M., Burton, R., Magni, P.A. and Lam, S., 2020. COVID-19: 20 countries' higher education intra-period digital pedagogy responses. *Applied Learning and Teaching*, 3(1), 1–20.

Cromdal, J., 2000. Code-switching for all practical purposes: Bilingual organisation of children's play. *In: Linköping Studies in Arts and Science*. Vol. 233, Linköping, Sweden: Linköping University Press, 131.

Dinsmore, J. and Wenger, K., 2006. Relationships in pre-service teacher preparation: From cohorts to communities. *Teacher Education Quarterly*, 33(1), 57–74.

Evans, C., Kandiko Howson, C. and Forsythe, A., 2018. Making sense of learning gain in Higher Education. *Higher Education Pedagogies*, 3(1), 1–45.

Foucault, M., 1991. *Discipline and Punish: The Birth of the Prison*. Harmondsworth: Penguin Books.

French, G., 2016a. Going pro: The use of point of view cameras in adventure sports research. *Outdoor and Environmental Education,* 19(1), 2–9.

French, G., 2016b. GoPro or no-no? *Horizons: Professional Development in Outdoor Learning,* 76, 18–21.

Fuller, R., Goddard, V.C.T., Nadarajah, V.D., Treasure-Jones, T., Yeates, P., Scott, K., Webb A., Valter, K. and Pyorala, E. 2022. Technology enhanced assessment: Ottawa consensus statement and recommendations, *Medical Teacher,* 44(8), 836–850.

Guo, P.J., Kim, J. and Rubin, R., 2014. How video production affects student engagement: An empirical study of MOOC videos. *Proceedings of the First ACM Conference on Learning @ Scale Conference,* 4–5 March 2014, Atlanta, USA, 41–50.

Harrison, D.J., 2015. Assessing experiences with online educational videos: Converting multiple constructed responses to quantifiable data. *International Review of Research in Open and Distributed Learning,* 16(1), 168–192.

Hatzipanagos, S., Tait, A. and Amrane-Cooper, L., 2020. Towards a post COVID-19 digital authentic assessment practice: when radical changes enhance the student experience. *EDEN Conference Proceedings,* 21–23 October, 2020, Lisbon, Portugal, vol. 1, 59–65.

Hodges, C., Moore, S., Lockee, B., Trust, T. and Bond, M.A., 2020. *The Difference Between Emergency Remote Teaching and Online Learning.* Boulder, CO: Educause Review.

Hodges, C. and Ocak, C., 2023. *Integrating Generative AI into Higher Education: Considerations.* Boulder, CO: Educause Review.

Howson, C. and Buckley, A., 2020. Quantifying learning: Measuring student outcomes in Higher Education in England. *Politics and Governance,* 8(2), 6–14.

Huber, E., Harris, L., Wright, S., White, A., Raduescu, C., Sandris Zeivots, S., Andrew Cram, A. and Brodzeli, A., 2024. Towards a framework for designing and evaluating online assessments in business education. *Assessment & Evaluation in Higher Education,* 49(1), 102–116.

Hussain, F.N., Al-Mannai, R. and Agouni, A., 2020. An emergency switch to distance learning in response to the COVID-19 pandemic: Experience from an internationally accredited undergraduate pharmacy program at Qatar University. *Medical Science Educator,* 30, 1393–1397.

Jaam, M., Nazar, Z., Rainkie, D.C., Hassan, D.A., Hussain, F.N., Kassab, S.E. and Agouni, A., 2021. Using assessment design decision framework in understanding the impact of rapid transition to remote education on student assessment in health-related colleges: A qualitative study. *PLoS One,* 16(7), e0254444.

Jones-Devitt, S., Pickering, N., Austen, L., Donnelly, A., Adesola, J. and Weston, A., 2019. Evaluation of the National Mixed Methods Learning Gain Project (NMMLGP) and Student Perceptions of Learning Gain. *Report to the Office for Students.* Sheffield: Sheffield Hallam University.

Kirk, D., 2010. *Physical Education Futures*. London: Routledge.

Kozaris, I.A., 2010. Platforms for e-learning. *Analytical and Bioanalytical Chemistry*, 397(3), 893–898.

Lee, A.V.Y., 2023. Supporting students' generation of feedback in large-scale online course with artificial intelligence-enabled evaluation. *Studies in Educational Evaluation*, 77, 101250.

Leibold, N. and Schwarz, L., 2015. The art of giving online feedback. *Effective Teaching*, 15(1), 34–46.

Leidner, S., Polkinghorne, M., Roushan, G. and Taylor, J., 2022. Evaluating student learning gain: What is the impact upon student learning resulting from the move to online teaching during the COVID-19 pandemic? *In*: Bilgin, M., Danis, H. and Demir, E. (eds.), *Eurasian Business and Economics Perspectives, Eurasian Business and Economics Society (EBES)*, Vol. 24. Cham: Springer, 3–10.

Lewis, C., Perry, R. and Friedkin, S., 2009. Lesson study as action research. *In*: Noffke, S. and Comekh, B. (eds.), *The SAGE handbook of Educational Action Research*. New York: SAGE, 142–154.

Lim, L.-A., Dawson, S., Gašević, D., Joksimović, S., Pardo, A., Fudge, A. and Gentili, S., 2021. Students' perceptions of, and emotional responses to, personalized learning analytics-based feedback: An exploratory study of four courses. *Assessment & Evaluation in Higher Education*, 46(3), 339–359.

Lockee, B.B., 2021. Online education in the post-COVID era. *Nat Electron*, 4, 5–6.

Loughran, J. and Hamilton, M.L. 2016. Developing an understanding of teacher education. *In*: Loughran, J. and Hamilton, M. (eds.), *International Handbook of Teacher Education*. Singapore: Springer, 3–22.

Mate, K. and Weidenhofer, J., 2021. Considerations and strategies for effective online assessment with a focus on the biomedical sciences. *FASEB Bioadv*, 4(1), 9–21.

McGrath, C, Guerin, B., Harte, E., Frearson, M. and Manville, C., 2015. HEFCE report. *Learning Gain in Higher Education*. Santa Monica, CA: RAND Corporation.

Mehanna, WN, 2004. E-pedagogy: The pedagogies of e-learning. *Research in Learning Technology*, 12(3), 279–293.

Meyen, E.L., Aust, R.J., Buj, Y.N. and Isaacson, R., 2002. Assessing and monitoring student progress in e-learning personnel preparation environment. *Teacher Education and Special Education*, 25(2), 187–198.

Montenegro-Rueda, M., Luque-de la Rosa, A., Sarasola Sánchez-Serrano, J.L. and Fernández-Cerero, J., 2021. Assessment in Higher Education during the COVID-19 pandemic: A systematic review. *Sustainability*, 13, 10509.

North, C. 2020. *Interrogating Authenticity in Outdoor Education Teacher Education*. Singapore: Springer.

Olasina, G., 2023. Using new assessment tools during and post-COVID-19. *Library Philosophy and Practice*, 7902, 1–28.

Oosterheert, I.E. and Vermunt, J.D., 2001. Individual differences in learning to teach: Relating cognition, regulation and affect. *Learning and Instruction*, 11(2), 133–156.

O'Sullivan, H., Polkinghorne, M. and Taylor, J., 2022. Investigating the impact of the COVID-19 pandemic on undergraduate education: Using learning gain as a measure to compare two student cohorts. *Businesses*, 2(2), 214–227.

Pettit, M., Shukla, S., Zhang, J., Sunil Kumar, K.H. and Khanduja, V., 2021. Virtual exams: Has COVID-19 provided the impetus to change assessment methods in medicine? *Bone & Joint Open*, 2(2), 111–118.

Polkinghorne, M, O'Sullivan, H., Roushan, G. and Taylor, J., 2021c. An innovative framework for Higher Education to evaluate learning gain: A case study based upon the discipline of marketing. *Studies in Higher Education*, 46(9), 1740–1755.

Polkinghorne, M., Roushan, G. and Taylor, J., 2017a. Considering the marketing of Higher Education: The role of student learning gain as a potential indicator of teaching quality. *Marketing for Higher Education*, 27(2), 213–232.

Polkinghorne, M., Roushan, G. and Taylor, J., 2017b. Evaluating student learning gain: An alternative perspective. *Higher Education Academy (HEA) Surveys Conference 2017*. York: Higher Education Academy, 857–869.

Polkinghorne, M., Roushan, G. and Taylor, J., 2021b. Seeking an educational utopia: An alternative model for evaluating student learning gain. *Further and Higher Education*, 45(6), 857–869.

Polkinghorne, M., Roushan, G. and Taylor, J., 2022. Understanding student learning gain: Using student-staff partnerships within Higher Education to inform the continuous improvement process. *In:* Bilgin, M., Danis, H., Demir, E. and Bodolica, V. (eds.), *Eurasian Business and Economics Perspectives, Eurasian Business and Economics Society (EBES)*, vol. 23. Cham: Springer, 3–17.

Polkinghorne, M., Taylor, J., Lamont, C. and Roushan G., 2023. Evaluating student learning gain: A case study based upon group-work. *Business Management & Change*, 21(1), 10–29.

Polkinghorne, M., Taylor, J. and Roushan, G., 2021a. Continuous improvement in education: Understanding the effectiveness of our business and management teaching. *Business Management & Change*, 19(2), 4–19.

Porter, W.W., Graham, C.R., Spring, K.A. and Welch, K.R., 2014. Blended learning in Higher Education: Institutional adoption and implementation. *Computers & Education*, 75, 185–195.

Prince, T., 2016. "Panopto" for lecture capture – A first time user's perspective. *Society for Information Technology & Teacher Education International Conference*, 21–25 March 2016, Savannah, USA, 2550–2565.

Richardson, V., 1997. *Constructivist Teacher Education Building: New Understandings*. London: Falmer Press.

Roohr, K., Liu H. and Liu, O., 2017. Investigating student learning gains in college: A longitudinal study. *Studies in Higher Education,* 42(12), 2284–2300.

Ruby, J., 1995. The moral burden of authorship in ethnographic film. *Visual Anthropology Review,* 11, 77–82.

Singaram, V., Naidoo, K. and Singh, S., 2022. Self-directed learning during the COVID-19 pandemic: Perspectives of South African final-year health professions students. *Advances in Medical Education and Practice,* 6(13), 1–10.

Sparrman, A., 2005. Video recording as interaction: participant observation of children's everyday life. *Qualitative Research in Psychology,* 2(3), 241–255.

Tight, M., 2021. Existing research on learning gain in higher education. *In:* Hughes, C. and Tight, M. (eds.), *Learning Gain in Higher Education (International Perspectives on Higher Education Research),* vol. 14. Bingley: Emerald Publishing, 1–16.

Tuah, N.A.A. and Naing, L., 2021. Is online assessment in Higher Education institutions during COVID-19 pandemic reliable? *Siriraj Medical Journal,* 73(1), 61–68.

Winslett, G., 2014. What counts as educational video? Working toward best practice alignment between video production approaches and outcomes. *Australasian Journal of Educational Technology,* 30(5), 587–502.

Innovative Applications of Technology to Support the Student Learning Experience

6

The following five case studies describe innovative applications of technology to support the student learning experience. Each case study presents the personal perspectives of those involved.

Case Study 6.1: Using Technology to Humanize Support for Students

LUCINDA BECKER

During this case study I will share three instances of how I have used technology to humanize my support for students: (1) through assignment instructions via screencast, (2) assignment feedback through audiofile and (3) a more wide-ranging project on humanizing and expanding the support offered within the VLE.

My use of technology in this way began during the COVID pandemic, when I responded to the loss of casual contact with students with a series of brief video screencasts (between two and ten minutes' long) that I created for a YouTube channel entitled 'Still Learning Together' (https://www.youtube.com/channel/UC3We0ibTxw_plzlO1P2JcgQ). In those

DOI: 10.4324/9781032635248-7

screencasts, which I released regularly over six weeks, I attended to what might be termed the hidden curriculum elements of my teaching (Orón Semper and Blasco, 2018; Çobanoğlu and Demir, 2014) ranging from guidance on grammar use and writing style, to advice on preparing for, and reflecting on, online lessons and exams (Becker, 2019).

Description

The screencasts were popular with over 1,000 YouTube hits over the six weeks of their release, and I came to realize that using rhythm in technology could be a useful way to provide consistency of layout, but also of expectation. Each of these screencasts used the same PowerPoint slide design, with the same opening page layout, and each began with a number, for example, 'five memory techniques', or 'three fixes for a comma splice'.

Anecdotally, students told me that they found it reassuring to know how many points to expect in each screencast. Further statistical analysis revealed that the topic and the number of points being covered were the key factors in deciding which screencast to view for some students. The YouTube analytics, and those gathered from our VLE, showed, rather surprisingly, that the length of the screencast was not a factor in how many students viewed the material to its conclusion. Students also liked the fact that, as one student commented, 'we knew it came from you' because of the consistency of design and the use of the numbered points. From this project, I could see that the human connection in the technology was important, especially during a pandemic.

I almost forgot about this approach in the crash back onto campus, but I was reminded of it later when I noticed a plethora of emails from students asking about a particular assignment on a 'Persuasive Writing' module that I was running. The assignment was not especially tricky, and I had put clear instructions on the VLE, but still, they did not seem to understand the requirements. Then I recalled that the location of the seminar in which I gave the instructions in person had moved last minute, and attendance had been poor, and so the students were not so much confused as anxious to get it right.

It took no more than 20 minutes to make a PowerPoint slide and then talk over it, producing a five-minute screencast of me telling the students exactly how to complete and submit the assignment. I put the screencast on our VLE and emailed the link to students via the announcement/email function. Such a brief task, yet it paid huge dividends as we received a higher percentage of first-time submissions for that assignment than in any previous year.

Based upon the success of this approach, which I used initially for a foundation-level assignment, I have now taken the same approach to the principal assignment on a final-year module. This is a film-based module entitled 'Shakespeare on Film', and it invites students to go beyond the text-based learning with which they are very familiar, and to instead consider the impact of another medium, this being film, on the representations, interpretations and adaptations of Shakespeare's texts.

During the module, students enjoy the experience of flexing their intellect in this way, and it is a popular and well-received module, but the assignments can be challenging. As part of the assignment, students are required to give an in-seminar presentation, sharing their analysis of a brief sequence of film. This can be nerve-wracking for the students who find standing up and presenting in front of their peers quite daunting, but the approach to content is relatively straightforward, and they see me demonstrating this type of analysis each week which they find to be helpful.

However, the more major element of their assignment feels more alien to students. They are asked to choose between short sequences from two films, and to make a comparative analysis of them. They may also create an overarching argument relating perhaps to the original texts, specific film-making techniques, directorial interpretation and/or even socio-cultural factors. Added to this, they are discussing a moving medium, with sound, which somehow makes a purely written set of instructions feel slightly less authentic. I give several guidance and instruction sessions on the assignment in class, but I noticed that this could result in students desperately scribbling down a series of notes in class, and then still coming to see me after the event for more 'clarification', which was often a need for reassurance as much as more instruction.

So, I am now taking the same approach with the third-year students as the foundation students, producing an instructional screencast on the assignment, but this time with an inset video of me through each PowerPoint slide. This new approach enables me to reflect upon the characteristics of the visual medium on which they are being assessed, and also offers both written and spoken channels of instruction.

Application

I thought perhaps students with an aural or visual learning preference might have been the main beneficiaries of this approach to instruction (Biggs *et al.*, 2014), but I am less sure now after trialing it, and seeing the responses from students. The feedback I received in the foundation class following the screencast was about how the students were relieved to hear my voice telling them what to do, just like in class, so I think perhaps it was more an emotional than neurological response (Cleveland-Innes and Campbell, 2012).

This fits with the responses I have received to feedback, and feedforward, on assignments delivered via audiofile. This was a leap of faith for me when we began some years ago to mark assignments in the fully anonymized setting of our VLE. I found this hard at first. Despite the benefits of student anonymity during assessment, I unexpectedly found myself feeling anonymous also. I wanted to give full feedback, and productive feedforward, to the students, but I felt hindered by the system, until I noticed the 'record' button during my first batch of online marking.

Since then, I have only ever given audio feedback in my overall assessment of an assignment, supported by the use of 'quickmarks', a standard note on the system that anyone can create, and sometimes I supplement this with the insertion of brief written feedback notes within the work itself. For anyone tempted to take this step, it might be useful to share some pointers from my experience.

I always use the full three-minute recording time that our VLE system allows. Already the audio feedback wins the day. I can say a significant amount more in three minutes of recording than I could possibly type in a feedback box in the same time period. I never use notes, but instead insert a 'quickmark' with the note 'audiofile', so that I, and later the students, can follow my train of thought through an assignment as I offer feedback. I very rarely re-record as students always forgive my stumbles, and because that is what makes the feedback more human. The student response to this feedback approach has been overwhelmingly positive, with one student memorably commenting that 'it is like having Cindy in my ear as I walk home'. This was from a student who listened to feedback via phone/earbud while walking.

For modules with multiple markers, our VLE analytics suggest that more students engage with the feedback, and for longer, with the audiofile feedback approach. However, there are potential hurdles and one niggling disadvantage. The hurdle exists for colleagues who struggle with such a spontaneous, and potentially exposing, method of supporting students. To hear your voice, and know that students will hear your recorded voice, with all the pauses, hesitations and verbal idiosyncrasies this might entail, can be intimidating. If, in trying to obviate this problem, the marker was to make notes prior to recording, this makes giving feedback a potentially far more onerous task than simply typing it, while also running the risk of making a rather monotone recording as the notes are read.

An unexpected outcome of this approach, and in some ways the potential disadvantage, arose from the fact that audio feedback can feel ephemeral. I had not realized this when I began to use the method. Several students have told me that they download the recording straight away so as not to lose it, even though they know that it is no more likely to be lost than a colleague's written feedback, which is also held in the same location on the VLE. Again, this is about an emotional response to technology, rather than an intellectual concern, although the two are inevitably linked.

Some students, while they might like audio feedback for its speedy and humanized delivery of feedback, can also find it more problematic in the longer term. When they want to return to my feedforward comments, perhaps weeks or months later, they might prefer a text-based version of the feedback. In some cases, students have used free, and nowadays very good, speech-to-text software to produce a written version, with no involvement from me, but this remained a concern for those unable to do this.

With this in mind, I am beginning to use this potential glitch to my advantage in my teaching, suggesting that students take time, sometimes with me in a seminar, to listen to their feedback audiofiles and then to summarize them into a series of brief bullet points, using the 'audiofile' quickmarks on their assignments to guide them. This is an activity that I plan to use more systematically with targeted groups of students in the future. It may be a way to reinforce the feedforward elements of the audiofiles, which is something that students can often overlook.

Impact

My most recent use of technology to humanize the support we offer to students is linked to the structure of our VLE. An institutional move from standard Blackboard to Blackboard Ultra has provided the opportunity, and the challenge, for us to make our VLE content more consistent and supportive. This is a project that has been evolving at my university for some time, but the move to Ultra prompted me to consider anew how I could use the system in the most human and supportive way.

Prompted by a link offered by our Technology Enhanced Learning Team, I discovered a method used by Leeds Trinity University which is called the 'PLP (pre-live-post) approach', in which they systematically and consistently offer their students weekly material to help them get ready for each week's live learning event, and another set of material to be used as an aid to reflection after the live event (www.timeshighereducation.com).

Using this as my basis, I have taken a slightly different approach. On a study skills module I convened for foundation-level students, the percentage attendance suggested that some weeks were more popular than others. Asking students why this was the case, they told me that some of the study skill topics were of less relevance to them than others. When I explained why the material might be relevant to them in the following term, they were clearly frustrated that the connection had not occurred to them. In another subject-based foundation-level module I had designed, students also sometimes struggled to see the connections related to how each week's material linked to the next, and to the overall module theme.

Although neither of these issues were causing significant problems in terms of statistical signifiers, as attendance remained high in both modules, and students were submitting their work as expected, it was still frustrating for me as a module leader. I think both issues link to students' understanding of the relevance, and connectivity, of what is happening in the classroom, and I think that both might have the same solution.

As a result, I have created two short screencasts for each week of the study skills module. These are simple in design and are based upon a PowerPoint slide for 'Getting ready for Week X' or 'Moving on from Week Y', with my voice-over talking for no more than three minutes. The content is also simple, i.e., in the first of these I explain the week's content, how it will help them now, and in future, and what they might think about, or do, before the seminar/workshop. In the second I talk more specifically about how the material might relate to their further learning, or an assignment, and what they can do to make the most of the week's learning.

Based on my earlier experiences, I have used the same slide design, and the same general title for each week, to provide a consistent resource that students can recognize readily. I also want to set up a rhythm to the screencasts, to help students get into the habit of consulting the resources each week. To aid in this, I have created a section on the VLE module entitled 'Weekly Support Videos'. In the first few weeks of term, I show/remind the class how to access the screencasts, with the dual purpose of increasing the number of hits, while also demonstrating that we care enough about their learning journey to offer this additional support. In this way I hope that the technological, online relationship will enhance the human, on-campus relationship, with the resulting synthesis being the best of both worlds.

Case Study Conclusion

I have yet to receive student feedback on some of these innovate uses of technology to support my teaching, but my expectation is that it will be similar to the positive feedback received previously. The support that I have developed, and offered, helps to ensure that students feel reassured and less anxious. That is, perhaps, the primary realization that I take from these projects, i.e., that technology provides educational tools and opportunities that can, and do, benefit students. We can use technology to inform, to assess, to feedback and to inspire our students, but we can also use technology to respond to their emotional needs.

If students are to learn how to be productive learners and successful graduates, we need to listen to their concerns and anxieties, and technology can have a key role to play in this respect, and in how we then respond as educators.

Case Study 6.2: Building a Bridge Between Analog and Digital with LEGO® Serious Play®

CAITLIN KIGHT AND HOLLY HENDERSON

The global COVID-19 pandemic had significant, long-lasting effects on teaching and learning in Higher Education (Marinoni *et al.*, 2020; Jensen *et al.*, 2022). For example, while blended and online learning techniques were implemented by *some* educators prior to the pandemic, their use skyrocketed among *all* educators during lockdown. At many institutions, the post-pandemic 'new normal' now includes a greater use of digital techniques than ever before (Ratten, 2023), though this may not be to the tastes of all learners or educators.

Entirely by chance, we found ourselves caught up in this educational sea change at precisely the moment we were initiating a collaboration designed to respond to a wholly distinct challenge. Our 'Serious Play, Serious Fun, Serious Skills' project was originally designed to introduce more creativity and innovation into Higher Education classrooms. Specifically, we aimed to harness the power of LEGO® Serious Play® (LSP) to improve the student experience, and increase employability, which had previously been identified by Schutz and Pekrun (2007) as being potential positive outcomes.

However, as our university pivoted to online learning during lockdown, we quickly reimagined our project as a means to address some of the challenges many Higher Education staff were reporting (Khan, 2021), including low student engagement, lack of cohesiveness and community, digital overwhelm and an increased need for pastoral support. We anticipated that LSP would lend itself well to this new context even though it was originally designed for use in face-to-face settings (Blair and Dröge, 2020). This is in no small part because it is inherently joyful, social and mindful, offering a tactile experience quite distinct from sitting at a keyboard. It seemed the perfect antidote to some of the biggest problems facing educators across Higher Education.

In adapting LSP activities for online use at that point in time, our facilitators gained insights that continue to influence their practice today. Below, we will reflect upon how, and why, LEGO® has helped us bridge the gaps between analog and digital teaching, and what we think this means for the future of teaching in an increasingly technological learning environment.

Description

While LSP was originally designed for use in business contexts (Peabody, 2015), it has subsequently been modified for application in a range of other environments, including therapy and education settings (Roos, 2006; James, 2013; Shipway and Henderson, 2023; Henderson and Shipway, 2023). LSP is, as the name suggests, inherently *playful*, a term associated with, among other things, lightheartedness, enjoyment, focus, enthusiasm and being in the moment (van Vleet and Feeney, 2015; Koeners and Francis, 2020). In other words, playing with LEGO® is *fun* – a characteristic lacking in much of the COVID-era online education practice we sought to reform.

Participants in LSP sessions undertake a series of 'builds' in response to prompts carefully designed to help students build understandings both literally and metaphorically (McCusker, 2014). Most sessions also involve elements of collaboration, or, at the very least, peer-to-peer sharing, which fosters connection and feelings of community. As a result, we anticipated that LEGO® could combat feelings of isolation and disengagement experienced during lockdown.

Nearly any topic can be explored in LSP sessions, and as a result, the technique can be used for not only discipline-specific topics, but also more universal 'soft skills' such as creative thinking, communication and team-work (López-Fernández et al., 2021). It can support these goals in a variety of ways, for example by facilitating icebreaking, brainstorming, reflection, planning, revision and evaluation. During the pandemic, we made good use of this flexibility, introducing LSP in both curricular and extracurricular contexts, i.e., wherever we felt that a playful, creative approach was needed to overcome barriers to learning.

Our team provided budding LSP facilitators with an introduction to the above principles, along with guidance on the practicalities of running LEGO®-based sessions online. As our LSP facilitators used this technique in their sessions, they amassed hard-won insights about the adaptations needed to successfully use the approach online for Higher Education audiences, and this wisdom was then disseminated both across the institution and with external colleagues.

During the lockdown period, we collectively delivered 150 sessions that reached over 4,000 students and some 430 staff. The breadth of this endeavor has ensured that LEGO® is now woven into the fabric of education at the University of Exeter, and that the techniques learned and honed during the pandemic act as a foundation for further innovations even now when we have resumed an overwhelmingly campus-based approach to teaching.

Application

There has never been a single approach to LSP delivery at the University of Exeter. The examples below capture our 'LEGO® journey', demonstrating the diversity of ways in which we have used LEGO® in both analog and digital contexts.

LSP for University of Exeter Business School (UEBS) Students

LEGO® first came to the institution via the Business School, where it was used to support team building among participants in the (on-campus) Exeter Scholar and Summer School programs. Subsequently, LSP was introduced as an icebreaker activity in a range of different modules. UEBS cohorts can comprise several 100 students apiece and, whereas groups like these are often taught only in large lecture theaters, our educators are always keen to provide students with an engaging, interactive learning experience. This became especially challenging during COVID, since online lectures can be impersonal and leave students feeling disconnected.

LSP was used to particularly good effect in our apprenticeship modules, in which student-built models explored topics as diverse as corporate governance and personal development. LSP was even incorporated into the School's Black History Month program as a means of supporting difficult conversations about race relations. This reflected a growing awareness of how many students were becoming 'fluent' in LEGO®-based discussions and were drawn to events because they featured LSP activities.

The Business School's innovative new Creative Quadrant building, designed during the lockdown period, now hosts a dedicated supply of LEGO® bricks, which demonstrates our ongoing commitment to using this tool to support engaging education.

LSP for Mental Health and Well-being

In response to reports relating to the poor mental health of students during the pandemic, we developed a series of LSP sessions to support well-being. Although there is a precedent for using LEGO® in formal therapeutic contexts (Reeve, 2021), we admit that we mostly just used LSP as an excuse to get students into a virtual room together so they would have a chance to socialize and swap self-care tips. Feedback was extremely positive; one student expressed relief at finally being offered a tangible mechanism for combatting the blues she was experiencing while living in isolation.

As we transitioned back to campus, we ran similar sessions at events designed to re-acclimatize students to campus-based life. LSP has also been embedded in the postgraduate research program, and academic personal tutoring scheme, in recognition of how this playful approach facilitates well-being by supporting interpersonal connection and mindful reflection.

LSP for Professional Development

Over the course of the lockdown, increasing digital fatigue manifested itself in the form of decreased attendance (by both staff and students) at any non-mandatory event. We noticed particular downturns in the levels of engagement with professional development, and so we introduced LEGO® to increase the appeal of these activities, and so inject an aspect of creativity and fun often missing from such sessions.

Among other things, LSP was used to explore writer's block and how to overcome it, literature reviews, positionality, communication skills and collaboration. Success in these internal sessions emboldened us to contribute to LEGO®-based workshops externally, and even at national and international conferences. LEGO® is now a regular part of development events at the institution, including both team and department away days for staff, as well as student-facing employability sessions.

Impact

Like colleagues and students at many other institutions, the University of Exeter's community has not experienced a 'return to normal' post-pandemic (Jensen *et al.*, 2022). Rather, we continue to work on establishing a *new* normal. There is a deeper appreciation for those aspects of education that we took for granted before the lockdown, in particular, the opportunity to:

- connect with and learn from others;
- build knowledge through immersive hands-on activities;
- pursue insights and abilities that support collaborative solutions to future global challenges;
- find joy in the learning process.

These are all facilitated by LSP, and so it is no wonder that interest in this technique has continued to grow. Our bespoke internal training has been delivered to hundreds of educators (both staff and students). Our LSP Facilitator Community of Practice comprises several dozen educators who regularly share resources, ideas and innovations, thereby supporting each other in continuing to adapt LEGO® activities for new audiences and topics. New members are added regularly, and the training is constantly evolving to support the changing needs and interests of our educators (Kight and Henderson, 2021).

For many, LSP has been a gateway to novel pedagogical approaches, and/ or a tool to make new or challenging ideas more accessible. For instance, LEGO® activities were one of several examples explored during a recent institution-wide workshop on transdisciplinary pedagogy. At another event, staff who had previously experimented with LSP decided to trial other playful approaches, such as sketchnoting, doodling and Zentangles, to further expand their repertoire of creative and joyful methods. For students who are used to a more 'sage on the stage' learning format, we found that the use of LSP during induction can gently introduce the more interactive, dynamic 'guide on the side' techniques favored at our institution (Kight et al., 2022).

One of the biggest appeals of LEGO® is its tactile nature. While we continue to implement the digital tools we discovered during the lockdown, including Mentimeter, Padlet and Mural, there is an undeniable zest for learning activities that allow students to put their devices aside. As was also the case during the pandemic, LSP therefore contributes to our pedagogy of compassion (Edgerley and Paddock, 2022), helping to reduce cognitive load, and restore a zest for learning.

Case Study Conclusion

The online pivot during the COVID-19 pandemic was intimidating for many because it challenged existing ideas about the form and function of education. Perhaps because LSP was such an effective technique in those circumstances, it continues to be a first port of call when staff and students are struggling with difficult topics and tricky learning situations.

Some of our most common requests are associated with the very same issues that LEGO® helped us tackle during lockdown, e.g., cohort-building, improving communication, supporting well-being and making complex topics more accessible. That colleagues continue to trust LSP to address these challenges testifies to its success in these areas, and to the glowing reviews provided by both staff and students.

This playful technique is an enduring symbol of our commitment to work toward a style of teaching which is very different from that which most of our educators grew up with. LSP is undeniably fun, but it is also inclusive, uplifting, engrossing and communal. It continues to support both teachers and students in enjoying the process of learning, and in developing a whole suite of skills and knowledge that can be applied outside of the classroom, no matter if that classroom is virtual, physical or a mixture of the two.

Case Study 6.3: Creating Online Social Connections for PGRs

CAROL AZUMAH DENNIS, PHILIPPA WATERHOUSE
AND INMA ALVAREZ

During March 2020, the COVID-19 global health crisis led to a series of international lockdowns. Campus universities in the UK were compelled to close or severely restrict onsite access. The case study we present emerges from the UK's largest, most well-established and highly regarded online and distance education university called the Open University, but it is also known as the 'Digital University' (Goodfellow and Lea, 2019). The Professional Doctoral (PD) program, which is our focus in this study, is a part-time doctoral program undertaken by mid-to-late career professionals whose thesis contributes to both theoretical knowledge and professional practice. It is one of the university's few hybrid programs and includes an annual in-person residential weekend which takes place at the start of each academic year, alongside online provision in the form of research supervision, research seminars and self-study research modules.

PD Postgraduate Researchers (PGRs) experienced the shock of the COVID-19 lockdown in several complex ways. Their annual face-to-face event, the only programmed occasion for them to meet their peers, their supervisors and their lecturers in person, was lost to them. However, the impact extended far beyond this. Their research projects, typically in education, health or social care settings, were significantly disrupted. If research sites were not closed during the crisis, then they were placed under lockdown instead, and extreme pressure in other ways, making it physically impossible, and ethically questionable, for PGRs to access the site, or to even research participants.

For some doctoral researchers their personal life was also thrown into turmoil. Those with school-aged children were home-schooling, and those working in the health and social care, or education sectors, saw their professional workloads intensify. During this time of isolation, anxiety and bewilderment, and using technology to facilitate delivery, PD leaders introduced Saturday morning drop-in sessions as a short-term emergency measure. Once the three planned sessions were completed, PGRs expressed a desire for ongoing contact which developed into Student-Led Seminars (SLSs) held on the second Saturday of each month.

This case study explores how PD PGRs developed the use of Microsoft Teams as a pedagogic platform during the COVID-19 pandemic. While there are several formal opportunities in the PD program for PGRs to present their work, these student-led sessions (SLS), initially envisaged as a short-term emergency response, assumed a distinct character in which PGRs spoke about their research, their research journey and their research project, in entangled autoethnographic terms.

Description

We used concepts associated with Cultural Historical Activity Theory (CHAT) to enable analytical purchase on this experience. In emphasizing the relationship between activity and consciousness, CHAT posits human action as motivated by the pursuance of desirable objectives. The objective may be an individually, socially or institutionally determined need. To achieve this goal, individuals use artifacts such as physical tools or socially, culturally and historically formed psychological signs (Clifford, 2022). The artifacts themselves make sense of, or otherwise mediate, the subject's relationship with the object(ive)s.

CHAT is most concerned with the relationships between subject, tool and object, providing an insight into 'who is doing what, why and how' (Hasan and Kazlauskas, 2014). A limitation evident in much of the literature surrounding education technology is the valorization of technology which is too frequently given agentic volition. CHAT disavows a technocratic perspective on the use of technology, i.e., technology does not independently transform human relations. Rather than being just about the technology, in this instance the technology was Microsoft Teams, it is instead understood to be part of a system of conscious sentient activity. Microsoft Teams once contextualized within CHAT becomes a tool, mediating a subjects' interaction with their environment and, in this instance, the accomplishment of a series of shifting objectives.

A key concept within CHAT is that contradiction defines activity systems. "Historically accumulating structural tensions" (Engeström, 2001, p. 137) collide or coalesce to form disturbances which compel the community to innovate. Activity systems are constantly working through contradictions. They are both disturbance and innovation, producing machines (Murphy and Rodriguez-Manzanares, 2008), which thrive on tensions, disturbances and local innovations (Cole and Engeström, 1997) as the rule and engine of change.

Prior to COVID-19, the PGR activity was accomplished through a blend of in-person (annual residential weekends) and online delivery (lecturer-led seminars plus a module website with teaching materials, activities and discussion forums). COVID-19 disrupted this activity system by changing the tools and objectives of the system. It is here useful to consider Leontiev's (1978) analysis of activities, actions, operations and changing objectives. His illustration focuses on the process of learning to drive. The ultimate objective of driving is to get from one place to another. In learning to drive, other objectives intervene, for example learning how to use a gear stick, learning to change gear while the car is in motion and shifting from conscious incompetence to unconscious competence in gear changing. Each objective is quickly replaced, or subsumed by another, once accomplished.

The outcome of the PD activity system is a complete doctoral thesis. Making use of a specific set of pedagogic tools such as blended learning, in-person annual residential weekends, online delivery in the form of lecturer-led seminars and the module website, which includes teaching materials, activities and discussion forums, together facilitate reaching this outcome.

With the arrival of COVID-19 the objective and available tools were changed. Thus, a new activity system was introduced featuring both a changed objective and a different set of tools. With lockdown announced, the objective, 'completing a doctoral thesis', became 'completing a doctoral thesis amidst a global pandemic'. The tool, 'blended learning', was no longer available, and 'online learning' was the only available mechanism for accomplishing our goal. A further objective was introduced to maintain a series of SLSs.

This newly negotiated activity system emerged from the previously established system. The crisis introduced several contradictions which created revised objectives, new tools and other embedded activity systems. Engeström (2014) identifies four sources of tension within an activity system. We are here focused on the second of his tensions which is when a contradiction between different nodes of an activity system occurs.

A changed environment necessitated a change in objective from 'complete a thesis' to 'complete a thesis amidst a global crisis.' This changed environment and objective also required a change in the available pedagogic tools, from 'blended learning' to 'online learning'. But this created contradiction between the 'pedagogic tool', which was the university's prescribed online teaching platform, and the 'subject' since the PD team were insufficiently skilled at delivering a residential event using the university's prescribed online teaching platform. Attempts to resolve this tension created conflict, the exploration of which is beyond the confines of this case study. Instead, the case study that we develop here focuses upon the reciprocal influences between the pedagogic tool, in this case Microsoft Teams, the revised objective of 'completing a thesis amidst a global crisis' and the subjects who were the PGRs.

With COVID-19, and its associated lockdown in our rear-view mirror, its legacies are beginning to unfold. As PGR leaders during the crisis, we recall the impact of the pandemic, the isolation, anxiety and bewilderment it invoked for PGRs and the PGR team. After securing a favorable opinion from the appropriate Human Research Ethics Committee, we organized three Focus Group Discussions (FGDs), two synchronous FGDs via Microsoft Teams and one asynchronous FGD via Padlet. We made use of the concepts and approaches associated with CHAT as a way of conceptualizing what was, and remains, a fast-moving highly complex set of interactivities. Rather than a faithful deployment of CHAT, we use CHAT as a practical device to examine the contours of contradiction created by the crisis.

Application

At the Digital University, the use of Microsoft Teams as a pedagogical tool is prohibited. Many of the PGRs at the Digital University are also members of staff, which reinforces this view. When we asked FGD participants about what difference the platform or tool made to their level of engagement, they almost inevitably made comparisons:

> Irrespective of the functionality of Adobe Connect … I've been told so many times, the learning platform is Adobe Connect and the

communication platform is Microsoft Teams, but at the end of the day, actually Microsoft Teams achieved what it needed to achieve.

FGD1, R2

The line of thought we pursue here is one that suggests that, by using Microsoft Teams in a student-led way, we introduced a different tool around which a new activity system could be developed. Our initial attempt at using Adobe Connect exposed a contradiction between the tool and the subject, making the accomplishment of the objective impossible.

Interestingly, PGRs also noted that not all PGR Team members were competent in the use of Adobe Connect:

It all depended on who was on the other side of using the technology. I think there were some people who were very aware of how to use Adobe Connect and how to use Microsoft Teams. But I think equally I've been in sessions where it was a nightmare where it didn't work and I don't necessarily think it's the technology, it's more [about] having the ability, and having been supported with how to use it.

FGD2, R2

Making use of Microsoft Teams not only avoided the need for technical competence in the use of Adobe Connect, but also had an unexpected outcome. In Microsoft Teams the seminars 'flew' in a way that they would not have done otherwise. Microsoft Teams facilitated a degree of student engagement, which the other platform does not enable or encourage in the same way (Chandler, 2022):

I do wonder in this instance, whether it kind of flew because also we were on Microsoft Teams. It was … a bottom-up request and being on Microsoft Teams, and the fact it was a Saturday, it just made it that little bit more informal and less 'teachy'. I felt more encouraged to ask questions. Also, I reacted and asked questions. I engaged in it…

FGD1, R2

Impact

Once the original objective of 'to complete a thesis' changed to instead become 'to complete a thesis amidst a global pandemic', the nature and level of student engagement also changed.

There are other online student-led spaces which might reasonably be considered pedagogic, and many of the PGRs have WhatsApp groups in which they discuss anything, and everything, relevant to their academic lives. An example of this is provided below:

> *WhatsApp was a life saver for me and still is. We have a WhatsApp group with all the people who started at the same time ... it is such a supporting group. We celebrate together, we cry together... this grew just by itself.*
>
> FGD2, R3

But these spaces are beyond institutional view and control, and while the WhatsApp group might well be analyzed as a tool within the PD activity system, with a different set of relationships surrounding and defining it, the SLS may be situated somewhere between the formality of a traditional 'present your research' session on the annual residential event and the informality offered by the WhatsApp space. The sessions removed formality, and required minimal functionality, which those involved recognized and valued:

> *We didn't need a high level of functionality. We just needed a platform that was accessible for everybody. Nobody needed to come in, and set it up in advance, as you do in Adobe Connect. It was the right platform, and I think we behave differently [when using it]. Certainly, in terms of the sessions that I attended, we behave differently in Microsoft Teams to how we behaved when we were in Adobe Connect.*
>
> FGD1, R3

While online meetings are often contrasted with in-person meetings, Microsoft Teams allowed a literal face-to-face encounter in which expression can be exaggerated and captured for later examination. Emotions can be conveyed through the use of chat and reaction emojis. This capacity was illustrated mid-way through FGD2 when a participant posted a heart emoji in response to a comment about the time- and travel-saving capacity of meeting online.

The enhanced communicative capacity of Microsoft Teams, i.e., the size of literally face-to-face images when cameras are switched on, and the use of reactive icons together meant that the tool influenced the subjects as it shaped how the PGRs behaved toward each other:

> *You're more attuned to quite small physical changes in people ... we have to act a bit sometimes on screen ... [to] emphasize your points, or nod your head, so that you're giving more encouragement. We were all there trying to support each other as well as learning, so I think that we tended to put our*

cameras on quite a bit, particularly when we talked. You engage differently in [Microsoft] Teams.

FGD1, R2

Case Study Conclusion

These SLS sessions were a valuable technology-enabled engagement for the PD program. They enabled the creation of a sense of community in the absence of an annual in-person event, and they enabled PGRs to articulate a sense of themselves at a time of tumultuous crisis.

Encoding this engagement in CHAT terms illustrates the fluidity of objectives as shaped by a changing context. As the environment changes, tools used to accomplish static outcomes evolve, as do the objectives that allow their accomplishment. The introduction of new tools modifies, and is then modified by, subjects which then creates new objects, even if these were not originally intentioned by the tool. What set the new activity system in motion was a contradiction between the newly defined objective and the exclusion of preferred tools. The change was slight, but also very significant.

My topic of research was not necessarily interesting for everybody in the group. But what was [interesting] was … 'How were we doing?' 'How were we surviving?' … the good things and the bad stuff. So OK, this is my research, but this is about me, and this is what I want to share with you ….

FGD2, R5

Case Study 6.4: Enhancing the Student Experience with Technological Added Value

MICK MARRIOTT AND ANNE KELLOCK

The technology used for the purpose of this case study is called Tinkercad Circuits. Tinkercad Circuits is an application published by Autodesk that allows students to create virtual representations of electronic circuitry. In this example, Tinkercad Circuits is employed across a range of computer science and software engineering undergraduate degrees at a post-1992 university in the UK. This technology is used with students because it allows a practical and applied approach that supports the development of skills required by employers in the sector.

The use of novel, and unfamiliar, tools and hardware can be intimidating and difficult for some students new to the discipline area (Al-Kandari, 2021). In addition, the equipment used can also provide challenges and barriers to students with different accessibility needs. By using appropriate and relevant tools, the engagement of all students can be achieved, while still using industry-standard tools and approaches (Allen *et al.*, 2003).

It has been our experience that the tools and technology used in a Higher Education setting are often used for the sake of it (Clement and Miles, 2018) and have little value in improving student experience and engagement (Schacter and Fagnano, 1999). For example, the overuse of apps and/or QR code quizzes to 'motivate' participation can become demotivating if used too often. In addition, the graduates identified here have historically been recruited and employed into industry, without being exposed to the technologies needed to undertake such roles. With that in mind, during our time in academia, we have strived to ensure that we are not just using technology for the sake of innovation, but instead only use it when it is applicable and appropriate to do so (Dror, 2008; Nichol *et al.*, 2023). This has been achieved by researching the correct and appropriate tools for each situation. We argue that the participative innovative technological approaches designed to engage students mentioned previously are often seen by those same students as boring gimmicks that do not enhance their learning experience.

Description

The product we are discussing, Tinkercad Circuits, is a free-to-use web application that runs on any browser. Registration is required to create an account with Autodesk, and this is also free. Tinkercad Circuits provides a simple approach to introducing students to electronics education (Aasvik, 2018). Using the interactive circuit editor, students have the opportunity to create, connect and program virtual projects using an extensive array of simulated components. They can rapidly create viable solutions to the challenges they have been presented with. For example, they can create a prototype circuit that allows the simulation of a lighting circuit, or the creation of an automated production line. This is a low-cost, and low-risk, environment for students to create their own solutions, and even try out some of the more eccentric designs they may produce, with no danger of personal harm that would arise from real-world experimentation. This may include using components beyond their usual use and/or testing components to destruction.

Accessible in 16 languages, and compatible with any internet-connected computer, Tinkercad Circuits stands as an unparalleled asset for teaching electronics. This is a web application that allows for the creation of 3D objects and virtual electronic circuit designs. The latter is utilized in this example. These virtual electronic designs can be robustly tested, and rapidly modified, to allow students to create workable solutions in a timely manner while not being hindered by specific usage issues, or by the availability of the correct physical components. It allows students to use specific micro controllers, for example Micro:bit and Arduino, which often form the basis of several common robotics platforms. These items of equipment are also widely used in both teaching and industry and thus are highly relevant to developing a student's practical experience.

The application also allows students to program their solutions using Scratch, Python or a combination of the two. These two programming languages enable students to use the software at diverse levels of aptitude. As this is used on a computing module, students use the pure code approach called Python, but there is also scope for using this software to assist students with a wide range of different skill levels. The security of this learning environment engenders confidence, and better develops the skills required by industry through a scaffolding approach that empowers students to succeed (Cunningham *et al.*, 1996).

In addition, Tinkercad Circuits allows for the easy introduction of new components, and electronic engineering principles, to students who have had little to no previous exposure to these in their studies to date. Students have provided feedback in this regard as to how these specific skills have supported their applications for graduate job roles. This is a key factor in using such software.

There is a raft of prewritten materials (https://www.tinkercad.com/lessonplans) for use if required, but experience of the product lends itself to an intuitive and easy-to-use teaching platform that does not require the use of these. It was very simple to create unique and applicable materials for students to use, manipulate and develop that were pertinent to the specific modules in question. Furthermore, Tinkercad Circuits has a large user base and support network for those academics needing inspiration and guidance.

Considering contemporary ways of working on and off campus, and recent global events, there is also the functionality to create classes for students to join and participate in remotely. While this has not been fully leveraged in this example, it is a useful backup resource should the need arise, and supports hybrid working (Bonk, 2020; Bülow, 2022). It also fully integrates with Google Classroom.

Application

There are three key reasons behind using this software: (1) good practice; (2) practical experience and creative application; and (3) cost-effectiveness. The following discussion details how the technology has been used, and justifies the approach taken. First, let's address the issue of good practice.

Good Practice

Tinkercad Circuits is an accessible application and allows users to hone their skills and abilities in a safe environment. This then leads to a growth in the confidence of students in their own skills, as there are minimal financial and safety-related repercussions from experimentation. This 'no-blame environment', and a trial-and-error approach, is well proven to encourage personal growth and increased confidence (Lee and Portillo, 2022). In addition, it can be difficult to read resistor values (very small, color-coded components) as well as manipulating fiddly components in non-simulated scenarios, issues that we have personally experienced ourselves (McNicholl *et al.*, 2020). Again, Tinkercad Circuits removes these barriers to student engagement due to the ease of viewing, and manipulation, of virtual components within the design interface.

Practical and Creative Application

As previously mentioned, following on from the students undertaking design work, and trialing different ideas, they can then use these tested designs to order any required physical components, to create the physical versions of their prototypes. These circuits ultimately make up the final robotic solution that the student presents for formative assessment.

The use of the application causes a 'buzz' in the classroom. Some students may have electrical engineering experience, while others have none, but all can quickly feel capable of creating viable designs and can also work on them easily outside of the academic setting. This promotes self-belief in their own abilities (Aldrich, 2005; Casey, 2019) and encourages further exploration of the problem domain, safe in the knowledge that they can try out outlandish ideas with no physical danger of harm, or damage to the components used.

Furthermore, the skills and techniques developed using this technology naturally lead on to more complex industry-standard tools such as Autodesk

Fusion 360. Designs that are created reside in the student's own account until deletion and can even be exported to the more advanced tool for future development and enhancement. Students can then use these experiences, and skills, to evidence their aptitude when applying for graduate roles within a portfolio of work.

Cost-Effectiveness

Tinkercad Circuits has been used within the Robotics module to allow 60 students to rapidly design, prototype and test their ideas, and to develop electrical solutions and designs that can then be created using physical components in a safe and no-risk environment. The rationale behind this was initially due to a shortage of viable physical components being readily available, as well as the overhead in staffing costs for constantly managing the physical inventory. Tinkercad Circuits overcomes this issue by synthesizing the experience for all users. In addition, it enables students with any physical impairments to be fully active within the module.

As previously mentioned, the selection of this tool has been carefully considered for its appropriateness and relevancy. While other technologies of a similar nature are available, Tinkercad Circuits uses the two main control boards that we have physical versions of within the department of computing. The zero-cost aspect was also a deciding factor in this current age of fiscal restrictions within Higher Education.

Skills Development

The benefit of employing suitable technology, and adhering to industry-standard tools and methodologies, is a proven trope (Allen *et al.*, 2003). This example provides key benefits including achievement, enjoyment and skills development. Beyond these benefits, engagement and interaction by students is clear to see, and is well evidenced by the results that the students achieved in their final formative assessment grades. The module feedback, based on the introduction of Tinkercad Circuits as an intrinsic part of the learning, showed quite clearly an increase in student enjoyment and satisfaction when compared to the previous two years' iterations of the module. Students commented that they felt more prepared for graduate employment because of the tasks they had undertaken, and by using the technologies they had been exposed to on the module.

As has been mentioned earlier in this case study, regarding the potential benefits, it was clear to see students' confidence and skills awareness grew exponentially thanks in part to the tools that they were exposed to. Without this confidence, it is considered that most of these students would not have received such good grades for their final mark. There is also a positive result regarding component inventory and stock management, in that it was not necessary to employ a technician to constantly maintain and update, and there was also no need for support staff to sort through thousands of individual components.

Moving forward, reflection and planning will be undertaken to integrate technological and industry-standard tools such as Tinkercad Circuits into more of our modules on the courses that we manage. This will ensure that students are fully prepared for the world of graduate work. As academics, we strive to use real-world tools, and we are not just using technology and applications as gimmicks, but because it is the current norm within Higher Education to do so.

We have learned that it is often better to show students the more practical and realistic approaches to solving problems. Using the actual tools that are applied in industry, and reinforcing that these do not always involve technology, is part of this process. They may be as simple as Post-it notes and pens to define and design systems. The only potential downside we can see to using this technology is that using Tinkercad Circuits relies on having an internet connection. Failure to have an internet connection will result in Tinkercad Circuits not being accessible to the students, and this could cause considerable disruption to any planned teaching, especially over an extended period.

Case Study Conclusion

Due to our respective backgrounds in the IT industry, and in education, our experience leads us to strive to ensure that our students and graduates are ready and able to join the world of work. As a result of the work undertaken that is documented within this case study, it is clear to us that the use of appropriate, and applicable, technologies is key to achieving this task.

It has also become apparent that many technologies and innovations, that are espoused by those who are well established within Higher Education and academia, are there only to show how cool and 'on-trend' the university is in regard to technology. As established educators, we recognize that there is a place for the correct use of technology where it is applicable, and relevant, to the subject being studied. Indeed, there are often a plethora of advantages.

The future direction for the technology demonstrated within this case study will hopefully lead to the provision of an offline version of the software. This will ensure that we will have a robust and reliable solution that can be leveraged in all areas of education in a globally accessible manner. Another view on anticipated direction is about using the right tools to deliver the teaching that we are trying to undertake with our students, and to ensure that it is applicable and appropriate, and not just done for the sake of using technology. We are also mindful of the continuing evolution of technology, and the need to ensure that we maintain contemporary and appropriate practices for our students moving forward, so that they learn skills relevant to their future employment.

Case Study 6.5 Using Synchronous Collaborative Platforms to Support Interdisciplinary Groups

UWE MATTHIAS RICHTER

This case study explores the use of synchronous online collaboration tools at Anglia Ruskin University (ARU) in the UK as part of the undergraduate 'breadth' module named *Where do you belong in this city?* which was delivered in semester 1 of academic years 2021–2022 and 2022–2023. The breadth of Ruskin modules (RM) (Brown and Acevedo, 2022) was introduced in 2021 for all Level 5 (second year) undergraduate programs at ARU. The core themes of these modules are interdisciplinarity, sustainability and employability, using wicked problems (McCune *et al.*, 2021) as a pedagogic approach.

The RM considered in this chapter addresses the core themes and learning outcomes developed through students working in mixed-disciplinary groups on a chosen wicked problem relating to urban life. To address this wicked problem, groups developed a digital artifact as part of a project, and then pitched sustainable solutions to different audiences and stakeholders. The group and project work were scaffolded to develop the employability skills sought after within employment according to the World Economic Forum (2023). The module aligns to the UNESCO learning objectives for the United Nations Sustainable Development Goals (UNSDGs) as defined by UNESCO (Barakat *et al.*, 2017). The primary focus was on SDG 11 which concentrates on making cities and human settlements inclusive, safe, resilient and sustainable. Like many other SDGs, this is a cross-cutting theme and so also links to other SDGs such as:

- SDG 3 – Ensure healthy lives and promote well-being for all at all ages;
- SDG 4 – Ensure inclusive and equitable quality education and promote lifelong learning opportunities for all;

- SDG 6 – Ensure availability and sustainable management of water and sanitation for all;
- SDG 7 – Ensure access to affordable, reliable, sustainable and clean energy for all;
- SDG 8 – Promote sustained, inclusive and sustainable economic growth, full and productive employment and decent work for all;
- SDG 9 – Build infrastructure, promote inclusive and sustainable industrialization and foster innovation;
- SDG 12 – Ensure sustainable consumption and production patterns;
- SDG 13 – Take urgent action to combat climate change and its impacts;
- SDG 15 – Protect, restore and promote sustainable use of terrestrial ecosystems, sustainably manage forests, combat desertification, halt and reverse land degradation and halt biodiversity loss;
- SDG 16 - Promote peaceful and inclusive societies for sustainable development, provide access to justice for all and build effective, accountable and inclusive institutions at all levels.

UNESCO identifies active and transformative pedagogies as part of Education for Sustainable Development. The key teaching methods suggested by UNESCO (Barakat *et al.*, 2017, p. 55) used in my module are:

- Collaborative real-world projects, such as service-learning projects and campaigns for different SDGs;
- Vision-building exercises such as future workshops, scenario analyses, utopian/dystopian storytelling, science-fiction thinking, and forecasting and backcasting;
- Analyses of complex systems through community-based research projects, case studies, stakeholder analysis, actors' analysis, modeling, systems games, etc.;
- Critical and reflective thinking through fishbowl discussions, reflective journals, etc.

Description

As I delivered the module fully online, I used a variety of learning technologies to support the delivery and learning process. I used the VLE as an asynchronous platform for content, resources and assignment submissions. Students had three hours of timetabled online synchronous seminars or workshop sessions. The synchronous platform used by ARU was Microsoft Teams and Microsoft Class Team (Gonzalez, 2018; Hewson and Chung, 2021). While all modules have had a VLE presence, the need to move to remote teaching during the COVID-19 pandemic led to an integration of the VLE and Microsoft Class Team for every module (Florjančič and Wiechetek, 2022).

While webinar tools such as Adobe Connect, Blackboard Collaborate and Zoom and collaborative platforms such as Google Drive have been available for more than a decade (I first taught using Adobe Connect in 1999), Microsoft Teams launched in 2017 developed rapidly (https://www.theguardian.com) during the pandemic, becoming a strong competitor to many of the more established synchronous tools. This led to complaints to the European Commission about 'anticompetitive behavior' because Microsoft included Microsoft Teams within its Office365 product. However, from an educational perspective, the advantage of Microsoft Class Team is that it integrates the webinar tool within the wider collaborative platform, which makes the use of Microsoft tools such as Office365, Stream (media library), Sway (digital storytelling and presentation) and SharePoint (integrated file directory) much easier. Furthermore, bespoke tools can be added such as private and public channels, the Insight app for learning/user analytics, Classwork for content, Assignments, Grades and Class Notebook which is a portfolio and collaborative tool. Additionally, Microsoft Class Team provides numerous applications that can be integrated such as Whiteboards, Polls and links to websites, such as the VLE. To avoid confusion with the VLE, I did not use Assignments, Grades and Classwork in Teams.

Application

I used a Waterfall Project Management approach (McCormick, 2012) for group work (https://business.adobe.com/blog/basics/waterfall) as it has designated stages and peer feedback at each one.

For the online module, I used Microsoft Teams for the three-hour timetabled sessions. The first half of the module involved tutor input and activities, while in the second half, time was dedicated to students' working in groups on their projects using their dedicated group channel. Student engagement in Microsoft Teams sessions varied from responses to questions and prompts in the text chat (students indicated their desire to provide audio responses using the 'Raise your hand' feature) and polls (using Microsoft Forms) to group work in breakout rooms. Group work was frequently assisted by collaborating on a Word document, PowerPoint slide or Microsoft Class Notebook set up in the General channel of the Microsoft

Class Team. However, I found it necessary to introduce students to these different engagement methods as they required different digital literacies. Clear instructions were provided during the Microsoft Teams meetings using PowerPoint slides, and I found that it was essential that these were repeated in the text chat and collaborative documents.

A colleague and I supported breakout room activities by 'room hopping', i.e., moving between breakout rooms, to ensure instructions were clear, and to provide any clarification and support necessary. One of the challenges of synchronous online learning that we experienced was with students being reluctant to communicate, especially using their cameras and voice. This experience is shared by other academic colleagues across the sector, often indicating a lack of belonging, especially during the pandemic (Mulrooney and Kelly, 2020; Abu *et al.*, 2021; Jisc, 2022). In some instances, students were completing tasks in a collaborative document without communicating in breakout rooms. I found that this behavior changed gradually over time, and students started using more active communication halfway through the module. To address these challenges, I introduced further onboarding, i.e., introductions to the technologies being used, and icebreaker activities, early in the second iteration of the module. I found that this approach helped to develop confidence, and trust, among students in terms of being able to communicate online, and it encouraged them to switch on their microphones and cameras during breakout activities.

I scheduled Microsoft Teams meetings in the General channel, which provided a permanent link for all sessions throughout the semester, which I also shared on the VLE. I preserved the chat and session recordings in the General channel and made these available to students. One drawback, however, was that the integrated polling tool available in Microsoft Teams, scheduled through the Microsoft Outlook calendar, was unavailable, and consequently I used Microsoft Forms. Students needed to log into Microsoft Class Team with their university account, as guest login limited their access to both the chat function and the collaborative documents. This could be confusing if students had more than one Microsoft Teams account, and I provided guidance to address these access issues.

I prefaced the project work with a short introduction to the Waterfall approach (https://business.adobe.com/blog/basics/waterfall; McCormick, 2012) and the Double Diamond (Renzi, 2021) project management approach. The Waterfall approach provided linear sequential stages, i.e., wicked problem choice; group formation; project planning; storyboarding; presentation of digital artifact and reflection, supported by peer and tutor feedback. This approach is ideal for managing small and time-limited projects. The formative feedback provided opportunities not only for groups to reflect upon their project progress, and amend their work where necessary, but also for tutors to keep project groups on track. I used a project plan, and a risk assessment, in combination with a group learning agreement, to manage how student groups worked together on key activities including communication, allocating project member roles and conflict management.

The Double Diamond approach provided more creative methods for project management using discovery, definition, development and delivery phases. For the discovery activity, I introduced the list of 'wicked problems', from which students could choose. I then formed groups based upon students' selection of their preferred wicked problem. I used a templated, scaffolded approach for wicked problems, which included a definition of the wicked problem, the desirable outcomes, the target audiences for the pitch and a selection of sources. In class, I used and supported techniques such as brainstorming, outlining and visualization such as flowcharting and storyboarding.

Once students formed groups, the definition stage involved identifying how the group would work together, i.e., group agreement, project roles, communication methods, how they would define the focus of the wicked problem and their completion of a project proposal that included a project plan and risk assessment. I supported the development phase of the digital artifact with practical introductions regarding the usability and accessibility of PowerPoint presentations, and the use of other presentation and media tools such as Microsoft Sway, Microsoft Flip (Microsoft, 2023), Yuja (www.yuja.com), Augmented Reality posters using ThingLink (www.thinglink.com) and podcasting using Anchor.fm (now Spotify for Podcasters, https://podcasters.spotify.com). The delivery stage included peer and tutor feedback on a draft version of the artifact, and a virtual gallery exhibition of the final assessed group artifacts alongside peer feedback for which a survey was used.

I provided templates of the project stages (e.g., group member roles, group agreement, project proposal, project plan, risk assessment and storyboarding), which I then shared in the General channel, with cross-group peer feedback in breakout rooms as part of the weekly Microsoft Teams sessions.

While group work, project work, analytical skills and critical thinking, as well as digital literacy, are all recognized employability skills (World Economic Forum, 2023), and most jobs involve working in groups, I found that a significant number of students disliked group work. It was therefore important for me to include scaffolding for group formation, and measures for conflict management and project work. I considered this to be part of creating a learning community for the online class and for the individual groups. However, in the 2023–2024 delivery, I included a formative assignment submission process for the documentation in each stage, where groups receive digital badges and tutor feedback on completion, and then share the documentation in the General channel for cross-group feedback.

Impact

As I taught the module online, using Microsoft Teams as a webinar platform was fundamental in providing engaging synchronous activities as timetabled sessions. However, I found that some students were reluctant to engage online for various reasons, including a lack of required digital skills, access and connectivity challenges and communication preferences, all of which I needed to address by developing the necessary digital literacy skills alongside creating a comfortable online learning space and community. I also had to accept that some students prefer to learn passively rather than actively.

While Microsoft Teams has similar functionalities to other video conferencing systems, being embedded in Microsoft Class Team provides an integrated experience for students rather than linking out to different platforms. Microsoft Class Team worked particularly well for project work, as the private group channels provided all the functionalities of the General channel. Students could meet and communicate in the chat, contact individuals and the whole group, add and collaborate on files, use other internal apps and link to external apps set up either by me or by themselves. Using Microsoft Class Team in dedicated timetabled slots allowed me to support students in their group channels, and/or use the General channel as a base for consultation and virtual office hours. Students identified the value of both group working and project management skills, for their further studies and future employment.

Case Study Conclusion

During the pandemic, ARU started to use Microsoft Class Team alongside the existing VLE. Active use of these technologies has continued after the pandemic to support, enhance and personalize learning and teaching, and provide flexibility in the delivery of, and access to, learning opportunities (McKenna, 2021). With working from home continuing in many employment settings, the digital skills students acquire from learning using these technologies have become essential for their future employment (Barber, 2021).

Technological literacy, working in groups and on projects, analytical and creative thinking, empathy and active listening, and leadership and social influence are all skills listed as the top 10 skills of 2023 by the World Economic Forum (2023, p. 38), and we manage to develop each of them through this module by using a synchronous online platform for collaboration.

References

Aasvik, M., 2018. *A First Impression of Tinkercad Circuits*. Trondheim, Norway: Norwegian Creations.

Abu, L., Chipfuwamiti, C., Costea, A., Kelly, A., Major, K. and Mulrooney, H., 2021. Staff and student perspectives of online teaching and learning; Implications for belonging and engagement at university – a qualitative exploration. *Compass: Journal of Learning and Teaching*, 14(3), 1–20.

Aldrich, C., 2005. *Review of 'Learning by Doing: A Comprehensive Guide to Simulations, Computer Games and Pedagogy in e-learning and Other Educational Experiences'*. Misenheimer, NC: Pfeiffer.

Al-Kandari, N., 2021. Students anxiety experiences in higher education institutions. *In: Anxiety Disorders – The New Achievements*. London, UK: IntechOpen.

Allen, E., Cartwright, R. and Reis, C., 2003. Production programming in the classroom. *ACM SIGCSE Bulletin*, 35(1), 89–93.

Barakat, B., Bengtsson, S., Muttarak, R. and Kebede, E., 2017. *Education for Sustainable Development Goals: Learning Objectives*. Paris, France: UNESCO.

Barber, M., 2021. *Gravity Assist: Propelling Higher Education Towards a Brighter Future*. London, UK: Office for Students.

Becker, L., 2019. Student screencasts within a learning partnership. *Student Engagement in Higher Education*, 2(2), 133–140.

Biggs, J., Boulton-Lewis, G., Boyatzis, R.E., Sternberg, R.J. and Zhang, L., 2014. *Perspectives on Thinking, Learning, and Cognitive Styles*. Florence, Italy: Taylor & Francis.

Blair, S., and Dröge, J., 2020. How to Facilitate the LEGO® Serious Play® Method Online. London: ProMeet.

Bonk, C.J., 2020. Pandemic ponderings, 30 years to today: Synchronous signals, saviors, or survivors? *Distance Education*, 41(4), 589–599.

Brown, E. and Acevedo, B., 2022. Interdisciplinary design for ambiguity: Work in a wicked world. *In:* Norton, S. and Penaluna, A. (eds.), *3 Es for Wicked Problems: Employability, Enterprise, and Entrepreneurship: Solving Wicked Problems*. York: Advance HE, 16–113.

Bülow, M.W., 2022. Designing Synchronous hybrid learning spaces: Challenges and opportunities. *In:* Gil, E., Mor, Y., Dimitriadis, Y. and Köppe, C. (eds.), *Hybrid*

Learning Spaces. Understanding Teaching-Learning Practice. Cham, Switzerland: Springer, 135–163.

Casey, R., 2019. Building your graduate's confidence in practice. *Practice*, 41(8), 394–396.

Chandler, K., 2022. Students' experiences of synchronous online tuition in health and social care. *Research in Learning Technology*, 30, 1–14.

Clement, J. and Miles, M., 2018. *Screen Schooled: Two Veteran Teachers Expose How Technology Overuse is Making our Kids Dumber.* Chicago, IL: Chicago Review Press.

Cleveland-Innes, M. and Campbell, P., 2012. Emotional presence, learning, and the online learning environment. *International Review of Research in Open and Distributed Learning*, 13(4), 269.

Clifford, S., 2022. The use and value of cultural historical activity theory in institutional educational technology policy. *Studies in Technology Enhanced Learning*, 3(1), 1–29.

Çobanoğlu, R. and Demir, C.E., 2014. The visible side of the hidden curriculum in schools. *Elementary Education Online*, 13(3), 776–786.

Cole, M. and Engeström, Y., 1997. A cultural-historical approach to distributed cognition. *In:* Salomon, G. (ed.), *Distributed Cognitions: Psychological and Educational Considerations.* Cambridge: Cambridge University Press, 1–46.

Cunningham, I., Hyman, J. and Baldry, C., 1996. Empowerment: The power to do what? *Industrial Relations Journal*, 27(2), 143–154.

Dror, I., 2008. Technology enhanced learning. *Pragmatics and Cognition*, 16(2), 215–223.

Edgerley, R. and Paddock, S., 2022. LEGO® Serious Play® from the heart, outwards – building compassionate campuses. *In:* Nerantzi, C. and James, A. (eds.), *Lego® for University Learning: Online, Offline and Elsewhere.* Genève, Switzerland: Zenodo, 95–97.

Engeström, Y., 2001. Expansive learning at work: Toward an activity theoretical reconceptualization. *Education and Work*, 14(1), 133–156.

Engeström, Y., 2014. Activity theory and learning at work. *In:* Taylor, J. and Furnham, A. (eds.), *Learning at Work, Excellent Practice from Best Theory.* London: Palgrave Macmillan, 67–96.

Florjančič, V. and Wiechetek, L., 2022. Using Moodle and MS teams in higher education – A comparative study. *Innovation and Learning*, 31(2), 264–286.

Gonzalez, J., 2018. *Build a Collaborative Classroom with Microsoft Teams.* Washington: Cult of Pedagogy.

Goodfellow, R. and Lea, M.R., 2019. Literacy and the digital university. *In:* C. Haythornthwaite, C., Andrews, R., Fransman, J. and Meyers, E. (eds.), *The SAGE Handbook of E-learning Research.* London: SAGE, 423–442.

Hasan, H. and Kazlauskas, A., 2014. Activity theory: Who is doing what, why and how. *In:* Hasan, H. (ed.), *Being Practical with Theory: A Window into Business Research.* Morrisville, NC: Lulu.

Henderson, H. and Shipway, R., 2023. Liminality, leisure, and Lego®: Using a leisure-based creative methodology to support children and young people. *Leisure Sciences*, 1–21.

Hewson, E. and Chung, G.W., 2021. Beyond the VLE: Transforming online discussion and collaboration through Microsoft Teams. *The Open, Online and Flexible Higher Education Conference* (OOFHEC), Madrid, 16–18 October 2019, Madrid, 36–47.

James, A.R., 2013. Lego® Serious Play®: A three-dimensional approach to learning development. *Learning Development in Higher Education*, 6, 1–18.

Jensen, T., Marinoni, G. and van't Land, H., 2022. *Higher Education One Year Into the COVID-19 Pandemic*. Paris, France: International Association of Universities.

Jisc, 2022. *Enhancing Student Engagement Using Technological Solutions*. Bristol: Jisc.

Khan, M.A., 2021. The impact of COVID-19 on UK Higher Education students: Experiences, observations and suggestions for the way forward. *Corporate Governance*, 21(6), 1172–1193.

Kight, C. and Henderson, H., 2021. Serious play: How LEGO® can help build learning communities and knowledge. *In: Enhance: Stories of Excellence in Education*. Exeter, Exeter University.

Kight, C., Pulman, S. and Walshe, K., 2022. Building bridges: Using LEGO® to foster communication, collaboration, and connection. *In:* Nerantzi, C. and James, A. (eds.), *Lego® for University Learning: Online, Offline and Elsewhere*. Genève, Switzerland: Zenodo, 73–74.

Koeners, M.P. and Francis, J., 2020. The physiology of play: Potential relevance for Higher Education. *International Journal of Play*, 9(1), 143–159.

Lee, J. and Portillo, M., 2022. Transferability of creative self-belief across domains: The differential effects of a creativity course for university students. *Thinking Skills and Creativity*, 43, 100996.

Leontiev, A.N., 1978. *Activity, Consciousness, and Personality*. New Jersey: Prentice-Hall.

López-Fernández, D., Gordillo, A., Ortega, F., Yagüe, A. and Tovar, E., 2021. LEGO® serious play in software engineering education. *IEEE Access*, 9, 103120–103131.

Marinoni, G., van't Land, H. and Jensen, T., 2020. *The Impact of COVID-19 on Higher Education Around the World*. Paris, France: International Association of Universities.

McCormick, M., 2012. *Waterfall vs. Agile Methodology*. Indiana: MPCS.

McCune, V., Tauritz, R., Boyd, S., Cross, A., Higgins, P. and Scoles, J. 2021. Teaching wicked problems in Higher Education: Ways of thinking and practicing. *Teaching in Higher Education*, 28(7), 1–16.

McCusker, S., 2014. Lego®, Serious Play TM: Thinking about teaching and learning. *Knowledge. Innovation and Entrepreneurship*, 2(1), 27–37.

McKenna, I., 2021. *The Power of Virtual Classrooms in a Post-Pandemic World*. Cirencester: Fosway Group.

McNicholl, A., Desmond, D. and Gallagher, P., 2020. Assistive technologies, educational engagement and psychosocial outcomes among students with disabilities in Higher Education. *Disability and Rehabilitation: Assistive Technology*, 18(1), 50–58.

Microsoft, 2023. *Flip*. Available at: https://info.flip.com/en-us.html (Accessed: 13 August 2023).

Mulrooney, H. and Kelly, A., 2020. COVID-19 and the move to online teaching: Impact on perceptions of belonging in staff and students in a UK widening participation university. *Applied Learning & Teaching*, 3(2), 17–30.

Murphy, E. and Rodriguez-Manzanares, M.A., 2008. Using activity theory and its principle of contradictions to guide research in educational technology. *Australasian Journal of Educational Technology*, 24(4), 442–457.

Nichol, D., Mulholland, K., Anderson, A., Taylor, S. and Davies, J., 2023. 'How was it for you?' The impacts of student-staff partnerships in developing online teaching and learning. *Further and Higher Education*, 49(9), 1276–1287.

Orón Semper, J.V. and Blasco, M., 2018. Revealing the hidden curriculum in Higher Education. *Studies in Philosophy and Education*, 37(5), 481–498.

Peabody, M.A., 2015. Building with purpose: Using Lego Serious Play in play therapy supervision. *Play Therapy*, 24(1), 30.

Ratten, V., 2023. The post COVID-19 pandemic era: Changes in teaching and learning methods for management educators. *International Journal of Management Education*, 21(2), 100777.

Reeve, J., 2021. Compassionate play: Why playful teaching is a prescription for good mental health (for you and your students). *Play in Adulthood*, 3(2), 6–23.

Renzi, J., 2021. *Double Diamond in Project Management*. Lyngby, Denmark: Technical University of Denmark.

Roos, J., 2006. Thinking from within. *In*: Roos, J. (ed.), *Thinking from Within – A Hands-On Strategy Practice*. London: Palgrave Macmillan, 1–24.

Schacter, J. and Fagnano, C., 1999. Does computer technology improve student learning and achievement? How, when, and under what conditions? *Educational Computing Research*, 20(4), 329–343.

Schutz, P.A. and Pekrun, R.E., 2007. *Emotion in Education*. Amsterdam: Elsevier Academic Press.

Shipway, R. and Henderson, H., 2023. Everything is awesome! Lego® Serious Play® (LSP) and the interaction between leisure, education, mental health and wellbeing. *Leisure Studies*, 43(2), 187–204.

van Vleet, M. and Feeney, B.C., 2015. Play behavior and playfulness in adulthood. *Social and Personality Psychology Compass*, 9(11), 630–643.

World Economic Forum, 2023. *The Future of Jobs Report 2023*. Geneva, Switzerland: World Economic Forum.

Conclusion

MARTYN POLKINGHORNE, GELAREH ROUSHAN AND UMA PATEL

In this book, we have collected a unique series of case studies that reflect the personal 'lived' experiences of those involved in developing and implementing technology to support teaching and learning across Higher Education.

The six case studies in Chapter 1 have shown us several examples of innovative applications of technology used to develop animation, simulation and visualization solutions that support the delivery of a high-quality student learning experience. Case Study 1.1 revealed the value of Virtual Field Trips (VFTs) for enhancing inclusivity and preparing students for in-person experiences, emphasizing the need for clear instructions, and teacher-student engagement, throughout the virtual journey. Case Study 1.2 demonstrated the effectiveness of Technology-Enabled Learning (TEL) platforms for engaging students, fostering essential skills development and reducing drop-out rates. This case study also highlighted the importance of personalized analytics and gamification elements.

Case Study 1.3 considered how Virtual Reality (VR) simulations in medical training have proven to be beneficial for skills practice, but challenges, such as accessibility and content quality, need to be addressed before wider adoption is likely. The case study has showcased the potential, and the limitations, of immersive technologies. Case Study 1.4 explored the integration of multi-cam and 360-degree immersive webinar designs for interactive learning, and emphasized the importance of audiovisual clarity, and user-friendly set-ups, in enhancing engagement and comprehension.

DOI: 10.4324/9781032635248-8

Case Study 1.5 focused on how the application of holographic technology can offer students an immersive learning experience. Challenges such as visual discomfort, and content availability, underscored the need for ongoing improvements and accessibility considerations. Case Study 1.6 highlighted the benefits of 3DVista Pro software in creating realistic learning environments, emphasizing the importance of collaboration, accessibility and continuous refinement to optimize student learning and assessment experiences. These case studies in Chapter 1 have demonstrated the transformative impact of innovative technologies within education. These case studies show how these technologies can offer immersive, engaging and inclusive learning experiences, fostering essential skills development, reducing drop-out rates and preparing students for real-world challenges. However, other challenges such as accessibility, content quality and the complexity of the technical set-up need to be addressed before widespread adoption can occur.

The five case studies in Chapter 2 have demonstrated the ways in which innovative applications of digital technology can be used to support online teaching, and, in doing so, deliver a more inclusive and engaging experience for the students. Case Study 2.1 focused on active digital education and the integration of the NILE learning platform to enhance co-creation among students. This process was supported with tools such as Padlet and Miro to facilitate collaborative learning, social interaction and skills development. The use of active digital education was found to foster metacognition, knowledge building and student agency. In Case Study 2.2, Microsoft Teams was used to support the delivery of pastoral care for students as it facilitated the streamlining of sessions which could then be offered in a more flexible manner. This also helped with the monitoring of student progress and the arrangement of group sessions, although there was a need for academics to be aware of the potential for digital fatigue among the students, and inclusivity challenges can occur. A balance of virtual and in-person engagement was therefore recommended.

Case Study 2.3 considered the application of a Microsoft Teams-centered learning ecosystem to improve student experience and satisfaction. Modules designed using Microsoft Teams received positive feedback from students but required both inclusive co-design and a significant investment of time. The personalization of learning experiences using plug-ins and AI integration are ways to further support student learning journeys in the future. Case Study 2.4 built a sense of student community using a blend of live events, static resources and social media. This approach fostered student engagement and connectivity, but it was necessary to be flexible and adaptable in terms of the use of multiple pedagogical tools and technologies to ensure inclusivity, particularly among harder-to-reach groups of learners.

Case Study 2.5 used OneNote to create digital escape rooms. This approach engaged students and enhanced their confidence, but needed to overcome various challenges including set-up time, usability issues and managing the expectations of learners. However, the asynchronous nature of the experience proved to be highly beneficial for those involved. These case studies in Chapter 2 have demonstrated the multifaceted applications of digital tools in education, showcasing how platforms like NILE and Microsoft Teams can enhance collaboration, streamline pastoral care and improve the student experience. They highlighted the importance of adaptability and inclusivity in utilizing digital technologies and the potential benefits of innovative approaches such as digital escape rooms. Despite encountering challenges, the case studies indicate that effectively integrating digital tools can lead to increased engagement, connectivity and confidence among students.

The six case studies in Chapter 3 have highlighted different examples of the innovative ways that digital technology can be used to support student engagement and inclusivity. Together, they provide a range of key learning points important for academics to consider. Case Study 3.1 explored the benefits and impact of using the BSEF (Blended Synchronous Education Framework) for teaching and highlighted the importance of adapting pedagogy for synchronous learning. Through listening to student feedback, and enhancing digital literacy, efforts were made to improve student engagement and representation. Case Study 3.2 evaluated a range of different approaches to supporting student engagement explored during the shift to online teaching. The importance of recognizing student needs was emphasized, and innovative teaching methods used positively impacted upon the student experience, which in turn helped develop their feelings of being connected.

Case Study 3.3 utilized learning analytics to address student engagement. This proved to be effective, with the targeted reminders being sent to students significantly improving course pass rates. The automation used reduced the administrative burden placed upon staff, while providing personalized support to students at risk of failing. Case Study 3.4 determined that workshops aimed at promoting equitable teaching practices revealed that hybrid participation generated a series of both challenges and successes. While initial workshops faced hurdles in creating safe discussion spaces, champions emerged who supported the roll-out of ideas and principles.

Case Study 3.5 discussed how weekly interventions, supported by targeted activities, enhanced student engagement. This proved to be especially effective during critical points such as assignment submissions. Feedback highlighted the importance of clear communication throughout. Case Study 3.6 described how implementing Studiosity to support student writing significantly improved attainment rates. The data indicated a clear correlation between Studiosity usage and academic success. These case studies in Chapter 3 have emphasized the importance of adapting teaching practices, and the leveraging of technology in partnership with students, to ensure that the potential benefits can be optimized. However, they have also reminded us of the need to carefully plan technological integration to prevent unintentional disengagement among students that may be unexpected, not easy to recognize and counterintuitive.

The five case studies in Chapter 4 have highlighted different examples of innovative applications of technology within Virtual Learning Environments (VLEs), which have been used to support the delivery of teaching and administrative processes. Case Study 4.1 discussed enhancing the PGR (postgraduate researcher) experience using a new system called ProGRess. ProGRess streamlined administrative tasks and provided real-time data for use by management. By listening to stakeholder groups regarding system functionality, and then providing training to stakeholders in how to use it, the system was well-received when implemented. Case Study 4.2 considered the implementation of guided flexible learning pathways using Moodle Book to address learning challenges. By organizing content in a structured, yet flexible, manner, students found it easier to navigate learning materials. The pathway provided students with a level of autonomy which they valued.

Case Study 4.3 focused upon implementing a Learning Design Framework (LDF) aimed at enhancing the student learning experience. It fostered a common language for discussing learning and teaching. Challenges that needed to be overcome included staff resistance and timetabling issues. Case Study 4.4 depicted the implementation of online exam proctoring using the Honorlock system. The system allowed students to complete exams remotely, with a minimal need for resits. Support was required to mitigate technical issues, and so implementation required the inclusion of time and resources from specialist staff such as learning technologists.

Case Study 4.5 described the efforts to enhance employability skills using the Riipen platform to facilitate experiential learning. This was achieved by connecting students to real-world business projects. The resulting learning improved student engagement and supported their future employability. The case studies presented in Chapter 4 have illustrated how we use technology to enhance both learning experiences and administrative processes. Examples such as the ProGRess system for postgraduate research administration, the use of Moodle Book for flexible learning pathways and the adoption of the LDF demonstrate the efforts to streamline operations and improve student outcomes. Additionally, initiatives including online exam proctoring with

Honorlock, and the use of the Riipen platform for experiential learning, highlight how innovative solutions can be implemented that enable us to adapt to changing educational demands.

The five case studies in Chapter 5 have provided examples of how innovative applications of technology can be used to improve teaching standards across the Higher Education sector. Case Study 5.1 demonstrated that implementing digital assessment solutions required careful consideration of internal factors such as strategic priorities, existing procedures and policies. Challenges included the need to address discipline silos, and to ensure seamless integration with existing systems. Case Study 5.2 considered student perceptions of learning. Understanding students' perceived learning trajectories beyond traditional metrics was found to be important, and by using online surveys it was possible to gain new insights into student experiences that could then be used to adapt teaching methods to cater to diverse learning preferences.

Case Study 5.3 explored the utilization of point-of-view videos to support teaching as they can provide students with immersive learning experiences and are particularly helpful when creating different perspectives of the same scenario from which students can observe, learn and reflect. Case Study 5.4 discussed delivering instructional training through short, episodic videos that enhanced user engagement and so allowed for a more personalized learning experience to be created. Analytical data on usage provided valuable insights for optimizing subsequent content, and delivery methods, as part of the continuous improvement process.

Case Study 5.5 reported on the development of a digital pedagogies framework that was used to enhance education quality and encourage the application of more consistent pedagogical strategies. Evaluating the framework's impact upon student engagement, attainment and satisfaction provided valuable insights that could be incorporated into future refinements. The case studies in Chapter 5 provide a clear emphasis on the importance of strategic planning, continuous improvement and stakeholder collaboration, when enhancing teaching and learning experiences in Higher Education through the integration of digital tools and pedagogies.

The five case studies in Chapter 6 have provided us with a useful understanding of how applications of technology can be used to support the student learning experience, and particularly regarding the integration of technology into educational settings. Case Study 6.1 illustrated the importance of using technology to enhance the support offered to students. By adopting a pre-live-post approach, and creating short screencasts, it was possible to improve student understanding of course materials, thereby reducing student anxiety, and enhancing the overall learning experience. Case Study 6.2 highlighted the importance of adapting pedagogical approaches. The example discussed related to LEGO® Serious Play® which was used to address the evolving needs of students. This technique supported creativity and collaboration and so helped make complex topics more accessible and enjoyable for students.

Case Study 6.3 underscored the significance of using online spaces effectively. Examples included the use of WhatsApp groups and Microsoft Teams to foster a sense of community among students. Such a sense of community was especially important during times of crisis, and these platforms provided opportunities for students to engage, collaborate and learn together within a positive, and supportive, environment. Case Study 6.4 emphasized the benefits of using technology to enhance learning outcomes. In this example, a safe and inclusive environment was created for students that enabled them to design and test their ideas. This approach fostered skills development and confidence building and promoted enjoyment in learning.

Case Study 6.5 demonstrated the importance of developing digital literacy skills alongside the integration of technology into education. Educators need to address challenges relating to digital skills gaps, but by doing so it is possible to create an online learning space for students that encourages their engagement. Across all the case studies presented in Chapter 6, the use of technologies has facilitated learning and helped students to develop key skills that are essential for success in the modern workplace, and which therefore will positively impact upon their future employability.

The Future

We cannot be certain how technology will be used across Higher Education in the future, but we can expect that any applications will be transformative in nature. While virtual learning may become more common, the current use of online learning platforms is likely to continue, with their functionality expanded so that they can offer higher levels of interaction, supported by more multimedia content. It is also reasonable to expect there to be greater provision for online group work, peer-to-peer communication and immersive activities.

The opportunity to use adaptive technologies to personalize learning experiences will become increasingly important as educators try to accommodate a wider variety of learning needs. Alongside this, it is likely that learning will become more mobile, and less structured, in terms of fixed timetabled requirements. Students will expect to be able to access more content, and to participate in a wider range of learning activities, at any time, and from any place. However, developments along these lines will also raise ethical issues relating to data privacy, and ironically, some technology applications intended to improve inclusivity may introduce new barriers for those on low incomes, and with restricted digital access. Furthermore, decision-making regarding entry into Higher Education, lessons taught, feedback provided and grades awarded may become more automated and data-driven over time, which will remove an important element of humanity from the process.

Technology already plays a significant role in supporting our provision of Higher Education, but in the future, it may be that technology becomes more and more essential, and there will be a temptation to respond to financial pressures by minimizing human intervention in student learning as a result. As we look to the future, we need to also keep an eye on the past and remember what we mean by 'a good education'. While technology can help us to accomplish this, we need to continue to inspire the learners of tomorrow to think critically, and perhaps we need to examine anew what it means to be a graduate in this modern era to ensure that we are providing students with the necessary tools.

Notes on Contributors

Dr Inma Alvarez is the Director of Postgraduate Research Studies at the Open University, UK. She is a Senior Fellow of the Higher Education Academy. She has over 30 years' experience teaching at Higher Education institutions in the USA, UK and Spain. She was previously Program Leader for the Doctorate in Education. Her current research interests include intercultural competence in language education, intercultural communication and technology-enhanced education. She is also interested in performing arts research, specifically in how these arts are documented and disseminated.

Dr Barry Avery is an Associate Professor and the Director of Learning and Teaching at Kingston Business School, Kingston University, UK. He is Senior Fellow of the Higher Education Academy. He teaches Information Technology to both undergraduate and postgraduate students. His research interests focus on the effective use of technology in education, particularly the way that assessment is used in peer-based learning communities.

Rachel Bancroft is Head of the Learning and Teaching Support Unit (LTSU) in the School of Arts and Humanities at Nottingham Trent University. She is Senior Fellow of the Higher Education Academy. She leads a multidisciplinary team of digital learning experts who give specialist advice and support for staff and promote effective practice for learning and teaching with technology. She has worked with learning technology in Higher Education for nearly 20 years.

Dr Anthony Basiel is a Lecturer in Computing Science at Solent University, UK, where he teaches User Experience and Interface Design. He is an Adobe

Certified Associate in Web Communications and Learning Technology. He has been researching and developing blended learning solutions for over a decade. Examples of his research projects are published on his website (abasiel.uk). Recently, he was the keynote speaker at the international education conference in Pakistan, ICE'23. His work on telepistemology has synthesized immersive 360^0 online seminar design with augmented reality.

Dr Lucinda Becker is the Professor of Pedagogy in the Department of English Literature and the Director of the School of Languages Foundation Year at the University of Reading, UK. She is Senior Fellow of the Higher Education Academy and has been awarded the Advance HE National Teaching Fellowship and the University of Reading Teaching Fellowship. She has a keen interest in Technology-Enhanced Learning and has been involved in several university-wide projects to develop this area of student learning. She is also a professional trainer and consultant in writing and communication skills.

Dr Liz Berragan is an Associate Professor of Health and Social Care Education at the University of Gloucestershire, UK. She is a Senior Fellow of the Higher Education Academy and has been awarded the Advance HE National Teaching Fellowship. She was awarded the esteemed Sigma European Recognition of Nursing Excellence in Education for her work and expertise focusing on simulation-based education. Her sustained positive influence and impact upon international nursing and healthcare research and education is widely recognized and celebrated. Working with students and colleagues, she transforms passive teaching approaches into authentic work-integrated learning. She is a registered nurse and academic whose career experience includes critical care nursing, military nursing and healthcare education spanning the NHS (National Health Service), MOD (Ministry of Defense), independent and voluntary healthcare sectors and Higher Education in the UK and overseas.

Dr John Blesswin A. is an Associate Professor in the Directorate of Learning and Development, SRM Institute of Science and Technology, Kattankulathur, India. He is a member of several academic committees and has contributed to academic standards at all university levels. He is the co-creator of the Technology-Enabled Laboratory (TEL) tool, which has been implemented across multiple courses and campuses. His expertise lies in the integration of technology into pedagogy, aiming to create dynamic and interactive learning environments. He is actively involved in research projects that focus on educational innovation, particularly in computer science and engineering.

Louise Bryant is the Doctoral College Administration Manager at Bournemouth University, UK. She is responsible for the leadership and management of the Doctoral College Postgraduate Research Administrators. Her role is particularly focused on strengthening consistency in administration, monitoring and progression data. She took a lead role in the development and implementation of ProGRess, the university's online postgraduate research administration and monitoring system. She has previously worked as a postgraduate research administrator in the Faculty of Health and Social Sciences and in Organizational Development at Bournemouth University, UK.

Dr Carina Buckley is the Instructional Design Manager at Solent University, UK. She is a Principal Fellow of the Higher Education Academy and co-host of the monthly Learning Development Project podcast. She is responsible for the development and implementation of the Solent University Learning Design Framework, which integrates the classroom and the Virtual Learning Environment into a student-centered, active and inclusive learning space. Her research interests encompass the role of collaboration and networks in building and maintaining community, with an emphasis on the value of writing for publication in building an academic field. She also explores ideas around leadership and professional identity in Learning Development.

Dr Helen Caldwell is an Associate Professor of Education at the University of Northampton, UK. She specializes in educational technology, teacher education and online learning. Her role involves leading postgraduate teacher education programs, including the MA Education. She has been the research lead on nine funded projects, the most recent of which are two three-year Erasmus+ projects on the theme of Digital Learning across Boundaries. She co-leads the Centre for Active Digital Education, and her research interests include technology-enabled learning, social innovation education and the use of immersive technologies for teaching and learning.

Rachel Challen is the Interim Head of Learning, Teaching and Student Experience in the School of Arts and Humanities at Nottingham Trent University, an Associate Professor in Educational Development and a Principal Fellow of the Higher Education Academy. Rachel brings over 20 years' experience of supporting colleagues in using technology in learning and teaching.

Shannon Delport is a Senior Lecturer at Central Queensland University, Australia, and Head of Emergency and Disaster Management Programs. She is Fellow of the Higher Education Academy. She has worked in emergency services for more than 20 years, serving in various roles related to health, emergency response and disaster management. She has a decade of experience as an academic and is committed to advancing emergency and disaster management and public health studies.

Dr Carol Azumah Dennis is a Senior Lecturer in Education, Leadership and Management, and the PRAXIS Director, at the Open University, UK. She is Senior Fellow of the Higher Education Academy. She was previously Program Leader for the Doctor in Education, program leader for Post-16 Teacher Education and Program Director for Postgraduate Taught provision. Her research interests center around post-16 policy, professionalism, and practice; leading and managing quality in vocational education; and teacher education, critical pedagogy, ethics and social justice.

Dr Angeline Dharmaraj-Savicks is a Senior Lecturer in Education Studies at the University of Portsmouth, UK. She is a Fellow of the Higher Education Academy. Her research focuses on education policy implementation and policy response to leverage social justice in marginalized communities in India. She holds a master's degree in education leadership and management and a doctorate from the University of Southampton, UK. Prior to this, she was running a school in the south of India catering to marginalized communities.

Amy L. Evans is a Teaching Fellow and Specialist Technician in Environmental Science at the University of Salford, UK. She is a Fellow of the Higher Education Academy. She is an experienced Geography and Biological Science Technician and Academic. She has a postgraduate certificate focused on environmental management from the Open University, UK. She also has a degree in Zoology and Conservation from the University of Wales, Bangor, UK. Technology and practical skills teaching have been a focus in Amy's academic career and fundamental to her approach in supervising students' practical projects.

Scott Farrow is the Head of Digital Learning at Edge Hill University, UK, where he provides strategic leadership on digital learning technologies for learning and teaching. He is a Senior Fellow of the Higher Education Academy. He is driven by a commitment to enhancing students' learning experiences, widening access and enabling access and inclusivity. He is a member of the Heads of eLearning Forum Steering Group and leads the Association for Learning Technology Northwest England Members Group.

Graham French is a Senior Lecturer in Education at Bangor University, UK. He is an accredited practitioner of the Institute of Outdoor Learning (IOL). He is the Chair of the IOL Cymru regional committee, chairs the North Wales region and sits on the national executive of the Association of Heads of Outdoor Education. His areas of expertise include adventure education and outdoor learning. His research interests include pedagogical models for physical education, adventurous activity education, equity in education utilizing outdoor learning to develop social capital and the impact and use of digital technologies and networked spaces in outdoor learning. He has previously directed the Postgraduate Certificate in Education (PGCE) program at Bangor University.

Tim Galling is the Technology Enhanced Learning Development Manager at Bournemouth University, UK. He currently specializes in the administration of Virtual Learning Environment, systems integration and learning analytics. Having initially studied web design and web application development, he found his way to learning technologies and has accumulated 18 years of experience in this field.

Dr Lynn Gribble is an Associate Professor, and an Education Focused Academic, in the School of Management and Governance at University of New South Wales – UNSW Sydney, Australia. She is an awarded educator recognized at the university, national and international levels. She has used her keen interest in transformative learning through engagement, belonging and personalization of each student's learning experience. She has extensively considered how to develop authentic assessment and has worked on university-wide feedback projects to enhance the student experience. She uses technology to connect with her students and personalize their experience. Her work on teaching innovation dissemination through 'The 4Cs (Classroom, Corridor, Campus, and Community) Practice Strategy' has been adopted and adapted both locally and globally.

Mary Joy Guevarra is a Learning Technology Specialist at Baringa Partners LLP and is a Certified Digital Learning Designer. In her current role, she plays a pivotal role in shaping the future of learning. Owning the overall Learner Experience of Baringa's internal Learning Management System, she leads the development, building and testing of core features and functionality. She brings her passion for learning and development, and technical expertise, to key projects and initiatives. She is currently exploring emerging technologies including AI and other tools, to create world-class learner experiences. Before joining Baringa, she spent four years in Higher

Education, including being an Assistant Technology-Enhanced Learning Developer and a Learning Technologist at Bournemouth University, UK.

Dr Andrina Halder is a Senior Lecturer at Guildhall Business School, London Metropolitan University, UK. She is a Senior Fellow of the Higher Education Academy. She has a background in Digital Marketing and Digital Business Transformation. She has an extensive leadership and teaching portfolio and supervises students for business consultancy projects and dissertation projects within Digital Marketing, Digital Business Transformation, Artificial Intelligence (AI), Customer Relations, and International Business Management disciplines. She designed and led a consultancy module in collaboration with the Riipen platform and is the lead academic supervisor for students who were working on industry projects through Riipen.

Mark Hancock is the Assistant Director of Digital Education at the University of Birmingham, UK. He is Senior Fellow of the Higher Education Academy. He has a wide portfolio of institutional digital education projects aimed at enhancing the student experience. He is responsible for academic engagement and the use of institutional digital education tools, and the pedagogic practice of those tools within teaching and assessment across the university. His role focuses on supporting the university's teaching framework expectations within the ecosystem of digital tools for education. He has led both college- and institutional-level projects in digital education and has a keen interest in scaling the ambition of digital assessment transformation within the Higher Education sector.

Dr Karen Heard-Lauréote is a Professor of Learning and Teaching and an Independent Consultant in the enhancement of educational practices. She is a Principal Fellow of the Higher Education Academy and has been awarded an Advance HE National Teaching Fellow of the Higher Education Academy. She is a widely published expert in teaching and supporting learning in HE and has over 15 years of experience as an academic in the UK and international Higher Education. She has held roles at the executive leadership team level focusing especially on organizational and cultural change projects.

Scott Hedger is a Learning Technologist in the Faculty of Science and Technology at Bournemouth University, UK. He is a Certified eLearning Instructional Designer. He is an experienced Technology Enhanced Learning (TEL) Developer. His role as a Learning Technologist is to bridge the gap between educators and technology to enhance the students' learning experiences. He excels at implementing innovative TEL tools, learning management systems and multimedia resources for dynamic and inclusive learning environments. He role models a strong dedication to continuous learning, and he is committed to sharing knowledge with the education community.

Dr Holly Henderson is a Senior Lecturer in Education Excellence at Bournemouth University, UK. She is a Principal Fellow of the Higher Education Academy and has been awarded the Advance HE National Teaching Fellowship. She is the Academic Lead for TeachBU pathway for staff to gain Advance HE Fellowship in all categories up to Senior Fellow. She is also part of the team that teaches the Postgraduate Certificate in Education Practice. She has experience in engagement, quality assurance and project management in various roles, including Research and Knowledge Exchange Development Framework Advisor, Education Incubator Research Fellow and Operations Manager for the London 2012 Olympic and Paralympic Games in Weymouth and Portland.

Dr Mike Howarth is an Education Technology Consultant who applies proven radio and video production methods to education and communication on a small screen. He has a Postgraduate Certificate in Higher Education. Mike worked for 20 years as a BBC Education producer to enhance eLearning engagement. His work draws on ten years of research experience as a dissertation tutor at Middlesex University, nine years as a video learning consultant at University College London and recently at the University of Hertfordshire Business School, UK.

David Hunt is a retired Learning Technologist from Bournemouth University, UK. He is Fellow of the Higher Education Academy and a Certified Practitioner member of the Association for Learning Technology (CMALT). He has a Postgraduate Certificate in Education Practice. He started working in Higher Education 2006 as an Information Learning Technology Staff Trainer, and Moodle Trainer, at Colchester Institute, UK. In 2012 he moved to Bournemouth University as a Learning Technologist for the Faculty of Media and Communication. After this he supported the Faculty of Health and Social Sciences. He has a keen interest in emerging technologies and has been involved in various projects to implement them within the educational environment.

Dr Simon M. Hutchinson is an Associate Professor/Reader in Environmental Science at the University of Salford, UK. He has held a range of roles delivering and supporting teaching and learning. He is a Senior Fellow of the Higher Education Academy. Field-based Active Learning strategies have been a particular focus throughout his academic career, which has embraced the use of Digital Visualization Tools to enhance accessibility and promote Equality, Diversity and Inclusivity (EDI) in environmental education.

Professor Dawne Irving-Bell leads on Scholarship at BPP University, UK. She is Principal Fellow of the Higher Education Academy and has been awarded the Advance HE National Teaching Fellowship. She holds a Collaborative Award for Teaching Excellence and a National Award for her outstanding contribution to teacher education. She established The National Teaching Repository, an Open Education Resource with proven reach and impact across the global Higher Education community. She is the editor-in-chief of *The Journal of Social Media for Learning* and is committed to raising the profile of the Scholarship of Teaching and Learning.

Rhys Coetmor Jones is the Director of Initial Teacher Education at Liverpool Hope University, UK. He formerly worked at Bangor University as a Physical Education subject specialist and director of the Postgraduate Certificate in Education program. His research interests include developing schools as learning organizations and the mentoring process in initial teacher education. Prior to teaching in Higher Education, he taught Physical Education in secondary schools in Wales, the USA and Australia.

Dr Helen Keen-Dyer is an Associate Professor in Emergency and Disaster Management at Central Queensland University, Australia. She is a Senior Fellow of the Higher Education Academy. She joined Higher Education with two decades of experience in emergency and disaster management operations. She is particularly interested in the preparedness (through a learning lens) of individuals, communities, emergency, and disaster management workers and volunteers for our increasingly complex world.

Dr Anne Kellock is Associate Head in the Sheffield Institute of Education at Sheffield Hallam University, UK. She is a Senior Fellow of the Higher Education Academy. She has 15 years of experience in learning, teaching and assessment in Higher Education. Currently, she teaches on the Postgraduate Diploma in Academic Practice focusing on contemporary issues in Higher Education. She leads a Special Interest Group on Creative and Innovative Research Methods. Her publications and research focus on children's perspectives on well-being in the primary school setting through visual and creative methods (in England and New Zealand), children's spaces and innovative approaches to teaching through Covid, among others. Her current research interests include postgraduate student experience, the use of technology to enhance learning and parental involvement in nursery settings.

Simon Kersey is the Practice Skills and Simulation Lead for the School of Health and Social Care at the University of Gloucestershire, UK. He previously worked as a senior lecturer in paramedic science at the University of the West of England (UWE), UK. He has spent the last 22 years involved in pre-hospital care, working across a wide variety of settings including the UWE Bristol Nightingale hospital project team, out-of-hours urgent care, Southwestern Ambulance Service Learning and Development project and as a Critical Care Paramedic for both Great Western and Midlands Air Ambulance. His current interests include simulation-based education, trauma studies, major incident response and patient blood management.

Dr Caitlin Kight is a Lecturer in Education Studies in the School of Education at the University of Exeter, UK. She is a Senior Fellow of the Higher Education Academy. She specializes in creative pedagogies, self-study and the intersection of social justice and education. Originally an ecologist studying avian bioacoustics, she maintains an interest in communication and science outreach. She is a fellow of the Dakshin Foundation and an editor and writer for the nonprofit educational magazines *Current Conservation* and *CC Kids*. She is the author of the natural history book entitled *Flamingo* (published by Reaktion books). Due to her interest in pedagogies of care and liberation, her research engages with the themes of social justice, sustainability and pastoral care.

Dr Fiona Knight is the Head of the Doctoral College (STEM) at Bournemouth University, UK. She is Senior Fellow of the Higher Education Academy. She has a Doctorate in Geochemistry and Mineralogy from Cardiff University, UK. In her current role she is responsible for the university's portfolio of postgraduate research degrees relating to science, technology and engineering related faculties. She has also served as the university's Head of Research and Knowledge Exchange Office. Prior to joining Bournemouth University, she was a Thematic Programme Manager at the Natural Environment Research Council (NERC). Her current research interests include postgraduate student mental health, research supervision and her lifelong interest in geology.

Dr Rebecca Lees is an Associate Professor and the Head of the Department for Accounting, Finance and Informatics at Kingston University, UK. She is

Senior Fellow of the Higher Education Academy. She undertakes research within the Higher Education environment with a focus on formative assessment practices and initiatives to develop students' employability skills and behaviors.

Dr Linda Lefièvre is an Associate Professor, and the Deputy Director of Education for Digital and Distance Learning, as well as Continuous Professional Development lead for the College of Medical and Dental Science at the University of Birmingham, UK. She is Senior Fellow of the Higher Education Academy. Her current roles include supporting colleagues with innovative and blended approaches to teaching and learning, as well as developing the portfolio of distance learning and short courses. She has extensive experience in digital assessment, having led initiatives that piloted and evaluated various online assessment platforms. She has been a Higher Education educator since 2010 and has a diverse teaching portfolio with a focus on human physiology teaching across different programs.

Dr Julie A. Lessiter is the Vice President of Texas State University (Round Rock) and was the former Vice President of Strategic Initiatives at Louisiana State University (Shreveport). She has a globally recognized Project Management Professional (PMP) Certificate. She is passionate about engaging students in immersive learning by integrating various technologies into classroom pedagogy. She is an advocate for learning-by-doing and encourages students to take knowledge and apply it to problem-solving across various technologies.

Allard Lummen is a Technology Enhanced Learning Developer at Bournemouth University, UK. His role is to maintain and update various online systems, such as the virtual learning environment Brightspace, video platforms like Panopto and Zoom and the ePortfolio platform Mahara. His primary focus centers on enhancing the delivery of video guidance for teaching staff and students. With a deep commitment to innovation, he continuously seeks innovative solutions to elevate the educational experience in the evolving digital landscape to make education more engaging and accessible for all stakeholders.

Raluca Marinciu is a Teaching Fellow of the Higher Education Academy at the University of Greenwich, UK, with a focus on employability, equal opportunities and AI in education. Originally from Sibiu, Romania, she advanced from a graduate role to Head of Employer Engagement at the university, managing key employer relationships and leading knowledge exchange projects. With a decade of experience, she is also pursuing a PhD and was recently shortlisted for the Unsung Hero of the Year award. Her research interests include student employability and the socio-economic landscape of employment opportunities.

Mike Marriott is a Senior Lecturer and Program Leader for Computer Science, and Computer Science with AI, degrees at Sheffield Hallam University, UK. He is a Senior Fellow of the Higher Education Academy. He has 20 years of professional experience in the IT industry. He ensures that the content and experience students receive enable them to apply their learning and adapt behaviors to match those required by businesses. He promotes employability and social mobility for all students by facilitating networks with businesses to ensure the curriculum remains relevant. He has previously managed teams of highly skilled technical experts in the IT industry and is now helping future IT professionals gain the skills and experience necessary to succeed in the industry.

Dr Selva Mary G. is an Assistant Professor in the Directorate of Learning and Development, SRM Institute of Science and Technology, Kattankulathur, India. She is an Advance HE Associate Fellow. She has been instrumental in redefining the pedagogical approaches within her institution, particularly in courses focused on programming and problem-solving. She co-developed the Technology-Enabled Laboratory (TEL) tool that aims to enhance learning experiences in practical computing courses. Her research interests include educational technology, curriculum development and student engagement. She has been involved in several initiatives aimed at fostering self-directed and reflective learning among students.

Sonya McChristie is the Learning Design Manager at the Centre for Enhancement of Learning and Teaching (CELT), University of Sunderland, UK. She is Senior Fellow of the Higher Education Academy. She has been working in Higher Education since 2008. Currently she is responsible for leading a team of learning designers who work with academics to produce high-quality, pedagogically sound learning materials. She is also the module leader for 'Designing Learning and Assessment in Higher Education' which is part of the Postgraduate Certificate in Higher Education at University of Sunderland.

David Meechan is a Senior Lecturer in Education at the University of Northampton, UK. He is a qualified Primary School Teacher and has international experience of learning development with not-for-profit organizations (NGOs). He has an MA in Early Years, an MA in International Development and a Postgraduate Certificate in Digital Leadership. He is an advocate of using technology to improve teaching and learning. His research interests relate to the use of technology and specifically exploring how AI is impacting education.

Dr Uma Patel is a Visiting Fellow at Bournemouth University and a co-principal investigator for the 'Contactless Transaction Literacy' project funded by the British Academy. She is a Senior Fellow of the Higher Education Academy and Honorary Research Fellow in Science and Technology Studies at University College London. She was the Program Leader for the Postgraduate Certificate in Education Practice at Bournemouth University. She has led and contributed to many educational research projects. Her work is informed by socio-material discourse analysis, digital identities and AI-enriched learning.

Rosemary Pearce is the Learning Development Manager in the Learning and Teaching Support Unit (LTSU) in the School of Arts and Humanities at Nottingham Trent University. She is Fellow of the Higher Education Academy. She has worked in a variety of roles in Higher Education for over a decade, including both teaching and professional services, and completed an Arts and Humanities PhD at the University of Nottingham.

Dr Martyn Polkinghorne is an Associate Professor of Business and Management at Bournemouth University, UK. He is a Principal Fellow of the Higher Education Academy and a UK Council for Graduate Education (UKCGE) Recognized Research Supervisor. He held a range of roles supporting teaching and learning for over 30 years, including Head of Innovation and Start-up Programs at the University of Plymouth, and Knowledge Transfer Programs Centre Manager, and Head of Education for Business and Management Programs, at Bournemouth University. His current research interests include small business management and the supervision of postgraduate research students.

Kelly Louise Preece is the Head of Educator Development at the University of Exeter, UK. She is Senior Fellow of the Higher Education Academy and has been awarded the Advance HE National Teaching Fellowship. During her 15-year career in Higher Education she has held roles as an academic, researcher and researcher developer. From 2015 to 2022 she led the Researcher Development Program for Postgraduate Researchers at the University of Exeter, UK. She adopted a holistic and inclusive approach to Researcher Development, designing training programs and learning inventions that support the researcher as a person.

Stephen Pyne is a Learning Technologist at the Anglo European Chiropractic University College, UK. He is Fellow of the Higher Education Academy, and a Certified Practitioner member of the Association for Learning Technology (CMALT). He has a Postgraduate Certificate in Education Practice. Stephen has over 10 years' experience in Technology-Enhanced Learning. He previously worked at Bournemouth University supporting faculty staff and students in adopting emerging educational technologies. He specializes in virtual worlds and immersive realities and has worked on various educational technology implementation projects to develop virtual reality simulations and immersive worlds in healthcare education.

Dr Sterling Rauseo is a Senior Lecturer in Strategy, Human Resource Management, and Organisational Behaviour, and a programme leader in the Greenwich Business School at the University of Greenwich. He is Fellow of the Higher Education Academy. Before pursuing an academic career, he held senior managerial roles in administration and finance. He is the Director of the Management Inquiry Group under the Centre for Research in Employment and Work (CREW), and a member of the governing board of CREW at the University of Greenwich. His most recent research areas are race and work, BAME (Black, Asian, and Minority Ethnic) graduate employability and career boundary theory, particularly underemployment among BAME university graduates. He was born and grew up in Trinidad and Tobago and has conducted research there and in the UK. His research has been funded by the British Academy, the University of Greenwich Development Fund and Centre for Research Employment and Work. His other research interests include the individual and organizational impacts of decision-making under high uncertainty, including institutional and organizational narratives to address the uncertainty.

Dr Uwe Matthias Richter is an Associate Professor for Digital Pedagogic Innovation at Anglia Ruskin University (ARU), UK. He is Senior Fellow of the Higher Education Academy. He first started working in education teaching German and cultural studies in America. He then taught adult education in Germany and the University of Limerick, Ireland, before joining ARU in 1993. In 2001, he joined ARU's Centre for Learning and Teaching as the lead on technology enhancement, online and distance learning. More recently, he has refocused his career on pedagogical research. He has taught undergraduate and postgraduate students in web design, computer tools, education and more recently a program on urban identity.

Dr Tom Ritchie is an Associate Professor/Reader and the Director of Student Experience (Chemistry) at the University of Warwick, UK. He is Senior Fellow of the Higher Education Academy. He studied at the Centre for the History of Science on a Collaborative Doctoral Partnership between the UK-based University of Kent and the Science Museum in London. He is an educator, a student experience consultant and an executive coach. He convenes multiple innovation and Education for Sustainable Development research modules in Chemistry and is developing a new module that examines the historical, ethical and cultural implications of AI in society. Alongside his teaching, he pursues a transdisciplinary approach to the student experience through his 'We are Chemistry' program, applying inclusive co-design principles to create a more holistic and student-centered educational ecosystem in Chemistry.

Dr Vivian Romero is a Senior Lecturer in Public Health at the University of Melbourne, Australia. She is a Fellow of the Higher Education Academy. She is the Deputy Chair of the Council of Academic Public Health Institutions Australasia Early Career Academics Committee. In her various roles and activities, she has focused upon helping students and practitioners create meaningful change by teaching and implementing action research methodologies.

Dr Gelareh Roushan is Professor of Digital Transformations and the Head of the Centre for Fusion Learning Innovation and Excellence at Bournemouth University, UK. She leads institutional projects in education enhancement and innovative pedagogies for Higher Education. She is Principal Fellow of the Higher Education Academy and a UKCGE Recognized Research Supervisor. She has led the successful achievement of AACSB (Association to Advance Collegiate Schools of Business) accreditation in her previous role in the Business School. She recently led the successful achievement of the bronze award in the Race Equality Charter. She has served on the Board of the UK Academy of Information Systems and serves as a mentor for AACSB International. Her current research interests include student learning and the use of technology-enhanced teaching methods, using digital transformation to develop staff capabilities and enhance the student experience.

Dr Daniel Russell is an Associate Professor at Kingston Business School, UK. He is a Senior Fellow of the Higher Education Academy. He holds a Doctorate in Computer Science from the University of Kent at Canterbury, UK. He has over 25 years of teaching experience with a particular interest in the mutual dependency of mathematics and information systems, and assessment approaches that foster learning.

Dr Claire Stocks is the Head of Academic Practice and Development, at the University of Chester, UK. She was previously Associate Professor of Educational Practice in the Learning and teaching Team at BPP University, where she was also the program leader for the Postgraduate Certificate in Learning and Teaching. She is a Senior Fellow of the Higher Education Academy. She has a Doctorate in the field of American Literature. She has been an academic developer for 19 years and has worked in several UK universities. Her research interests include supporting professionals who move into Higher Education and the broader development of novice academics.

Dr Helen Clare Taylor is a Professor of English and the Provost and Vice Chancellor for Academic Affairs at Louisiana State University (LSU) (Shreveport), USA. She has a PhD in medieval literature. She is a Board Member of Louisianna State Exhibit Museum. She has held various leadership roles at LSU Shreveport and now serves as its Chief Academic Officer. Her teaching focuses upon English and liberal arts, and her current research interests include devotional literature by, and for, medieval women.

Dr Julia Taylor is the Head of the Doctoral College at Bournemouth University, UK. She is Senior Fellow of the Higher Education Academy. She has a Doctorate in Media History. In her current role, she is responsible for the university's portfolio of postgraduate research degrees. She was previously Research and Enterprise Operations Manager for the university following an earlier career as a commissioning editor in the electronic publishing sector. Her current research interests include the early years of the BBC, broadcasting magazines, postgraduate student mental health and the development of effective postgraduate research supervision.

Dr Janis Wardrop is an Associate Professor and the Director of Education at the Centre for Social Impact at the University of New South Wales, Australia. She is Senior Fellow of the Higher Education Academy and a winner of the Vice Chancellor's Award for Teaching Excellence. She is a leading educator in the School of Management and Governance. She specializes in developing students' learning capabilities to meet the challenges of the 21st-century workplace through innovative curriculum and course design. Her passion is to support others in their development. Her work on transforming the student experience in large core courses is widely noted, as is her development of other academics as a 'guide on the side'.

Dr Philippa Waterhouse is a Senior Lecturer in Health at the Open University, UK. She is Senior Fellow of the Higher Education Academy and a UKCGE Recognized Research Supervisor. Her PhD considered Social Statistics and Demography. Her current research interests center on the individual's occupancy of multiple roles, and specifically considers the work-family study interface with a focus on student well-being, and the work-family balance of women in sub-Saharan Africa.

Tracey Webb is the Learning Technology Team Manager at Bournemouth University, UK. She is Fellow of the Higher Education Academy and a Certified Practitioner member of the Association for Learning Technology (CMALT). She has over 30 years of experience working within the education sector including in Higher Education, learning development and the charity sectors. She has worked with several different virtual learning environments and contributed to the production of an institutional 'Digital Pedagogies' framework to support the adoption of technology-enhanced learning tools, environments and pedagogies.

Dr Emma Whewell is an Associate Professor in Learning and Teaching at the University of Northampton, UK, where she co-leads the Centre for Active Digital Education. She is a member of the Primary Physical Education European Network Group and the All-Party Parliamentary Group on a Fit and Healthy Childhood. She joined the University of Northampton in 2006 as part of the Initial Teacher Training team. She is the Program Leader of the Sports Development and Physical Education degree and has an MA in Education and a Doctorate for her research on the formation of identity in newly qualified teachers. She is an experienced teacher educator whose research focuses upon teacher identity, mentoring and digital pedagogies.

David Wooff is Professor of Educational Practice, and the Director of Apprenticeship Quality and Regulation for BPP University and the wider BPP Education Group. He is Senior Fellow of the Higher Education Academy, Fellow of the Chartered College of Teaching, Fellow of the Society of Education and Training and Fellow of the Royal Society of Arts, and also a Trustee and Director of the Frank Field Education Trust. He has published widely in technology education and teacher training. His current interests include the Scholarship of Teaching and Learning, the impact and benefit of apprenticeships and work-based learning.

Glossary of Terms

- ADE – Active Digital Education;
- AI – Artificial Intelligence;
- AMME – Aggregate Measure of Module Engagement;
- AR – Augmented Reality;
- AY – Academic Year;
- BSEF – Bioecological Student Engagement Framework;
- BU – Bournemouth University;
- CDIO – Conceive Design Implement Operate;
- CHAT – Cultural Historical Activity Theory;
- CL – Collaborative Learning;
- COVID-19 – COronaVIrus Disease of 2019;
- CQ – Central Queensland;
- D&E – Design and Engineering;
- DL – Directed Learning;
- DPF – Digital Pedagogies Framework;
- DVT – Digital Visualization Tool;
- E&DM – Emergency and Disaster Management;
- EAL – English as an Additional Language;
- EDI – Equality, Diversity and Inclusivity;
- ES3 – Earth Sciences, Environmental Sciences and Environmental Studies;
- FGD – Focus Group Discussions;
- GEM – Geography and Environmental Management;
- GenAI – Generative Artificial Intelligence;

- GL – Guided Learning;
- HE – Higher Education;
- JISC – Joint Information Systems Committee;
- LAI – Learning Analytics Insights;
- LDF – Learning Design Framework;
- LMS – Learning Management System;
- LOTF – Linear-on-the-Fly;
- LSP – LEGO® Serious Play®;
- LSUS – Louisiana State University in Shreveport;
- LTI – Learning Technology Integration;
- LV – Live Facilitator;
- MCQ – Multiple-Choice Questions;
- NGS – Next-Generation Sequencing;
- NSS – National Student Survey;
- PD – Professional Doctoral;
- PGCLT – Postgraduate Certificate in Learning and Teaching;
- PGR – Postgraduate Researcher;
- PLD – Personalized Learning Designer;
- POV – Point of View;
- PSRB – Professional, Statutory, and Regulatory Bodies;
- PTA – Postgraduate Teaching Assistant;
- QAA – Quality Assurance Agency;
- RDP – Researcher Development Program;
- SLS – Student-Led Seminar;
- SOL – Solent Online Learning;
- SUTE – Student Unit Teaching Evaluation;
- TEF – Technology-Enhanced Feedback;
- TEL – Technology-Enabled Laboratory (Ch. 1);
- TEL – Technology-Enhanced Learning (Ch. 5);
- UDL – Universal Design for Learning;
- UK – United Kingdom;
- UKAT – UK Advising and Tutoring;
- UKRI – UK Research and Innovation;
- UNESCO – United Nations Educational, Scientific and Cultural Organization;
- UNSDG – United Nations Sustainable Development Goals;
- UoS – University of Salford;
- UPLC-MS – Ultra Performance Liquid Chromatography-Mass Spectrometer;
- VFT – Virtual Field Trips;

- VLE – Virtual Learning Environment;
- VR – Virtual Reality;
- VR-HMD – Virtual Reality-Head-Mounted Display;
- WP – Widening Participation;
- XR – Extended Reality.

Index

ABC toolkit 111
academic: integrity 22, 136, 137, 159, 160; literacies 136; misconduct 150; writing 137
academic writing of students 114–120; *see also* Studiosity
Action and Participation Plan 115, 117
Active Digital Education (ADE) 52, 53, 56, 57
active learning 64, 110
activity-based learning 22
adaptive technologies 230
Adobe Acrobat 71
Adobe Connect 70, 71, 206, 207, 217
Advance HEs Professional Standards Framework 77
adventure education (AE) postgraduate initial teacher education (ITE) program 172; *see also* Point-of-View (POV) cameras
Advertising Management program 29
aerial photography 14
aggregate measure of module engagement (AMME) 111–114; activity based on 112–113; classifying students' engagement level 111–112, 114
agile approach 127, 149
AI-generated Avatars 103, 105–109

Anchor.fm 219
andragogical approaches 172
Anglia Ruskin University (ARU) 215, 216, 220
anticompetitive behavior 217
anxiety 15, 116, 125, 127, 204, 206, 229
Arduino 211
Artificial Intelligence (AI) 32, 69, 114, 120, 145
Audacity 71
audience response tool 93
Augmented Reality (AR) 20, 40, 44, 219
authentic teaching 69, 72, 74
Autodesk 209, 210, 212
Autodesk Maya 40

Bangor University 172
'Beyond Science' 68
Bioecological Model of Human Development 85
Bioecological Student Engagement Framework (BSEF) 85–87, 91; benefits and impact 89; ecosystem 88–89; exosystem 89; macrosystem 89; mesosystem 88, 90; microsystem 88, 90
Biotechnology Education Laboratory 38
Blackboard Collaborate 54, 217
Blackboard Ultra 196

Black History Month program 200
Blackmagic ATEM 33
blended learning 34, 36, 140, 205, 206
Bournemouth University (BU) 31, 126, 132, 169, 177, 182, 186
BPP University 75, 78
Brightspace 177–179; advantages 180–181; incorporated self-assessment questions into 178; knowledge quizzes in 180, 181; quiz tool 145–147; success of 182; survey and feedback on 180, 181; VLE 145, 177, 182
Business Management program 110

Calendly 67
Canvas 71; LMS 109, 111, 117
Canvas' SpeedGrader 116
care pedagogy 97, 101, 102
ChatGPT 160
Chemistry Department, University of Warwick 64
City University 37
Class Notebook 76, 80, 217
classroom proxemics 33
'clickable' icons 14, 44
climate emergency 13
co-creation 55, 56, 64, 141
Code of Practice for Research Degrees 126, 129
cognitive loads 15, 54, 96, 97, 99, 150
collaborative learning (CL) 8, 54, 56, 80, 135, 140, 142, 144
collective knowledge 56
comma-separated value (CSV) files 110
communities of practice 53
community building 71–74, 93–94
Computing Science User Experience and Interface Design 36
Conceive-Design-Implement-Operate (CDIO) frameworks 22
confidence 24, 26, 33, 46, 54, 56, 57, 60, 65, 79, 87, 90, 97
constructivist approach 29, 56
constructivist epistemology 172
continuous improvement process 167, 171–172

COVID-19 pandemic 13, 14, 28, 32–34, 57, 59, 62–64, 75, 92, 98, 140, 144, 148, 159, 202, 203
CQUniversity Strategic Plan 2024–2028 133
Creative Quadrant building 200
critical thinking 24, 25
Cultural Historical Activity Theory (CHAT) 204–206, 209
cultural norms 57
Cyber Collaboratory 38

data: accessibility 18, 24, 47, 63, 132; analysis 129; governance and approval 163–164; privacy 231
data-driven decisions 167
Data Visualization Lab 38, 40
decolonization 106
Department of Design and Engineering (D&E), Bournemouth University 144
Department of Law, Bournemouth University 144
Department of Media Production 28
Digital Animation: program 38, 40; students 40–42
digital: assessments 86, 162, 163, 165, 166; badges 28, 220; cameras 14; collaboration 57; environment 52, 53, 56, 57; escape room 76–80; laboratory books 76; learning environment 92, 124–133, 182; literacy 32, 87, 90, 141, 142, 144, 164, 182; pedagogy 162; tools 70, 90, 103, 182–184, 202
digitalization 160, 162
Digital Pedagogies Framework (DPF) for student learning experience 182–183; automated reporting 184; benefits of 186; challenge in 184; designing 183; developing 185–186; students' engagement 185; using JISC Online Surveys tool for data collection 184
Digital University 203, 206
digitization 159, 165
directed learning (DL) 140, 142, 144

Directorate of Learning and Development, SRM Institute of Science and Technology 20
disruption 139–140
distance learning 62, 73
DJI Mini 2 drones 14
DNA structure 39
Double Diamond approach 219
double marking 161, 163

Earth Sciences, Environmental Sciences and Environmental Studies (ES3) 12, 13
education: globalization of 1; hybrid 63; inclusive 13, 102; internationalization of 1; online 64, 199; students' perception on 166, 170–171
e-learning techniques 34
'ELE' Moodle platform 69, 70
Emergency and Disaster Management (E&DM) online postgraduate offerings in Central Queensland University (CQUniversity) 133–139; online pedagogical model for 135–139; shift in students' enrollment patterns 134; target people for 134
Emergency Remote Teaching approach 160
emerging technologies 26, 28–32
emoji reactions 94, 208
emotional belonging 105, 108
English as an Additional Language (EAL) 52–57
ePortfolios 76
equality 103, 104
Equality/Equity, Diversity and Inclusivity (EDI) 15, 18, 19, 103, 135
equity 103, 104, 108
Equity Compass Tool 103–109
ethical issues 231
European Commission 217
Exeter Scholar and Summer School programs 200
experiential learning 30, 32, 46, 77, 151, 152, 154; see also Riipen digital learning platform

Extended Reality (XR) 20
eye tracking glasses 29, 30

Facebook 28
face-to-face teaching 34, 95, 99, 102, 110, 150
Faculty of Media and Communication 28, 29
fieldwork: carbon footprint of 13; definition 12; students' participation in 13
15-CATS module 64
film-in-a-film approach see meta-film approach
Focus Group Discussions (FGDs) 206
formative assessments 33, 46, 95, 111, 212, 213
formative learning objects 137
Foucauldian technique 104–107

gamification 77
gamifying teaching 79
GenAI-supported feedback 164, 165
General channel 218–220
Generative Artificial Intelligence (GenAI) 150, 159–162, 165
Geography and Environmental Management (GEM) modules 14
globalization of education 1
Google 28
Google Cardboards 28
Google Classroom 88, 211
Google Drive 217
Google Meet 88
GoPro Hero series 173
'GoPro MAX 360-degree' action cameras 14
green screen technology 180, 182
guided flexible learning pathway pedagogical model 135–137; additional lessons in 138; in Moodle Book 138, 139; students' feedback on 137–138
guided learning (GL) 140–141

Harvard system 77
higher education providers (HEPs) 124, 125

'history of the now,' concept of 105–108

holographic 3D representations 38–42; collaboration with Digital Animation students 40–42; negative impact on students 41, 42; students gaining positive learning 41, 42; to study cell and molecular biology 39–41

Honorlock software 145; benefits of using 148, 150; challenges in 150; integration with Brightspace VLE 145; licensing and pricing model 150; participation in mock exams 147; students' access to online exams 145–146, 149; technical issues in 147–149; technical support for students 148–149; training for admin staff 146; web access restrictions and whitelisting of online publications 146

hot spots 43, 44, 48

Human Research Ethics Committee 206

hybrid education 63

hybrid teaching 32, 34

identity 105–108

immersive learning 39, 40, 42, 43, 90, 139

immersive teaching 33

immersive technology 41, 43; for health and social care education 43, 44

in-class discussion 27, 45, 95, 110, 114

inclusive co-design 68

inclusive education 13, 102

inclusiveness 62

inclusivity 15, 62, 103, 179

individual learning 24, 96

inequalities 103

informal learning 71

information technology (IT) 127–131

Innovation 101 64, 65, 68

in-person teaching 160, 170

Insight app 217

Insta 360 Pro AR camera 36, 37

instructional video guides 178–182

intellectual property rights 144

Intelligent Agents 29

interactive digital artifacts 30

interactive experiential learning 30

interdisciplinary collaboration 46

internationalization of education 1

Java 23

Joint Information Systems Committee (Jisc) Online Surveys tool 167–169, 171, 184; data collection and analysis 169–171; student engagement in 169–171

Kahoot 88

Kingston University 109; Kingston Business School 109

knowledge construction 53, 57

languages speaking practice 94–96

learning: analytics 136; behaviors 97–99, 101; experience 15, 19, 21, 24, 97, 141

Learning Analytics Insights (LAI) program 100

'learning by doing' 52

Learning Design Framework (LDF) see Local Development Framework (LDF) for learning design

learning ecosystems 63, 65; benefits for students 63

Learning Management System (LMS) 53, 97–101, 109–114, 134, 136, 137; Blackboard Learn 53

Learning Technology Integrations (LTIs) 117

Learning Tools Interoperability (LTI) 117

learning types model 108

Leeds Trinity University 196

LEGO@ Serious Play@ (LSP) 198–200, 203; bespoke internal training for 202; for mental health and well-being 201; for professional development 201; tactile nature of 202; for University of Exeter Business School (UEBS) students 200

lifelong learning 21, 24, 25

Linear-on-the-Fly (LOTF) testing 110, 114

live documents 53
Liz Thomas Associates 119
Local Development Framework (LDF)
  for learning design 140–141; benefits
  142, 143; collaborative learning 140,
  142, 144; directed learning 140, 142,
  144; fitting into timetabling system
  143; guided learning 140–141;
  implementation 141, 142; lessons
  learnt from 143–144; for students'
  engagement 141; students' mistrust
  144; teething problems in 144
logical reasoning abilities 22
Louisiana State University in
  Shreveport (LSUS) 38, 39
LSP Facilitator Community of
  Practice 202
LSUS Cyber Collaboratory 38

marketization of higher education
  166, 171
media-based learning 41
Media Skills Passport 28, 29
mental health 59, 62, 64, 201
Mentimeter 103, 106, 108, 202
Meta 28
metacognition 56
meta-film approach 36
Micro:bit 211
Microsoft Class Team 216–218, 220
Microsoft Flip 219
Microsoft Forms 218
Microsoft Outlook calendar 218
Microsoft PowerPoint 39, 71, 105
Microsoft Stream 71
Microsoft Sway 75, 217, 219
Microsoft Teams 57–63, 70, 71,
  75–79, 147–149, 204–208, 216–218,
  220; centered learning ecosystem
  approach 64–69; challenges and
  issues 59–62; channels 66–67;
  dissertation meetings 58, 60, 63;
  pastoral care support sessions
  using 59–63; protection of privacy
  and confidentiality 60; for student
  empowerment and engagement 57,
  58, 62
minoritized communities 103, 104, 106

Miro 54–56
Moodle 100
Moodle Book 134–139
Moodle LMS 134, 136, 137, 139
Moodle.org 134
motion graphics 40
multi-cam desk 32, 34, 37, 38
multiple-choice questions (MCQs) 28,
  111–113
Mural 71, 202

National Health Service 34
National Strategic Vision 43
National Student Survey (NSS) 142, 161
newsfeed 92–93
Next-Generation Sequencing (NGS)
  technology 38
NILE 53–56; Blackboard Collaborate
  in 54, 55; co-creation process 56;
  module 53–54; Padlet and Miro in
  54–56
Nursing and Midwifery Council
  procedures 30

Oculus 28
Office365 78, 217
Office for Students' Condition of
  Registration 125
OneNote 75–79
one-on-one communication 100
online Academic English sessions 93
online assessment platforms 160,
  161; analytical capabilities in 165;
  challenges in 162, 165; diversity
  and differences in 163, 164;
  incorporation of GenAI into 161,
  162; integrating feedback into 164;
  integration capability 163; student
  engagement on 165–166
online collaborative spaces 53
online communications 36, 93
online education 64, 199
online eReading list 137
online feedback provision 160–162,
  164–166; need for frequent 162;
  utilizing GenAI for 162
online learning 52, 53, 65, 93, 98, 99,
  134, 135, 171, 198, 205, 206

online learning ecosystem 63–69;
Calendly 67; development of 64;
Innovation 101 module 64, 65,
68; student feedback 67–69; using
Microsoft Teams 64–69; Virtual
Learning Environment Moodle 67
online marking 162
online platforms 88, 164, 165, 178
online presence, approaches on 92,
95–96; community building in
large-group online sessions 93–94;
self-interview recordings 94–95;
use of news items for student
engagement 92–93
online proctoring technologies
144–145, 149–150; *see also* Honorlock
software
online streaming 34
online teaching 28, 32, 95, 160
Open University *see* Digital University
Otter.ai 71

Padlet 54–56, 103, 106, 108, 202, 206
pandemic lockdowns 10, 28, 32, 37, 60,
63, 148, 203
Panopto 71, 77
pedagogical model for Postgraduate
Researchers (PGRs) 69, 70; live
element of 70–73; social element of
71, 72; static element of 70–73
Pedagogies Innovation Lab (PIL)
26–32; 3D scanners in 27; advantage
32; avatars in 30, 32; barriers 27–28;
at Bournemouth University 31;
construction of website 30; creation
of marketing materials 30; designing
student-facing workshops 27, 29;
eye tracking glasses 29; micro
formative quizzes 31; module
28; students on eye tracking data
29; test environment for learning
technologists 26–27; training
midwives to conduct urinalysis
30; virtual and non-virtual control
groups 31; virtual worlds in medical
training 30, 31
peer-led approach 143
Personal Academic Tutoring project 115

Personalized Learning Designer
(PLD) 98; automating processes for
reminders and support 101, 102;
creating 'personalization at scale' 98;
generating emails 100, 102; process
map for 99; rules 99, 101; student
academic performance analysis 100;
tracking student engagement 98, 102
personal tutoring 58–60, 62
physical education (PE) postgraduate
initial teacher education (ITE)
program 172; *see also* Point-of-View
(POV) cameras
plagiarism detection engine 22
podcasts 71
Point-of-View (POV) cameras:
developing student teachers'
observation abilities 177; engaging
in professional development exercise
176; for practical PE and AE sessions
172–177; student feedback 174–176
Postgraduate Certificate in Education
Practice course 103
Postgraduate Certificate in Learning
and Teaching (PGCLT) program
75–80; asynchronous curriculum
delivery on 75, 76, 80; challenges 79;
criticisms 79; digital escape room to
77–80; OneNote notebooks 75–80
postgraduate researchers (PGRs)
administration 124; challenges of
124, 131; online monitoring systems
of 125–126, 129; phases of System
Development Lifecycle 128–130;
progression and engagement of
PGRs 125–127, 132; ProGRess
system for 126–133; research degree
supervision and supervisors for 125,
127, 132, 133
Postgraduate Teaching Assistants
(PTAs) 72, 75
postmodernist approach 87
pre-live-post (PLP) approach 196
preplanned communication schedule 136
Professional, Statutory, and Regulatory
Bodies (PSRB) 144
Professional Doctoral (PD) program
for PD Postgraduate Researchers

(PGRs) 203–206; Cultural Historical Activity Theory (CHAT) 204–206, 209; use of Adobe Connect 206, 207; using Microsoft Teams as pedagogic tool 204–208

professional practice learning 43, 44, 48

'Programming for Problem Solving' course 20, 22, 24

programming skills 22

ProGRess bespoke online system 126–127; automation of administrative tasks 132; coding 129; deployment 129–130; design 129; feedback from PGRs 130–131; functionality of 128; implementation 131–133; maintenance 130; project planning 128; requirement and data analysis 129; testing 129

Protein Data Bank 40

Public Sector Equality Duty 103

'push and pull' communications 98, 99

PyMOL 40

Python 23, 211

QR codes 88

quality assurance 125, 132

RCSB.org 40

real-life experiences 48, 153

remote learning 62, 91

Researcher Development Program (RDP) for Postgraduate Researchers (PGRs) 69; campus-based students engagement with webinar program 73; learning experience 70, 71, 73; 'multiple ways of doing' 69, 70; pedagogical model for 69–75; qualitative feedback 72

rhizomatic learning 56

Riipen digital learning platform 151–155; assessment tasks and feedback in 153; benefits of 154; challenges in 155; facilitating employability 152–154; helping business project owners 154–155; integrating educators, business organizations and students 151–153; internships in 152; student's perspective on 153, 154

room hopping 218

Ruskin modules (RM) 215

SCORM packages 70

Scratch 211

screencasts 193, 195, 197

scripting technologies 114

self-assessment 36, 46, 178

self-directed learning 22, 24, 46

self-directed learning objects 135–136, 138

self-interview recordings 94–95; students feedback 95

self-managed learning tasks 28

self-report caring 97

sensemaking 111, 114, 137, 138

sense of belonging 58, 63, 65, 85, 92, 97

'Serious Play, Serious Fun, Serious Skills' project 198

service-level agreements (SLAs) 148

SharePoint 217

'show and tell' approach 26, 33

simulation technology 30, 43; for health and social care education 43, 44

Sketchfab 40

Skype for Business 70

smartphone cameras 14

social distancing 57, 60

social ecology 88

social justice 103, 108

Socratic discussion model 35–38

Socratic method 35–36

soft skills 34, 38, 199

Solent Online Learning (SOL) Standard 140

Solent University 36

SRM Institute of Science and Technology 22, 24, 25

staff development workshops, learning technologies for 102–109; AI-generated Avatars 105–109; aim of 103; Equity Compass Tool 104–109; Foucauldian technique 104–107

statutory external reporting requirements 127

'Still Learning Together' 192–195, 197; audiofile feedback approach for 195–196; 'Persuasive Writing'

module 193; 'Shakespeare on Film' 194; student feedback on 197; 'Weekly Support Videos' 197
Stream 217
stress-testing 47
student-centered learning 32, 44
student engagement 1, 5, 11, 13, 29, 84, 109–114; Bioecological Model of Human Development for 85; Bioecological Student Engagement Framework (BSEF) for 85–91; microsystems to improve 86–88; 'show not tell' teaching for 34; in synchronous learning 85–89; see also aggregate measure of module engagement (AMME)
student learning experience 182–183
student learning gain 166–167, 172; changes in 167; concept of 167; discussions with teaching team 170; evaluation 167; perception of personal learning 170–171; pilot tests using Jisc Online Surveys tool 168–171
Student-Led Seminars (SLSs) 204, 205, 208, 209
students attendance in online participation 109–114; see also aggregate measure of module engagement (AMME)
students' perception on education 166, 170–171
students visibility in large-group online sessions 93–96
Student Union 186
Student Unit Teaching Evaluation (SUTE) 136–138
Student Voice Committee 87
Studiosity 114, 115; aspects of 115–116; disclaimer in 116; feedback on academic writing quality 115–116; improvement of International Foundation Year (IFY) students' performance 119; Learning Tools Interoperability (LTI) standard 117; referrals and interventions 116–117; services 116; success of 118; 'Write it Right' activity 117–118, 120; Writing Feedback service 116, 118
sustainable development 133

synchronous online collaboration tools for interdisciplinary groups 215–221; challenges of 218; Double Diamond approach 219; Microsoft Class Team 216–218, 220; Microsoft Teams 216–218, 220; Office365 217; SharePoint 217; Stream 217; Sway 217; Waterfall Project Management approach 217–219
System Development Lifecyle 128–130

tap-to-check-in system 110
teacher education programs 172
teacher-student engagement 17, 57
Teaching Excellence Framework (TEF) 88
teaching from home 33
teaching practices 26, 27, 75, 77, 108, 139, 172, 184
teaching standard improvement 159
Technology Enabled Laboratory (TEL) tool for problem-solving skills 20–25; architecture 21–22; dynamic color-coding system in 22; engagement and feedback mechanisms 23, 24; improvement of accessibility 24; integrated Conceive-Design-Implement-Operate frameworks into 22; as multifaceted educational resource 23; objectives 20; participation of learners 24; programming languages in 23; student motivation and confidence 24; success of 25
Technology-Enhanced Feedback 164
Technology Enhanced Learning (TEL) development team 177, 182, 196
Technology-Enhanced Learning research 104
ThingLink 14, 77, 219
third-party apps 67
3D printed models 41
3Dvista.com 43, 44
3DVista Pro virtual tour software 43–48; ability to track students' performance and feedback 46–47; accessibility challenges 47; assessment on social work apprenticeship degree program 45; benefits 45, 47; in health and social education 44, 46–48; helps in

students' professional practice skills
46; improves student performance
and engagement 46–48
3D visualizations 41
360-degree camera 32, 36, 37
360-degree immersive webinar design
35–38
Tik-Tok 177
Tinkercad Circuits and student
experience 209–211, 215;
cost-effectiveness 213; good
practice 212; practical and
creative application 212–213; skills
development 213–214
transdisciplinary approach 35
transformative learning behaviors 97
turbulence and perturbance 139–140
Turnitin 116

UKAT's Framework for Advising and
Tutoring 115
UK civil aviation rules 14
UK Equality Act 103
UK Office for Students 84, 133, 166
UK Research and Innovation (UKRI) 133
UK Student Engagement Survey 84
Ultra Performance Liquid
Chromatography-Mass
Spectrometer (UPLC-MS) 38
UNESCO 215, 216; teaching methods
by 216
United Nations Sustainable
Development Goals (UNSDGs) 133,
185, 215–216
Unity 44
Universal Design for Learning (UDL)
52, 53, 57, 139, 184
University College, London 33
University Language Programme 94
University of Birmingham 160
University of Exeter 69, 71, 200, 201
University of Northampton 53
University of Salford (UoS) 13, 14
University of Sunderland 114–117,
119, 120
Unreal 5 game engine 44

videogaming 41
virtual classroom 54, 55, 77

virtual field trips (VFTs) 12–20; digital
visualization tools to develop 13,
18, 19; ES3 students' participation
in fieldwork 12–13; Geography
and Environmental Management
modules 14–15; GoPro Max action
cameras 14; student feedback on their
experience 15–19; teacher-student
engagement 17; ThingLink online
visual learning platform 14; useful for
physical disability and neurodivergent
students 18; visual aids and media
in 16
Virtual Geoscience Trainer 13–14
Virtual Learning Environment (VLE)
26, 28, 29, 47, 86–89, 92, 127, 140,
144, 149, 160, 163, 175, 176, 178–180,
185, 196, 216–217, 220
Virtual Learning Environment Moodle 67
Virtual Reality (VR) 14, 28, 31, 38, 40,
43, 44, 47
Virtual Reality-Head-Mounted Displays
(VR-HMDs) 27, 28, 30
virtual simulations 46
virtual tours 44
virtual 'walk-throughs' 14
virtual whiteboards 71
VR360 technology 43
VR glaciated landscapes 14

Warwick Award for Teaching
Excellence 68
Waterfall Project Management
approach 217–219
webinar designs 34–35
web links 14
WhatsApp groups 207–208
White, David 91
wide-angle web camera 33
widening of participation (WP) 85–88,
90, 115
World Economic Forum 215, 221

X 71, 72, 74

YouTube 28, 177, 193
Yuja 219

Zoom 71, 105, 147, 149, 217